"Readers will appreciate Mr. Gentile's scholarly approach to a major question within the Body of Christ. He enthusiastically presents compelling evidence for The Gift that is available to every believer."

Ted Haggard, senior pastor, New Life Church, Colorado Springs

"Ernest Gentile has written an excellent, biblically based introduction for anyone seeking to know about the baptism with the Spirit. Pastor Gentile's years of experience in the local congregational setting have given him insight into the real and practical issues that many pastors are confronted with when leading their churches into a fuller relationship with the Holy Spirit. He has effectively interpreted the most relevant biblical texts in an articulate, compelling and yet winsome and nonthreatening way. He communicates effectively the importance of developing a closer relationship with the Holy Spirit of God. I would highly recommend *The Glorious Disturbance* for use by pastors, seekers and students preparing for ministry."

Cecil M. Robeck, Jr., professor of church history and ecumenics, director of the David du Plessis Center for Christian Spirituality, School of Theology, Fuller Theological Seminary

"In my estimation, speaking in tongues is one of the foundation stones of the first church and should be in today's church. Ernest Gentile speaks from three proven arenas: He speaks as a pastor with more than forty years of experience who knows what people need and what the Holy Spirit can do. Second, he speaks as a scholar and a disciplined man of skilled research. Last, he speaks from personal experience. Great job, Ernest!"

Frank Damazio, senior pastor, City Bible Church, Portland, and president, Portland Bible College

THE

GLORIOUS

DISTURBANCE

UNDERSTANDING AND RECEIVING THE BAPTISM WITH THE SPIRIT

ERNEST B. GENTILE

Chosen Books

A Division of Baker Book House Co
Grand Rapids, Michigan 49516

© 2004 by Ernest B. Gentile

Published by Chosen Books
a division of Baker Book House Company
P.O. Box 6287, Grand Rapids, MI 49516-6287
www.bakerbooks.com

Printed in the United States of America

Library of Congress Cataloging-in-Publication Data
Gentile, Ernest B.
      The glorious disturbance: understanding and receiving the baptism with the Spirit / Ernest B. Gentile.
          p.   cm.
      Includes bibliographical references and indexes.
      ISBN 0-8007-9323-4 (pbk.)
      1. Holy Spirit. 2. Baptism. I. Title.
BT121.3.G474 2004
234′.13—dc22   2003022703

To
Joseph Gentile

Good and True Friend, Dedicated Christian
My One and Only Brother

CONTENTS

Diagrams and Charts   9
Introduction   11

Part 1: Astounding Holy Spirit Miracles Introduce a New Era
Did Jesus Really Need the Holy Spirit Baptism?

1. Jesus' Preparation: Inner Spiritual Development   21
2. Jesus' Ministry: What He Learned, Lived and Taught   39
3. Jesus' Promise: The Holy Spirit Will Come   55

Part 2: A Glorious Disturbance Interrupts Pentecostal Festivities
Howling Wind, Blazing Fire and Supernatural Tongues

4. The Miracle of Pentecost: God's Gift Arrives   71
5. Great Balls of Fire! "Whoa! Me on Fire?!"   93
6. Speaking in Tongues: Is This Really Necessary?   105
7. Answers to Pesky Questions: Reasons People Give   123

Part 3: The Baptism with the Holy Spirit
A Marvelous Gift for All

8. The Peter Pattern: A Prescription for Success   139
9. The Baptism with the Holy Spirit: Every Believer Linked to Pentecost   157

Part 4: Holy Spirit Activity Recorded in Acts
 The Power of Pentecost Sweeps On

10. Amazing Episodes in Acts: Luke Tells It as It Was   179

11. More Episodes: The Rain Keeps Falling   193

12. The Spirit for All People: The News Spreads
    Everywhere   211

13. Why the Fuss over Acts? Let's Read It Right   221

    Appendix: The Church Body's Diverse Views on the Baptism
      with the Holy Spirit   229
    Notes   243
    Bibliography   263
    Subject Index   273
    Scripture Index   280

DIAGRAMS AND CHARTS

Herod's Temple 76–77
Map: Countries Represented at Pentecost 91
Scriptural Overview of the Peter Pattern 141
Summary of New Testament Baptisms 143
The Threefold Pattern 144
Spirit Empowerment Activity in the Book of Acts 172
Maintaining the Peter Pattern 175
The Threefold Purpose of Acts 181
Illustrations of the Peter Pattern in Acts 182–3
Comparison of Experiences in the Groups 240

INTRODUCTION

For sixty years I have been speaking in tongues—and listening to the theological debates about whether this is done by some mental gymnastics, the power of the devil or the power of the Holy Spirit. Rarely has a subject so divided sincere followers of Christ. The Holy Spirit, our greatest Helper, has been our biggest battleground!

This is a book about the Holy Spirit and why it is all right to speak in tongues. The title, *The Glorious Disturbance,* refers to that awesome Day of Pentecost recorded in Acts 2 when—for the first time—people were baptized with the Holy Spirit and spoke in tongues. Throughout the history of the early Church, people continued to experience that outpouring—and it continues today as people all over the world enjoy this amazing miracle and have a wonderful new appreciation of their Savior Jesus Christ because of it.

I have now lived long enough to see this appreciation grow in regard to Holy Spirit activity. Take seminaries, for example. Back in my early days, not very many Pentecostals attended accredited seminaries. They were not particularly welcome. Since the professors invariably had not had the experience, they were usually outspoken against it.

Today, so many seminary students are Pentecostal or charismatic that if they were removed, some schools would be out of business! Some well-known professors speak in tongues. More Ph.D. dissertations have been written on the baptism of the Holy Spirit and the Pentecostal movement and charismatic renewal than we could imagine.

Likewise, I am encouraged when I attend prayer summits and pastoral prayer meetings in various cities. It is not uncommon for prophecies to be given or for denominational ministers to lift their hands and pray fervently for the Holy Spirit to work in their lives. Some may even pray out in tongues—and none of the other ministers seems surprised or upset.

Thus, the renewal that is touching all parts of the globe is bringing with it a new climate of tolerance and understanding. A strong segment of Christians now speaks in tongues and is involved in some type of charismatic activity. These believers come from almost all branches of the Christian Church and, according to some experts, number more than five hundred million.[1] Many of the fastest growing churches in the country believe in the power of the Spirit as described in the Acts of the Apostles.

I would be remiss not to mention here an individual who was a key figure in helping build tolerance for Holy Spirit discussion and experience in our day. David DuPlessis (1905–1987) was a man from South Africa whom the world came to call "Mr. Pentecost." He had an amazing ability to discuss the Holy Spirit and introduce people (especially denominational church leaders) to a personal encounter with this heavenly Personality.[2]

One of his favorite ways of presenting the subject in high-level denominational meetings or seminary settings was to use the example of frozen meat. He explained that many could analyze the nutritional content of the meat, could tell what part of the animal the steak came from and could even determine the origin of the steer itself, but they never had anything more than frozen meat to serve hungry people!

DuPlessis then compared the frozen meat to our understanding of God and the Holy Spirit. While the common people wait for something nourishing and tasty to eat, the leaders are giving lectures on biblical nutrition. Let the meat thaw! That does not lessen the nutritional value! Let it be made ready for consumption! Bring the meat (the theology) to the fire of the Holy Spirit and see how excitedly people will respond. They can learn about the intricacies of nutrition after their hunger has been met.

Indeed, the meat is beginning to thaw. And yet, with all of this growing understanding and acceptance, there is no doubt that confusion—even animosity—still exists. Over the centuries renewals have swept over certain churches or certain locations, but the Body as a whole has failed to embrace all that the baptism with the Spirit offers the new believer. Those who speak in tongues are often, as in times past, ridiculed and ostracized and ejected from the mainstream of church life.

On a recent trip to Brazil I talked with an evangelical missionary. Since I knew that his denomination did not approve of the present-day expression of the charismatic gifts, his strong belief in them surprised me. He explained that if his headquarters found out about how his team was ministering, they would be recalled. But, he said, it is impossible to work in the jungles and other primitive areas without the Holy Spirit's power to cast out devils and heal the sick. His approach is to serve God in the power of the Spirit, and let the folks back home do their own thing.

AUTHOR'S INTENT

This book is concerned with clearing just such confusion and misconceptions that still exist in the Church today on the subject of baptism with the Holy Spirit and speaking in tongues. We will learn what the Church of Bible days believed about the Holy Spirit and how it experienced Him—and how those experiences can take place in our day. The 290 verses in the New Testament that mention the Holy Spirit will be the foundation of our discussion, but we will look particularly at the book of Acts (where the Holy Spirit is mentioned more than in any other book). In a way it will be both an intellectual inquiry and an experiential pursuit. I wish to blend scholarship and everyday usefulness. My strong desire is to lead the reader into the presence of and personal experience with the Holy Spirit Himself.

To do this, I will first invite you to share part of my own journey so you know where I am coming from. Although it will lengthen this introduction, I hope it will help you better understand my presentation of a normal, practical Pentecostal theology of the Holy Spirit of God. Not everyone will share the same agony and ecstasy that I experienced, but I can assure you that God has promised you a wonderful gift that will bring you great joy!

AUTHOR'S PERSONAL TESTIMONY

I had two introductions to the Holy Spirit and a very meaningful water baptism (by submersion) all before the age of fifteen years—and before knowing much about the Bible or theology. Both experiences were transforming and down-deep satisfying. I have had many experiences with the Holy Spirit during my 62 years as a Christian, but these two spiritual encounters (along with my water baptism) have been basic to my successful Christian life. I want to describe them for you here. Little did I realize then, that the question of one, two or three experiences helps fuel the great debate on the Holy Spirit.

First Encounter

My first major encounter came at the age of twelve. Every week I listened to the best-known radio preacher of the 1940s, Charles E. Fuller (founder of Fuller Theological Seminary). One Sunday his straightforward message of salvation touched my heart. Dropping to my knees by our living room couch, I repented of my sins and invited Jesus Christ into my life. Assurance of salvation flooded my heart as I was "born again" by the wonderful work of the Holy Spirit.

For two years I lived as a person who knew Christ and had experienced the grace of God. Because I was not established in a local church, I was not baptized in water, my Bible knowledge did not increase greatly and I was not an active witness.

One day in high school, while tossing my books into a locker, I heard a commotion near by. Another student, one of the few African-Americans in our school, was excitedly sharing about Jesus Christ to one of my "spiritually resistant" friends. Amazing! This was what I should be doing, but I just lacked the gumption to do it. I had to meet that young man.

After I introduced myself, he threw a bold, authoritative question at me: "Have you been filled with the Holy Ghost?" I stammered that I was not sure. His next statement floored me. "Well, if you're not sure, you haven't been!" Having no extensive Bible knowledge, I accepted the statement as perfectly logical. From that point on, diligent Bible study filled my time.

Second Encounter

My new friend invited me to hear his uncle preach at the Stevens Street Mission in the skid row area of Spokane, Washington. Not too many showed up that night, but Brother Smith preached an amazing sermon. His one theme riveted my attention, and his flamboyant style drove the message home. The text was Acts 2:4 and the theme was the importance of being filled with the Holy Spirit to gain power in one's life—a classic message and typical of the sermons preached in Pentecostal churches at that time.

Wanting that power desperately, I ran to the altar at the conclusion of his sermon. My second Holy Spirit encounter was about to happen!

I was the only outsider present that night, so the sparse crowd concentrated its prayers on this spiritually hungry, fourteen-year-old boy who wanted help. The prayers went on for about an hour. I knelt and, following their instructions, lifted up my hands and tried to praise the Lord audibly. I asked for the Holy Spirit. I gave up everything wrong that I knew was in my life. Finally, gripped by a sense of desperation, I told God I would not leave that night until I was filled with His Spirit!

The older folks seemed to take turns praying with me. They would urge me to say "Glory!" or "Hallelujah!" Finally I got to the point where I could hardly speak (how many times can you say "Glory! Glory!"?) and literally fell back on the floor, whether from exhaustion or the Holy Spirit, I do not know. Everyone sat down and watched me. All was quiet, and my eyes were closed. They must have wondered what had happened.

A powerful, peaceful presence of the Holy Spirit settled upon me. Although perfectly still on the outside, my inner being was alive with faith and expectancy. This was an infilling of the Holy Spirit! My prayer was simple: "Lord, the Bible says that people spoke in tongues when they were baptized with the Spirit. And, Lord, these people believe that you can speak in tongues when you are filled. Lord, I believe this is the Holy Spirit! I am going to open my mouth and speak in tongues!"

It felt as though a volcano erupted inside of me. I started to say "Hallelujah!" but the sound was swept away by a torrent of words that I had never learned. The miracle tongue flowed unabated as the Spirit gave utterance. Finally, I arose from the floor—unable to speak in English! This was the most exciting experience of my entire life!

Catching the last bus home, I burst through the front door speaking in tongues and scared my poor mother half to death! (My father was in the Army and overseas at the time.) The next day in high school, I had to speak slowly and carefully or this new, strange, wonderful language of the Holy Spirit would burst forth. I never questioned that this experience was anything but the Spirit since Jesus was more real than ever before and prayer to God had become so exhilarating.

Fervent witnessing for Christ became my passion. The skid row "street meetings" held near the mission became my delight. We stood in the gutter, testified, sang and preached to the people who gathered there. I guess that is where I learned to preach and be bold for God. What a difference the Holy Spirit baptism made!

I discovered quickly that not everyone was excited about the Pentecostal doctrine of Holy Spirit baptism and speaking with other tongues. The Christians at my school were, like their home churches, quite divided on the issue. The Pentecostals said that the evangelicals did not have the Spirit, and the evangelicals said that speaking in tongues was from the devil! Regretfully, both sides were wrong, and the enemy had a field day keeping us separated. If we all could have pulled together, we would have made a mighty impact on the student body. (Now, thank God, most of us recognize the error of those unfortunate attitudes.)

ORDER OF PRESENTATION

Now, back to this book. The first part deals with Jesus and the Holy Spirit. His ministry, His teachings and His promise regarding the Holy Spirit are an important foundation for proper understanding. I propose that Jesus was the prototype Spirit-filled man—as well as the divine Son of God. As the Son of man, He was our example of dependence on God's Spirit. As the Son of God, He was the Lord of glory.

The second part presents the astounding Day of Pentecost, attended by howling wind, blazing fire and miracle tongues. The fire and tongues will particularly hold our attention.

Then, in the heart of the book, we explore the baptism with the Holy Spirit. We seek to understand the apostolic Church of Bible times as well as today's Pentecostal-charismatic renewal. The exciting episodes in the Acts of the Apostles are discussed, and we examine why some scholars see them as important history but not relevant to today's Church. Some key principles of hermeneutics, the art and science of Bible interpretation, will guide us to sound answers.

Contemporary scholarship does raise persistent questions and challenges concerning the baptism with the Holy Spirit and speaking in tongues. Logical answers exist, however, for every argument and pesky question, and I will share them with you. Since I wish to keep the flow of the book moving, I tend to put academic information in the endnotes.[3]

THE THESIS OF THE BOOK

In the following pages, I will pursue the thesis that there is really only
one theology of the Holy Spirit in the New Testament. Many books
have been written trying to explain Luke's charismatic approach, John's
prophetic approach and Paul's Christological approach. Actually, the
insights of all three biblical writers—inspired by the same Spirit—give
a unified presentation. The problem comes either from starting with
Pauline theology and then trying to make the teachings of Luke fit in,
or from starting with the Acts and then making an awkward transition
to the many Holy Spirit references in the epistles.

The best approach is to start with the gospels and the life of Christ,
then proceed to the Acts with its graphic descriptions of the early Church
and finally approach the teaching of the epistles. In other words, Jesus'
life is the sterling example, followed by the apostles' and finally the
Spirit-filled life portrayed in the epistles.

We simply cannot eliminate or alienate any part of the New Testament—not if we consider God to be the one author! My argument will
be that Peter and Paul were Pentecostals, in the sense that they were
bonded to the one Body of Christ and each other by the working of the
Holy Spirit. My sincere desire is that you share that same experience. It
is definitely available to you—a precious gift from God awaiting your
acceptance.

We are all somewhat skittish about how this term *Spirit-filled* is used.
I cannot help but admire the simplified approach of classical Pentecostal
scholar Gordon Fee when he stresses that *Spirit-filled Christian* would
have been a redundant expression in New Testament times, something
like saying Scandinavian Swede. Back in Bible days, Fee says, it would
have seemed impossible to be a Christian apart from the empowering
presence of the Holy Spirit. The very meaning of *Christian* is someone
whose life has been changed and filled by the Holy Spirit.[4]

An important last thought before we start: I will promote strongly
what I call "the Peter Pattern," a Christian-life paradigm given by the
apostle Peter on the Day of Pentecost. Acts 2:38 says: "Repent, and let
every one of you be baptized in the name of Jesus Christ for the remission of sins; and you shall receive the gift of the Holy Spirit." The early
Church followed this basic prescription for Kingdom living:

- Conversion (Salvation: new birth, believing in Christ)
- Water baptism (Sanctification: burial of the old lifestyle)
- Baptism with the Holy Spirit (Service: endowment of power)

This dynamic threefold approach is used by the Spirit to initiate the convert into a vital role in the Church and the Kingdom of God. After that, the Christian will find that salvation, sanctification and service will continue their power to enable the Christian to walk with the Lord in ever increasing faith.

PART 1

ASTOUNDING HOLY SPIRIT MIRACLES INTRODUCE A NEW ERA

DID JESUS REALLY NEED THE HOLY SPIRIT BAPTISM?

1

Jesus' Preparation
Inner Spiritual Development

In This Chapter

- Learn how an obscure village became world famous
- Consider the two main ingredients of Jesus' education
- Understand the meaning of Jesus' boyhood statement in the Temple
- Find out why Jesus performed no miracles before age thirty
- Read about the impact of the messianic Scripture on Jesus

The small town, some would call it a rural village, was of no significance to the world, the nation or the province. One spring supplied the town's water. The population numbered possibly several hundred, but certainly no more than several thousand. Located in the hills of Galilee, nestled in a sheltered basin on a hillside thirteen hundred feet above sea level, the obscure town was not mentioned in the Hebrew Scriptures, the writings of Josephus or the Talmud. No main road of international trade passed through it, although it was a short distance from a caravan route to Egypt. It lay thirty miles from the Mediterranean and fifteen miles from the Sea of Galilee.

The ridge above the town provided an excellent vantage point for the activities of northern Israel. The observer could trace the magnificent, scenic panorama of Mt. Carmel on the west, the beautiful lower valleys, Mount Tabor nearby in the east and finally up to the snowy peak of Mt. Hermon in the north. Jewish children watched from a distance as Roman legions marched in shining symmetry and the stately retinues of royal personages passed in review. Pilgrim processions also moved to and fro, and Egyptian and Midianite caravans lumbered along.

Not totally secluded, these villagers were neighbors of the booming city of Sepphoris. With an estimated ten thousand inhabitants and a main colonnaded street with shops, it was clearly visible three miles north (an hour's walk). Serving as the unofficial capital of Galilee, this bustling commercial, military, political and cultural city ran just behind Jerusalem in importance. As a child, Jesus was exposed to the bustling work and trade going on there. Sepphoris's fame was short-lived, however, for the Romans burned the city to the ground to squelch rebellion. This would have happened when Jesus was a young man. Not mentioned in the gospels, the city is hardly remembered.

In contrast, there was no reason for the village of our story to be remembered in history, except that a certain man lived and worked there for about 25 years. When He died, His followers ensured that it would never be forgotten. How it all happened was truly miraculous—a work of the Holy Spirit.

Jesus was the man and Nazareth was the town. The two became famous together: Jesus of Nazareth. When He died by crucifixion on a Roman stake, they tacked to His beam those words, adding five more:

Jesus of Nazareth
The King of the Jews

DIVINE YET HUMAN

More books have been written about this man of humble beginnings than any other person in history. Rightly so, since Jesus has had a greater impact on history than any other. Secular historians, unfortunately, miss the basis for His greatness, but four devoted disciples, recording Jesus' life story, draw back the curtain just far enough to disclose the secret of His powerful life: His divine birth and the baptism with the Holy Spirit. Jesus has always been a stumbling block to secular historians. His life has been like the great, imperishable anvil upon which critics have worn out their flimsy hammers through the ages.

The Bible describes Jesus as both Son of God (divine) and Son of man (human). The great mystery of His life is how He, the living Word of God by whom the worlds were created, assumed our human form and natural limitations. John declared: "In the beginning was the Word, and the Word was with God, and the Word was God" (John 1:1). The New Living Translation gives a sharper edge to the translation: "In the beginning the Word already existed. He was with God, and he was God." The term *the Word of God* is a wondrously descriptive name given to Jesus that shows Him to be the divine method of self-expression.[1]

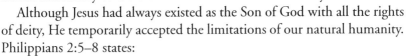

Jesus was physically conceived by the direct action of the Holy Spirit. This incarnation of the eternal God in human form was His finest effort to communicate Himself to humanity. Jesus was God, but for our sakes He determined to go an incredible route of humility. For our salvation He chose to take on our human nature, to live His life on earth through that nature and finally to die the worst kind of human death by crucifixion.

Although Jesus had always existed as the Son of God with all the rights of deity, He temporarily accepted the limitations of our natural humanity. Philippians 2:5–8 states:

> Let this mind be in you which was also in Christ Jesus, who, being in the form of God, did not consider it robbery to be equal with God, but made Himself of no reputation, taking the form of a bondservant, and coming in the likeness of men. And being found in appearance as a man, He humbled Himself and became obedient to the point of death, even the death of the cross.

The New Living Translation gives this wording:

> Though he was God, he did not demand and cling to his rights as God. He made himself nothing; he took the humble position of a slave and appeared in human form. And in human form he obediently humbled himself even further by dying a criminal's death on a cross.

verses 6–8

The New American Standard Bible says that He "emptied Himself, taking the form of a bondservant." G. Campbell Morgan points out that "the change was not in the essential nature or personality, but in the method of manifestation."[2] This means that Jesus the Word set aside one form of manifestation, His divinity, and took up another form, humanity, in which His equality with God would be subordinated for a time.

He became human and He stayed human, not claiming any special privileges as He underwent this incredibly humbling process. And, as professor John Rea has said: "In this position of humility He depended completely upon the Father and the Spirit (John 5:19–20)."[3]

It was in this limiting human form that Jesus could demonstrate successful living. He showed by personal example how we might seek, find and depend upon the Holy Spirit—the only way we can live godly lives. Jesus was not lacking or insufficient; rather, He was constrained under divine mandate to minister and function as the Son of man for our example.[4]

Part 1 of this book describes how Jesus, the Son of man, learned to depend on the Holy Spirit as His helper and guide, and, thereby, became our model of "the Spirit-filled life." The Jewish title of *Messiah* (the Spirit-anointed One) rightfully rests upon Him. Gentile Christians generally use the Greek form of the word, *Christ,* but the meaning is the same. Now we bear the name *Christian,* indicating that we, His followers, are endued with His Holy Spirit. We gather together as the Spirit-filled messianic community!

This chapter introduces Jesus of Nazareth and the development of His human, conscious need of the Holy Spirit. During this time (before His thirtieth year when He received the baptism of the Spirit), the Holy Spirit worked powerfully through the agency of His divine birth to develop character traits as well as a relational experience with God.

All this occurred in the humble setting of Nazareth. Jesus developed there like a root in dry ground (see Isaiah 53:2) without public acclaim or fanfare. There He matured, attended a synagogue school, related to other growing children and worked as a carpenter (see Mark 6:3). All this was God's supreme self-denial and self-abnegation as Jesus submitted to His own creatures. Living a life of redemptive purpose, He died as the sacrificial Lamb of God and provided redemption for all who believe; He conquered death, hell and the grave as our Savior, Lord and God.

THE MAN OF THE SPIRIT

Let us now begin at the beginning to learn how Jesus lived the Spirit-filled life as our inspiring example, the prototype man of the Spirit.

Background

The young couple returned home after an exile of approximately four to six years: Mary the mother, approaching her twentieth year with Joseph her ever-loyal, protective husband. The boy Jesus also came with them, now walking, talking and finding interest in all about Him. Possibly another child or two had joined the family by this time.

The parents were understandably apprehensive as they approached Mary's hometown of Nazareth, for they had left hurriedly in a state of great concern—watched closely by a curious and somewhat critical community. A quick review of developments before their return, especially noting the activity of the Holy Spirit, gives important perspective for Jesus' later ministry.

Miracle Births

The young couple's amazing adventure was intertwined with that of an elderly couple living in the hill country of Judea (tradition says in Hebron, the burial place of the founders of God's people—Abraham, Isaac and Jacob). Both women, apparently cousins, had unusual conceptions that linked them and their sons together in a fascinating series of events, all of which showcased the miraculous power of the Holy Spirit and the activity of angels. The older couple were Zacharias and Elizabeth, a godly, priestly couple who found themselves childless in old age, a cause for great concern in that Jewish society.

The story begins in the first chapter of Luke. God's angel Gabriel announced that the elderly pair would have a son. The boy would be the prophetic herald of the Messiah, the Spirit-endowed One, to Israel. His name was to be John ("God is favorable"), and he would be known as "John the Immerser" (today we call him "John the Baptist") because he would submerge repentant Jews in the Jordan River. John would be filled with the Holy Spirit from his mother's womb!

In Galilee, some eighty or so miles north, Gabriel also visited Mary with a startling announcement: She would conceive and bear the Messiah supernaturally, for God Himself was going to create the divine seed within her womb. "The Holy Spirit will come upon you, and the power of the Highest will overshadow you; therefore, also, that Holy One who is to be born will be called the Son of God" (Luke 1:35). Mary, a virgin, would also be a mother, even as foretold by Isaiah the prophet (see Isaiah 7:14). The mechanics of that miraculous conception continue, by divine decree, to remain a mystery, even as they were to Mary herself.

A complication soon developed! The ensuing pregnancy became known to Mary's fiancé, Joseph, creating profound embarrassment for this devoted, upright man. His anguished conclusion was to terminate the engagement quietly. Not wanting to make her a public example, Joseph decided not to subject Mary to a trial and the accusation of adultery. The angel, however, came and forcefully clarified the situation: "That which is conceived in her is of the Holy Spirit" (Matthew 1:20).

Mary, desperately in need of counsel and encouragement, heard that her elderly cousin Elizabeth, incredibly, had conceived a child in old age. She hastened southward on a three-day journey to isolated Hebron. On arrival, as Mary greeted the older woman, Elizabeth was filled with the Holy Spirit and prophesied. Mary also became inspired and prophesied. Three months later, Elizabeth gave birth to her son, John, and her husband, Zacharias, was suddenly filled with the Holy Spirit (see Luke 1:67) and he, too, prophesied!

Mary returned to Nazareth, continuing to advance in her pregnancy as questions surfaced in the community. Joseph and Mary were married quietly during this period, and a Roman decree provided an escape from embarrassment. Joseph was required by Roman law to return to Bethlehem, his hometown, to register for taxation. The trip was long and arduous for Mary, and upon arrival in Bethlehem the weary couple discovered that no room in the city was available—and baby Jesus was now due! Their desperate search ended in an animal shelter where Mary gave birth to the Son of God. Angelic hosts sang, shepherds arrived breathless and livestock looked on with curiosity. Only God would conceive of such an extraordinary, defenseless and trusting entrance into human affairs.

The Child Grows

Eight days later Jesus was circumcised, and a month later He was taken to the Temple in Jerusalem for dedication. While Jesus and His parents were there, the Holy Spirit came upon an old prophet named Simeon. Led by the Spirit, he found the family and confirmed prophetically that the child was indeed the Messiah (see Luke 2:25–35).

(Notice throughout our story the frequency of Holy Spirit operation.)

Returning to Bethlehem, the family occupied a house for approximately two years. Meanwhile, led by a miracle-star, dignitaries from a distant land traveled toward them. Arriving in Jerusalem, they consulted with King Herod about a newborn king. Following the advice of the court advisors, they journeyed on toward Bethlehem, the predicted birthplace of the Jewish Messiah. The star appeared again, leading them to the very house (see Matthew 2:10–11) where these "wise men" from the East startled the young couple.

Furious that this potential rival could replace him as king, Herod ordered his soldiers to kill all male babies in the Bethlehem area who were two years old and under. Warned by God, the young couple escaped immediately to Egypt with their infant son. The Reader's Digest commentary *Jesus and His Times* suggests: "To reach this haven would have required a lengthy journey across sun-baked desert wastes. Joseph would probably have taken his family from Bethlehem west to the shores of the Mediterranean, then followed a coastal road to the borders of Egypt. . . . We know that a young Jewish family could have found a welcome in Egypt. We can suppose that Joseph could have found work as a carpenter or as a laborer, if necessary, in that rich land."[5]

A few years passed, and God informed Joseph that he could now return to Israel. Fearful of Herod's son (who now reigned in Judea) and warned of God, Joseph led his family to Nazareth, where Mary (some four to six years before) had miraculously conceived Jesus by the power of the Holy Spirit.

The Boyhood Years

Joseph, the protector, now settled into the role of provider. Working as the town carpenter (a term of general meaning: woodworker or builder, perhaps even stonemason and blacksmith)[6], he cared for a growing family that eventually had five boys and at least two girls (see Matthew 13:55–56). The family put down their roots in the Jewish community life of Nazareth. Luke 2:39–40 summarizes Jesus' early boyhood: "They returned to Galilee, to their own city, Nazareth. And the Child grew and became strong in spirit, filled [increasing or filling up] with wisdom; and the grace of God was upon Him." He grew strong in body, mind, emotions and spiritual consciousness—a healthy, vigorous little boy whose wisdom kept pace with His bodily growth.

Only a few sentences tell us of this early time, but we know that His childhood was attended by diligent, loving care. Jesus entered earthly life heralded by angels as the divine infant. Now, as a human child, He was subject to all natural conditions and restrictions, and supervised carefully and zealously by God's appointed guardians. Mary and Joseph, typical Jewish parents, would have taken their assignment joyfully and seriously, engulfing this special child in a rigorous, religious atmosphere. Alfred Edersheim, Jewish historian, gives this description of education in the Jewish home.

> Education begins in the home, and there were not homes like those in Israel; it is imparted by influence and example, before it comes by teaching; it is acquired by what is seen and heard, before it is laboriously learned from books; its real object becomes instinctively felt, before its goal is consciously sought. What Jewish fathers and mothers were; what they felt towards their children; and with what reverence, affection, and care the latter returned what they had received, is known to every reader of the Old Testament. The relationship of father has its highest sanction and embodiment in that of God towards Israel; the tenderness and care of a mother in that of the watchfulness and pity of the Lord over His people.[7]

Jesus' education began in the home with Mary's influence, reinforced by Joseph's teaching of the Torah and vocational skills. From His earliest awareness Jesus was trained through sight, hearing and example to recognize God as Father and the maker of the world. He would have been taught to develop His memory, since forgetfulness or neglect of God's laws could prove fatal. Like all other Jewish children He was taught the importance of worship and prayer.

Every Jewish boy was required to learn a trade; accordingly, Joseph brought Jesus early into the carpenter's shop to learn the skills that would later enable Him to support the family (see Matthew 13:55; Mark 6:3).

When the New Testament speaks of Jesus assuming the role of a servant or being subject, it refers partially to His growing up as a normal Jewish boy under parental authority and guidance, subject to the human learning process. Unlike the Romans and Greeks, the Jews considered hard work and manual labor to be honorable, and this dependency on labor for a living would have been a vital aspect of Jesus' training.

According to Edersheim, at age five or six Jesus (like other Jewish children) was probably sent to the synagogue school. This could have begun for Jesus upon His family's arrival in Nazareth. The synagogue study started with the book of Leviticus, ordinances with which every Jew ought to be acquainted.

On the Threshold

The Bible's mysterious silence covering His early life is suddenly interrupted in His twelfth year. Like a bright shaft of sunlight breaking—for just a moment—through clouds, the episode of Jesus visiting the Temple is dropped into Luke's gospel (see 2:41–52). Another eighteen years of silence follow this brief interlude.

Joseph and Mary took Jesus with them to Jerusalem for the Passover Feast; we do not know if this was Jesus' first such pilgrimage. We do know that Jesus was "on the threshold of adult life." I. Howard Marshall explains further: "At the age of 12 a boy was prepared for his entry to the religious community which took place when he was 13."[8] With puberty, a boy became a "son of the law" or "son of the covenant" and began to observe the Jewish ordinances, including the wearing of phylacteries as a reminder. This custom continues in the present-day bar-mitzvah ceremony.

Jesus and His Times comments on the family approaching Jerusalem:

> As Jesus and his family crested the nearest of the ridges of hills that helped to protect Jerusalem on the north, the rural lad would have seen spread before him, perhaps for the first time since his infancy, one of the major cities of the age—one that would be described by Pliny as "by far the most famous city, not only of Judea, but of the whole East." . . . Above it all stood the Temple—the jewel and heart of Jerusalem and of the Jewish nation. . . . [T]he sanctuary was an awesome, thrilling sight. Radiant on the Temple Mount, it stood isolated from the city by a courtyard large enough to hold about 20 football fields. Its walls gleamed like snow on a mountaintop, according to

Josephus, and so much gold covered its sides that, had the sun been shining brightly, the boy's eyes might have smarted from the glare.[9]

Pilgrims who visited Jerusalem for the feasts were required by law to stay two days, and this was undoubtedly all that Joseph and Mary intended. Nothing of special interest would detain them after that, unless it was the opportunity to spend extra time in the Temple courts listening to the learned rabbis who were holding special teaching sessions on the Torah. Joseph and Mary remained the required time, and then joined a caravan headed homeward, assuming that their responsible oldest child was also in the group with relatives or friends. During their first day's journey of about twenty miles, the increasingly anxious parents began an intensive search for Jesus that lasted three days: one day's journey out, one day's journey back to Jerusalem and the third day in Jerusalem.

Once the Passover Feast was over, Jesus had quickly made His way to the area where the leading Temple rabbis were teaching. Seemingly, the lad forgot the trip home, for He hungered to hear the most brilliant, most learned, most spiritual of all Israel's teachers. Surely, if there were answers to the questions burning in His mind, these venerable scholars, whose lives were immersed in the study of the Scripture, must have had them!

W. Phillip Keller describes the scene:

> For three full days He plied them with questions. His insight into spiritual truth astounded them. Where would a youth of twelve gain such a broad grasp of God's Word? Surely no second-rate rabbi in Nazareth could impart such spiritual understanding! They in turn put difficult questions to Him . . . questions that they themselves had never resolved . . . questions tinged with doubts, misgivings, and perhaps even skepticism. Swiftly, surely He replied, dispelling their doubts and assuring them of the absolute veracity of God's Word.
>
> So engrossed were student and scholars in their discussions that the days sped by. Where Jesus slept and who provided His meals has often interested me. Did no one stop to wonder where His parents might be? It is a measure of the depth and intensity of their dialogue that secondary considerations hardly entered their thoughts. Suddenly Mary and Joseph showed up in the temple searching for the lad.[10]

J. W. Shepard comments that ". . . they found Him on the morning of the third day sitting at the feet of the Doctors of the Law on the Temple

Terrace. There the Midrash or Academy of Jerusalem established popular session on feast days and sabbaths, allowing all classes of Jews to sit as learners and propound questions."[11] Alfred Plummer suggests that: "Jesus probably sat on the ground, while the Rabbis sat on benches or stood."[12] A. T. Robertson draws this picture:

> Picture this eager boy alive with interest. It was his one opportunity in a theological school outside of the synagogue to hear the great rabbis expound the problems of life. This was the most unusual of all children, to be sure, in intellectual grasp and power. But it is a mistake to think that children of twelve do not think profoundly concerning the issue of life. What father or mother has ever been able to answer a child's questions?[13]

As a learner, Jesus sat before a group of Israel's best teachers. His were not mere boyish inquiries but surprising, probing questions as might be discussed in ancient academies, amazing questions that could not be answered adequately in the small synagogue in Nazareth, questions that had built a great reservoir of reflection in His mind. Time ceased to be important as He alternately sat spellbound and shared insightful answers. The mystified teachers must have been spellbound themselves! J. W. Doeve suggests of the teachers: "Their amazement must relate to his deducing things from Scripture which they had never found before."[14]

The Amazed Parents

Jesus' parents were astonished at the scene—"their eyes fairly bulged in surprise"! Jesus, however, "is not surprised at their coming back for Him, but at their not knowing where to find Him."[15] At first Mary's mild rebuke seems appropriate and Jesus' reply unsympathetic. Much more, however, is involved in Jesus' immediate response, for messianic consciousness now grips Him, and the call of God rings in His spirit. His first recorded words are prophetic. Look at Mary's question and Jesus' seeming surprise as He answers:

> "Son, why have You done this to us? Look, Your father and I have sought you anxiously." And He said to them, "Why did you seek Me? Did you not know that I must be about My Father's business?"
>
> Luke 2:48–49

Mary's reference to Joseph as Jesus' father was deftly pushed aside as Jesus referred with pointed meaning to His heavenly Father and the priority of His demands. The various Bible versions do not translate Jesus' answer consistently, and this is because the Greek text does not say specifically either "about My Father's business" or "in my Father's house" (NIV). Either meaning could be implied: the latter because of the context, and the former because of Jesus' time in life. The Jewish New Testament states it well: "Didn't you know that I had to be concerning myself with my Father's affairs?" However worded, Jesus' reply meant that He was bound by heaven's commission.

At this time in His life Jesus, like every other Jewish boy, was expected to choose His vocation. Most boys selected the trade or profession of their fathers, one in which they were partially trained. Jesus was already a carpenter's apprentice. Even though He had great spiritual aptitude, we can assume that He was not being pushed by His parents toward rabbinical training.

Thus, Jesus' statement was one of major importance to His parents. He was announcing that He would not be pursuing Joseph's profession as the primary focus of His life. Rather, the business of His heavenly Father would be His life's work. Raymond E. Brown suggests this meaning: "He is merely saying that his presence in the Temple and his listening to the teachers is indicative of where his vocation lies, namely, in the service of God who is his Father, not at the beck and call of his natural family."[16] It was a confusing moment for the parents; they "did not understand the statement which He spoke to them" (Luke 2:50).

The two following verses add: "Then He went down with them and came to Nazareth, and was subject to them, but His mother kept all these things in her heart. And Jesus increased in wisdom and stature, and in favor with God and men."

From this point, Jesus pursued two vocational goals: the secondary one as a workman would occupy eighteen years of His life and the primary one as Messiah only three and a half years. Being subject to His parents entailed development of His professional skills. Being faithful to His heavenly Father meant development spiritually. Both tracks developed well, we know, for our text says that Jesus increased in wisdom (mentally) and stature (physically), and in favor with God (spiritually) and men (socially). The young man "increased," which means, "He kept cutting His way forward, as a pioneer cuts his way through the undergrowth of a jungle."[17]

The Servant of Nazareth

Although the Bible gives no more information about Jesus' development in the next eighteen years, it is obvious that He became a well-rounded, disciplined man of integrity. We do not know when Joseph died; various commentators suggest that it occurred soon after the Temple experience because he is not mentioned again in the Bible text. Jesus succeeded naturally to Joseph's position, becoming both the carpenter of Nazareth and the provider for a household of eight (Mary, Jesus and at least six other children).

As I have mentioned, this shows the practical meaning behind Philippians 2, where Paul speaks of Jesus humbling Himself, making Himself of no reputation, taking the form of a servant and coming in the likeness of men. Jesus was God manifest in the flesh, the Son of God who became the Son of man. Jesus was divine because He was born of God; born of Mary, He was also human.[18]

In Hebrews 1 we are told that, as the Son of God, Jesus was superior to the angels; as the Son of man, He was not as great as the angels. Hebrews 2:17 adds that Jesus was made like His brethren ("in every way," NIV), and that He was perfected through suffering (see 2:10). He was "our brother" (2:11–12) and partook of the same things we do (2:14).

Small wonder that Paul exclaimed in 1 Timothy 3:16: "And without controversy great is the mystery of godliness: God was manifested in the flesh. . . ." For our study, the next phrase in this text as expressed in the New American Standard Bible and the New International Version is particularly notable: We are told that Jesus was "vindicated" in or by the Holy Spirit. This means, I believe, that His ministry was proven or declared authentic by the Holy Spirit's activity.[19]

The theme of our ensuing chapters will be that Jesus was proven/approved/authenticated in His later earthly ministry by the power of the Holy Spirit upon and within Him. Acts 10:38 confirms this thought: "God anointed Jesus of Nazareth with the Holy Spirit and with power, who went about doing good and healing all who were oppressed by the devil, for God was with Him." Also notice Acts 2:22: ". . . Jesus of Nazareth, a Man attested by God to you by miracles, wonders, and signs which God did through Him in your midst."

Life in Nazareth, Void of the Miraculous

Jesus' boyhood and young manhood were not marked with miraculous happenings, apart from the common blessings of devout living. His parents, siblings, friends and relatives never saw Jesus perform a miracle until His thirtieth year, which was after His baptism with the Holy Spirit. If He had healed the sick or performed other miracles beforehand, His fame would have broken out immediately and the divine plan been thwarted. He would have had to perform His ministry as a begotten, divine Son rather than an *anointed,* begotten, divine Son. This would have robbed the Church of our sterling example of the perfect prototype "Spirit-filled" Son of man.

Nevertheless, the Spirit worked powerfully through His divine nature to produce the godly qualities and attributes that would be the foundation for His later ministry. His personality and poise undoubtedly drew people to Him, but His reputation in Nazareth was that of "the carpenter's son." He grew up among them and His kindly ways and deep piety were simply taken for granted as marks of a superbly spiritual man. Through His obedience to parents and the will of God, Jesus not only was "filled" with wisdom and favor (see Luke 2:40), but He continued to progress and mature in these aspects of development (see Luke 2:52).[20] Fulton J. Sheen comments: "Human development of the God-man unfolded in the village so naturally that not even the townspeople were conscious of the greatness of Him Who dwelled in their midst."[21]

His was a hard, plain life in a small, rural, insignificant village—harsh country living with simplicity of meals, dress and manners. It was an inauspicious beginning for the King of the earth and Savior of the world. Later, a doubter expressed everyone's attitude: "Can any good thing come out of Nazareth?"

Jesus assumed responsibility for His family and sat as head of the household—offering family prayers; explaining life, nature, the Jewish feasts and customs; sharing His own spiritually awakening thoughts from Scripture; working at grinding, physical labor. Somehow, He also prepared for the call to messianic ministry burning in His heart. Some commentators picture Him laboring at His workbench with a borrowed scroll of Scripture spread out beside Him. Perhaps so. It was probably at this time that He developed His lifelong habit of "prayer-walking" in the solitary hills.

Invisibly and personally, the Holy Spirit was at work—just as happens in the life of a person who is spiritually "born again."

e.g. name identity
team

Mary's Secret

Was Jesus ever told about His virgin birth in Bethlehem? No one knows for sure, of course, but it does seem logical that the whole story was explained to Him. Mary must have made Him aware of the astonishing activity of the Holy Spirit. Surely Jesus heard about Zacharias and Elizabeth and their miracle son—especially about the prophecy concerning John's being a forerunner of the Messiah. Jewish children were named with prophetic conviction and challenged to live up to parental expectations. To be named by an angel, as John and Jesus were, could hardly go unmentioned. Jesus must have known when John began to live in the wilderness, awaiting the call of God to introduce Him. It is possible that Jesus could have met John and talked to him about these things.

If Mary could conceive and bear Jesus at the approximate age of fifteen—and handle the responsibility connected with it—does it not seem likely that Jesus would be capable, as a teenager, of hearing about those awesome developments? The episode of Jesus in the Temple would undoubtedly prompt Mary to pass on the whole, grand story, if she had not already done so.

Surely it was important for Jesus to hear Joseph tell the secret kept deep in his heart: his perspective on the divine conception out of wedlock, the flight into Egypt, the prophecy by aged Simeon in the Temple. Such things Jesus should know, especially since unwarranted criticism might come against Him and the parents from time to time. As a developing young man, divinely captive to human limitations, Jesus had to acquire knowledge gradually.

The Messianic Consciousness

Jesus, in His teens and then in His twenties, sat in the synagogue along with the other devout men and women of Nazareth. He prayed, chanted Scripture portions and listened to the homilies and explanations. Undoubtedly He was asked to read the Torah from time to time.

One biblical topic—the coming Messiah—was of great interest to every Jew, and Jesus would not have been an exception. When would the Messiah come? When and how would the Kingdom of God come? The reading of messianic Scripture passages in the synagogue, such as the four "Servant Songs of Isaiah,"[22] must have particularly stirred His heart, creating deep and serious contemplation. Surely awareness dawned within Him that He was that One upon whom the Spirit would come. This consciousness, along with every blossoming human faculty, surged toward maturity of His total being.

Consider how He might have pondered the following Scriptures, knowing that these would be fulfilled in the Messiah!

- "The Spirit of the LORD shall rest upon Him" (Isaiah 11:2).
- "Behold! My Servant whom I uphold, My Elect One in whom My soul delights! I have put My Spirit upon Him" (Isaiah 42:1).
- "GOD and His Spirit have sent Me" (Isaiah 48:16); "The Lord GOD has sent Me, and His Spirit" (NASB); "And now the Sovereign LORD has sent me, with his Spirit" (NIV).
- "The Spirit of the Lord GOD is upon Me" (Isaiah 61:1).

Jesus later quoted copiously from the Psalms, so we might assume that they were the source of some of His deepest reflections, the life-giving food for His soul. Can you imagine the feelings of this sensitive young man as He grew more mature and attuned to the Holy Spirit—and read such passages as the messianic Psalms[23] or tried to apply the profound Psalm 40:6–8 to Himself? Consider, too, how He must have pondered deeply the prophetic passages that described the Messiah as the Righteous Branch of David.[24]

Jesus, man of the Word, overcame the devil in the wilderness by quoting from Deuteronomy from memory. His Sermon on the Mount showed remarkable understanding of the commandments of God and their deeper intent. His discussions often began with "Have you not read," thus demonstrating an amazing grasp of Hebrew Scripture. All this biblical information—along with His profound reflections—brought completeness and continuity to Jesus' spiritual foundation.

As Jesus approached His thirtieth year, the messianic Scriptures had bonded with times of prayer and reflection, bringing Him to an indisputable conclusion: He could do nothing apart from the power of the Holy Spirit upon Him. As He has been subject to His parents and then to His family responsibilities, so He as the Messiah must now be totally subject to the leadership of the Holy Spirit.

Things natural and spiritual came together in brilliant comprehension, and Jesus, Son of God and Son of man, readied Himself for the divine call.

He knew, every part of Him knew, two stunning realities: one, He was the divine Son of God who would die for the sins of the world; and, two, He was the awaited Messiah, the One upon whom the Holy Spirit would reside. It was probably at the point that He reached the height of realization, that He heard the heavenly summons.

REVIEW QUESTIONS FOR CHAPTER 1

1. Name six Jewish adults in whom the Holy Spirit worked during the time of Jesus' birth and early infancy.
2. Why do you think the Messiah grew up in such an obscure village?
3. What were the two main ingredients of Jesus' education? Does this have a counterpart in education in American homes and schools?
4. How would you describe the interaction of the boy Jesus with the Temple teachers?
5. Why was it necessary for Jesus to be subject to parents and human limitations?
6. How do you think the messianic passages in Isaiah affected Jesus?

2

JESUS' MINISTRY
WHAT HE LEARNED, LIVED AND TAUGHT

IN THIS CHAPTER

- Find out how John knew when to start preaching
- Learn what two things persuaded John that Jesus was the Messiah
- Read what the Hebrew Scriptures taught Jesus about the Spirit
- Consider what it means to be born again
- Discover what it means to blaspheme the Holy Spirit

*E*ighteen years of labor as a craftsman have passed from the time of Jesus' episode with the teachers in the Temple. He has reached His thirtieth year, still working and living in Nazareth; the siblings have grown up. Cousin John, also thirty years old, lives a severe, ascetic life in the desert. Both men

*await the word from God that will ignite their ministries—and bring renewal
to Israel and salvation to the nations.*

*It is a moment of great consequence. The time line of mankind's human
history is about to be intersected by the prophetic purposes of almighty God.
Two young men, prepared by God, will be used by the Holy Spirit to close one
divine era and open another.*

THE CALL

Luke, beloved physician and historian, realizing that the Call that brought
Jesus and John together was world-shaking in dimension, established for
posterity exactly when it took place. Luke also showed God's disregard for
the high and mighty of this world in His choice of the humble.

> In the fifteenth year of the rule of Caesar Tiberius—it was while Pontius
> Pilate was governor of Judea; Herod, ruler of Galilee; his brother Phillip,
> ruler of Iturea and Trachonitis; Lysanias, ruler of Abilene; during the Chief-
> Priesthood of Annas and Ciaphas—John, Zachariah's son, out in the desert
> at the time, received a message [the Word] from God.
>
> Luke 3:1–2, MESSAGE

The young man John—gaunt from a spartan diet of locusts and wild
honey, bronzed by the sun and wind—prayed much in his solitary abode.
His manner of life "in the Spirit" had become as normative as his abstinence
from alcoholic drink. The prophetic word, given at the time of his birth
by his father, undoubtedly hung on him heavily. Even his name, meaning
"the Lord is gracious," was reason for serious reflection.

He waited in the desert, God's careful choice for his preparation. George
M. Lamsa, native of that part of the world, gives this description of the wilderness. It becomes easy to see why God placed John in such a setting.

> Even though the desert lacks trees, villages, and the attractions which make
> life happy and important in populous centers, it has its own natural majestic
> beauty. The celestial bodies pour on it their limitless light of majestic glory.
> The blue sky with its brilliant stars looks like a painted ceiling. It is in these
> beautiful spots that the Arabs and other Nomadic people live. . . . Living in
> these wide open desert spaces, one is impressed by the vastness of the heavens

contrasted with the smallness of the earth and life is revealed in its proper proportion to the universe. Away from the material things of organized civilization, the dweller of the desert feels that God is near, God is everywhere. God is seen in the natural and mystical beauty and his presence is felt to a far greater extent here than by the inhabitants of the cities.[1]

The Call was a word from God, a divine summons that dropped like a blazing meteor from heaven upon the solitary figure waiting in the wilderness of Judea. John's experience was a repeat of Ezekiel 1:3: "The word of the LORD came expressly to Ezekiel . . . in the land of the Chaldeans . . . and the hand of the LORD was upon him there."

I had an experience at a popular restaurant that could somewhat illustrate John's Call. Since there was a thirty-minute wait, I was handed an electronic device that would summon me when a table was available. This was my first experience with such a gadget, so I walked away wondering how I would know when the time had come. I need not have worried! When the table was ready, the caller vibrated in my hand and a series of red lights began flashing. A table was ready!

John had no electronic gadget, but he did have a sensitive, prophetic nature attuned to the Holy Spirit. He prayed. He waited in an environment stripped of distractions and filled (especially at night) with awe-inspiring, mind-stretching displays of divine pageantry. Suddenly, in the Spirit, the buzzer and lights went off. When this happens, a person knows—and nothing can disprove it. There was no question; it was time to begin.

That summons, coupled with Gabriel's announcement and Zacharias's prophecy, included the following instructions to this thirty-year-old firebrand of the desert. He was to go public in a big way!

- The Messiah was about to appear in Israel, and John must announce His coming and prepare His way
- John would be called "the prophet of the Highest"
- The Baptist was the fulfillment of Isaiah 40:3–5; he was "the voice" in the wilderness, crying out, "Prepare the way of the LORD!"
- John was to go before the Messiah in the spirit and power of Elijah, turning hearts of the fathers to the children, the disobedient to the wisdom of the just—to make ready a people prepared for the Lord

- John was to call Israel to repentance, both the lowly and the high-and-mighty, by preaching throughout the Jordan Valley and immersing the repentant in water
- His message? The Kingdom of God is at hand! He was to bring salvation knowledge, to give light and to give guidance
- John was to announce that his baptizing in water was a precursor to the Messiah's "baptism with the Holy Spirit and fire"
- John would recognize the Messiah because he would see the Holy Spirit come upon Him in the waters of baptism and remain on Him
- He was to bring a new definition of who Israel was (see Luke 3:8)
- Finally, John must gradually fade from the religious scene and the Messiah must take center stage

John headed for the busiest places he could think of. Since he would preach repentance to Israel, what better place to station himself than at the busy caravan crossings of the Jordan? The travelers would carry his message far and wide—and the river furnished a great baptismal font! This would much better suit his purpose than Jerusalem or the Temple.

JESUS' DUAL BAPTISM

They were two humble men—one a manual laborer, the other a desert dweller—and both were tough and strong. Jesus and John were also both single and possibly knew each other.[2] They were the products of miraculous births. They were men of prayer and knew the sacred Scriptures in personal ways unknown to the rabbis. Now, both (each in his own place) realized that it was God's time to visit His people.

Thousands of Jews flocked to the waters of Jordan to be baptized by the impressive prophet with uncut hair and clothes of camel's hair and a leather belt. Known as the Voice, John proclaimed his uncompromising message to the crowds with extraordinary results. He also waited patiently for a particular figure to appear, the Messiah, the One upon whom the Spirit would descend (see John 1:32). Finally, Jesus did arrive at the Jordan . . . and waded out into the water toward the Baptist.

They faced each other: the greatest prophet of the old era, a Nazarite filled with the Spirit since birth, and the greatest prophet of the new era, the Messiah, conceived of the Spirit and now to be baptized with the Spirit. The immersion in the Jordan was a sacred moment. Luke recorded it happening "while He [Jesus] prayed" (Luke 3:21). With trembling hands, the Voice lowered the Word into the water. Righteousness was being fulfilled in Jesus' act of submission to all the prophets and the Scriptures.

A twofold confirmation left no doubt in John's mind that this was the Messiah, bearer of the Holy Spirit. First, the Spirit descended as an alighting dove upon Jesus. Heaven's anointing oil, the actual Spirit, invisibly flowed over Jesus making Him the Christ—the Anointed One—in the fullest sense of the word. The bird, both a vision and a prophecy, was seen by Jesus and John only, but described later by John (see John 1:32). (Ever since, the dove has been considered a symbol of the Holy Spirit. Actually, for Jesus the dove was more a symbol of sacrifice and a sign of His own impending death since such birds were the prescribed sacrifice of the poor. The joyous moment had the shadow of the coming Cross cast upon it.)

Second, the Father's voice from heaven affirmed Jesus: "You are My beloved Son; in You I am well pleased" (Luke 3:22). Jesus surely stood enraptured for a moment in the Jordan, overwhelmed that He was indeed the Son of man and the Son of God:

- Divinely conceived
- Sanctified by immersion in water
- Anointed by baptism with the Holy Spirit

Thus, a pattern was given us in Jesus (the prototype) that would be foundational to the experience of the early Church:

1. spiritual birth
2. water baptism
3. baptism with the Holy Spirit

WHAT JESUS LEARNED ABOUT THE SPIRIT FROM SCRIPTURE

Before continuing with our discussion of Jesus' ministry and teaching, it seems appropriate to pause and note some of the verses about the Holy Spirit in the Hebrew Scriptures that would have influenced Him. I am impressed by the variety of thought on the Holy Spirit given in 108 verses of the Old Testament.

Jesus learned well from the life experiences of the Hebrew saints. It is obvious, however, that Jesus moved past the less interactive, sovereign miracles of those times into a warmer, personal relationship with the Holy Spirit. Thomas L. Holdcroft observes: "[I]n general, the Old Testament ministry of the Spirit was restricted to the sovereign works of God. He was not the promised one of the New Testament era whose provisions were to be claimed by the believer."[3]

"Filled with the Spirit"

The expression *filled with the Spirit* is used in both Old and New Testaments. Along with the expressions *put the Spirit within* and *the Spirit entered,* it means to be influenced, directed, empowered by the Spirit. We read of this experience happening to the following individuals:

Bezalel, an artisan (Exodus 31:3; 35:31)

Joshua, leader of God's people (Deuteronomy 34:9; Joshua 27:18)

God's people themselves (Isaiah 63:11; Ezekiel 11:19; 36:26–27; 37:14)

Ezekiel, a prophet (Ezekiel 2:2; 3:24)

"The Spirit Came Upon"

This terminology, along with the phrases *poured upon* and *fell upon,* emphasizes the immediacy and urgency of the experience. It shows God blessing from His superior position. It also shows the Spirit's presence to be an overwhelming experience. The following experienced this:

God's people (Leviticus 8:12; Isaiah 32:15; 40:13; 44:3; Ezekiel 39:29; Joel 2:28–29; Zechariah 12:10)

Elders (Numbers 11:17, 25–26, 29)

Balaam, a practitioner of divination (Numbers 24:2)

Judges: Othniel (Judges 3:10); Gideon (Judges 6:34); Jephthah (Judges 11:29); Samson (Judges 13:25; 14:6, 19; 15:14)

Saul, a king (1 Samuel 10:6, 10; 11:6; 19:23)

Saul's messengers (1 Samuel 19:20)

David, anointed as king (1 Samuel 16:13)

Prophets: Elisha (2 Kings 2:9, 15); Amasai (1 Chronicles 12:18); Azariah (2 Chronicles 15:1); Jahaziel (2 Chronicles 20:14); Zechariah (2 Chronicles 24:20); Ezekiel (Ezekiel 11:5)

The Spirit in the Prophets

The prophets, God's spokesmen in the Old Testament, were the most common recipients of divine visitation. Hebrews 1:1 says: "Long ago God spoke many times and in many ways to our ancestors through the prophets" (NLT). (See 2 Samuel 23:2; 1 Chronicles 28:12; Nehemiah 9:30; Micah 3:8; and Zechariah 7:12.)

Divine Characteristics of the Spirit

The Scriptures gave Jesus insights about the divinity of the Holy Spirit. He is:

Omnipotent (Psalm 104:29–30; Micah 2:7; Zechariah 4:6)

Omniscient (Isaiah 40:13)

Omnipresent (Psalm 139:7)

In addition the Holy Spirit is portrayed as being:

Good (Psalm 143:10; Nehemiah 9:20)

Generous (Psalm 51:12)

Tangibly present in the world (Genesis 1:2; 6:3; Psalm 51:11; Isaiah 4:4; 59:19; Haggai 2:5)

Other expressions clearly refer to the Holy Spirit:

Breath of God (Genesis 2:7; Job 27:3; 33:4; 34:14; Isaiah 40:7; 42:5; Ezekiel 37:9–10)

Hand of the Lord (Ezra 7:6, 9, 28; 8:18, 22, 31; Isaiah 31:3; Ezekiel 37:1)

Wisdom (Proverbs 1:23)

The Messianic Prophecies

As discussed in chapter 1, Scripture declares that the Messiah would have the Spirit. (See Isaiah 11:2; 42:1; 48:16; 59:21; and 61:1.) Matthew quoted Isaiah 42:1 as applying to Jesus: "I have put My Spirit upon Him; He will bring forth justice to the Gentiles."

People Can Rebel against the Spirit

Ever since Adam's fall, the human race has been in some form of rebellion against God. The prophets were constantly challenging Israel for having "abandoned" God. (See Genesis: 6:3; 1 Samuel 16:14; Psalm 106:33; and Isaiah 63:10.)

As Jesus pondered the work of the Spirit in creation, in the lives of the great leaders of Israel, in the amazing prophets and miracles, and particularly the messianic prophecies, a consciousness of dependence was awakened within Him. Without the Holy Spirit, He could do nothing.

This realization was critical to Jesus' ministry. No sooner had He received the Holy Spirit than that dependence was tested in the greatest battle of His life.

JESUS' RELIANCE ON THE SPIRIT

Newly anointed of the Spirit, Jesus was directed into the solitary wilderness. Mark says the Spirit "drove Him," which suggests urgency. For the next forty days Jesus fasted and prayed alone. That is, He had no human companionship but "was with the wild beasts" (Mark 1:13). As A. T. Robertson points out, "It was the haunt at night of the wolf, the boar, the hyena, the jackal, the leopard. It was lonely and depressing in its isolation and even dangerous."[4] Angels, however, did come and minister to Him. The whole scene seems reminiscent of Daniel in the lions' den—or might it have been more like Adam (before sin) in control of the animals in the Garden?

Jesus was led to that forsaken place for a specific reason: "to be tempted by the devil" (Matthew 4:1). The meeting of Jesus and Satan was a battle of inestimable importance: If Jesus should fail, if He should give in to temptation even for a moment, all would be lost. The evil spirit hurled temptations that no man before was able to withstand. And in each case, the Son of man, empowered by the Holy Spirit and the Word of God, overcame them.

The personal strength derived from thirty years of maturing in the Spirit coupled with the empowering of the Spirit at Jordan enabled Jesus to trust totally in God and conquer the enemy bent on His destruction.

Jesus' coming ministry would be geared to expelling the powers of evil, so it was most fitting that at the very beginning of ministry He vanquish the archenemy Himself. As Mark 3:27 states: "No one can enter a strong man's house and plunder his goods, unless he first binds the strong man, and then he will plunder his house." If the very root of evil and rebellion could be conquered, then all evil forces must succumb as well. Scriptures like Zechariah 4:6, used by saints through the ages, would have directed Him: "'Not by might nor by power, but by My Spirit,' says the LORD of hosts." As we know, Jesus—despite His weakened physical condition—prevailed by using God's Word in the power of the Spirit. As Henry Swete has said: "[I]t cannot be doubted that the Spirit which urged the Lord to the conflict with Satan strengthened Him for it and carried Him through."[5]

Proclaiming Freedom

"Then Jesus returned in the power of the Spirit to Galilee" (Luke 4:14).

The impression given by the accounts of Matthew, Mark and Luke is that Jesus left the wilderness and returned immediately to Galilee. Actually, the first four, perhaps five, chapters of John must be inserted before that point, as is noted in any harmony of the gospels. Jesus ministered publicly and privately, speaking to Nicodemus and the Samaritan woman at the well among others. But, when He did begin ministry in Galilee, He came in "the power of the Spirit"—the secret of His great success. "News of Him went out through all the surrounding region. And He taught in their synagogues, being glorified by all" (Luke 4:14–15). Then, Luke tells us, He came to Nazareth, where He had been brought up.

Announcement in Nazareth

The news must have swept through the town like a wind-driven fire. Jesus was in Nazareth! The beloved carpenter, known and esteemed by all, would speak in the synagogue and perform the miraculous. There must have been great excitement on that Sabbath when the whole town turned out to hear their now famous local boy speak. W. Phillip Keller says of Jesus at this time: "At the end of His first year of public ministry He was easily the most popular person in Palestine."[6]

At the synagogue, Jesus was asked to read a passage of Scripture and make comment. He chose the messianic passage from Isaiah 61. (Interestingly, I. Howard Marshall states that this passage "may well have been spoken by him as his typical 'synagogue sermon' in a variety of places.")[7]

"The Spirit of the LORD is upon Me,
Because He has anointed Me to preach the gospel to the poor;
He has sent Me to heal the brokenhearted,
To proclaim liberty to the captives
And recovery of sight to the blind,
To set at liberty those who are oppressed;
To proclaim the acceptable year of the LORD."

Luke 4:18–19

Stopping mid-sentence after the words, "To proclaim the acceptable year of the Lord," Jesus rolled up the scroll.[8] He sat down as the custom was and began to speak. He startled His hometown friends with three thoughts. First, He made the text from Isaiah His personal ministry statement—what His preaching and ministry was to accomplish—and the fact that it would be possible because "The Spirit of the LORD is upon Me." The focus of His Spirit-enabling would be on:

1. Proclamation: Good news! This is God's acceptable time
2. Healing: He would heal the brokenhearted and restore sight to the blind
3. Liberation: He would set free the captive and the oppressed

Second, He said something about this text that no other rabbi had said: "Today this Scripture is fulfilled in your hearing." He made the Scripture personal! He said it was happening before their very eyes!

The crowd marveled at His gracious words—until He made His third point: that prophets are not accepted in their own countries, giving Elijah and Elisha as examples of prophets who ministered to non-Hebrews. The people were so angered at this they threw Him out of the city with the intention of hurling Him down a cliff. He passed through the mob and went His way.

Jesus' Ministry in the Spirit

Jesus' preaching and teaching would be characterized by "authority"— something woefully lacking in the rabbis and religious authorities of that day. That authority would be His because of an awareness of the Spirit's presence and His unwavering dedication to do only the will of the Father.[9] It is possible to preach with consciousness of the anointing of the Spirit, and what a difference that empowerment makes!

Acts 10:38 gives this summary of Jesus' activity: "God anointed Jesus of Nazareth with the Holy Spirit and with power, who went about doing good and healing all who were oppressed by the devil, for God was with Him." Paul indicated that the works of the Spirit wrought through Jesus were the vindication of His ministry (see 1 Timothy 3:16).

Let's look briefly at this ministry in action.

Anointed Preaching

Jesus said: "It is the Spirit who gives life; the flesh profits nothing. The words that I speak to you are spirit, and they are life" (John 6:63). John the Baptist said: "For He whom God has sent speaks the words of God, for God does not give the Spirit by measure" (John 3:34).

Jesus learned the secret of preaching with anointing. Paul later described this preaching as "of the Spirit; for the letter kills, but the Spirit gives life" (2 Corinthians 3:6). Jesus did not concentrate on laborious, textual examination; He fed the people with a current Word that would help them in their life experiences. His substance was significant, of course, but the uniqueness and forte of His proclamations lay in the force of Holy Spirit delivery.

Miraculous Works

First John 3:8 declares: "For this purpose the Son of God was manifested, that He might destroy the works of the devil." Even more importantly, Jesus revealed the works of the Father:

"The words that I speak to you I do not speak on my own authority; but the Father who dwells in Me does the works. Believe Me that I am in the

Father and the Father in Me, or else believe Me for the sake of the works themselves."

John 14:10–11

Jesus performed many healings and miracles that are not recorded in the gospels (see John 20:30; 21:25), but 35 specific miracles are.[10] They describe bodily cures—how He healed a paralytic, a blind man, a woman with a hemorrhage. They tell of overcoming forces of nature—how He calmed a storm and fed thousands with one little boy's lunch. They show Him curing demoniacs and raising the dead. Miracles were used of God to authenticate Jesus' mission of healing and liberation; to prove He was from God; and, of course, to express God's sympathy for the suffering.

Joyful Worship

Jesus enjoyed God. One interesting example occurred when the seventy disciples returned from a mission where they had successfully exercised power over unclean spirits. They were jubilant! Luke 10:21 states: "In that hour Jesus rejoiced in the Spirit and said, 'I thank You, Father, Lord of heaven and earth, that You have hidden these things from the wise and prudent and revealed them to babes.'" Jesus demonstrated what it means to worship in the Spirit (John 4:23–24). He had more than mere human joy over the success of His disciples; this rush of exaltation came to Him "in the Spirit."

Since Jesus worshiped in the Spirit, it seems logical that He also prayed in the Spirit. Sometimes the question is raised—because praying in the Spirit in 1 Corinthians 14 is associated with speaking in tongues—whether or not Jesus spoke in tongues. The Bible does not say whether He did or He did not speak in tongues, so any comments would have to be conjecture. I think that He very possibly did, but not for public observation or record since tongues were particularly reserved for the Age of the Holy Spirit. This gift of the Spirit—never manifested in the Old Testament—was to be uniquely identified with the Church. As Jesus told His followers: "And these signs will follow those who believe: . . . they will speak with new tongues" (Mark 16:17).

When Jesus ascended to the Father and poured out His Spirit on the Day of Pentecost, tongues of fire settled on all of the disciples—just as the dove had settled on Jesus. The tongues of fire were then transformed into

Spirit-empowered languages not learned by the disciples. This, then, became the normative experience and manifestation of the baptism with the Holy Spirit in the early Church. Although Jesus may not have spoken in tongues (because the time had not yet come), He does now speak in tongues through the Spirit in His disciples! More on this in Part 2 of the book.

Jesus' Teaching on the Spirit

Some 290 verses in the New Testament refer specifically to the Holy Spirit. Fifty-nine of those verses are in the four gospels, so Jesus obviously shared His experience of the Spirit in teaching. Seven things about the Spirit are mentioned below that seemed important to Jesus.

Necessity of Spiritual Birth

Jesus answered and said to him, "Most assuredly, I say to you, unless one is born again, he cannot see the kingdom of God. . . . Unless one is born of water and the Spirit, he cannot enter the kingdom of God. . . . That which is born of the Spirit is spirit. . . . So is everyone who is born of the Spirit."

John 3:3, 5–6, 8

In a discussion with Nicodemus, a Pharisee, Jesus presented a new approach to the Kingdom of God. The Jews of that day, probably because of the Roman occupation, were politically oriented. Jesus made it clear that there must be an inner change of heart, accomplished by the Holy Spirit. This was more than a metaphor; Jesus was describing reality. It happens because the human heart is impregnated by the Spirit of God (see Romans 8:1–11). We are born physically into natural life. We are born spiritually into the life of the Spirit, which is life in the Kingdom of God.

Worship in Spirit and Truth

"But the hour is coming, and now is, when the true worshipers will worship the Father in spirit and truth; for the Father is seeking such to worship Him. God is Spirit, and those who worship Him must worship in spirit and truth."

John 4:23–24

A Samaritan woman talked with Jesus by a well, and she attempted to provoke an argument over worship. Jesus made it clear that neither the Samaritan temple nor the Jewish Temple held the real answer. True worship involves the Holy Spirit. I would like to quote from my book *Worship God!*

> If we interpret Jesus' expression "in spirit and truth" to mean heartfelt worship, or sincere worship, or worship with a right motive, etc., the meaning becomes confused. Sincere, motivated people are in all religions. The Samaritan woman is a good example. However, capitalize Spirit (as many leading commentators suggest) and it becomes immediately apparent that Jesus referred to a Spirit-enabled worship that mankind had not yet experienced "for the Spirit was not yet given" (John 7:39). Spirit-enabled worship did exist at that time ("and now is"), because Jesus presented it to the Father. An unusual confirmation of this is found in the Gospel of Luke [10:21, as explained above]. . . . The hour that "is coming" took place later on the day of Pentecost when the Holy Spirit came upon the church for the first time. Jesus meant that true worship—exemplified in His own life—would become possible within the church, and it actually happened.[11]

Blasphemy of the Holy Spirit

"Therefore I say to you, every sin and blasphemy will be forgiven men, but the blasphemy against the Spirit will not be forgiven men. Anyone who speaks a word against the Son of Man, it will be forgiven him; but whoever speaks against the Holy Spirit, it will not be forgiven him, either in this age or in the age to come."

Matthew 12:31–32

The Pharisees were slandering Jesus because He cast evil spirits out of people. They said He did it by the power and authority of Beelzebub (a title indicating the ruler of demons). These were religious professionals who were hardened toward the things of God. The text implies that they knew that Jesus performed miracles by the Holy Spirit, but they still argued that it was by the devil's power. This deliberate blasphemy is unforgivable, so Jesus issued a strong warning; rebels must know that there is a point of no forgiveness. (See also Mark 3:28–30 and Luke 12:10.)

Prophetic Expectation

Jesus foretold that there would be times in which persecuted Christians would be brought into courts of law against their will, times in which they would be expected to defend themselves without time for preparation. Jesus assured His followers that they were not to worry in that event because the Spirit of the Lord would give wisdom and prophetic words adequate to the challenge. (See Matthew 10:20; Mark 13:11; and Luke 12:12.)

Inspiration of Scripture

Jesus believed that the men who wrote the Bible did so by the inspiration and enlightenment of the Holy Spirit. Note Matthew 22:43: "He said to them, 'How then does David in the Spirit call Him "Lord," . . . ?'" Also, Mark 12:36: "For David himself said by the Holy Spirit. . . ."

Association of Spirit with Father and Son

Jesus associated the Father, Son and Holy Spirit. The classic text is Matthew 28:19: "Go therefore and make disciples of all the nations, baptizing them in the name of the Father and of the Son and of the Holy Spirit."

Promise of the Spirit

"He who believes in Me, as the Scripture has said, out of his heart will flow rivers of living water." But this He spoke concerning the Spirit, whom those believing in Him would receive; for the Holy Spirit was not yet given, because Jesus was not yet glorified.

John 7:38–39

The Holy Spirit was active in the Old Testament period; the Bible makes that clear. Jesus' intention here was to clarify that the Holy Spirit functioned in ancient times in accordance with the dealings and purposes of God. The New Testament era was a new time, one in which everyone could have the Holy Spirit living within. In Old Testament times, God moved sovereignly from time to time by His Spirit, usually on prophets, priests or kings. When God launched the Church Age, He did so by filling His believers with the Holy Spirit, regardless of who they were.

We end here our narrative of events in Jesus' life—how He was prepared as a young man, how He fulfilled all righteousness in His submission to water and Holy Spirit baptisms, how He lived and taught by dependence on the Holy Spirit. Jesus surrendered in death the way He had lived life, under the direction and guidance of the Holy Spirit. Look at His obedience—and the importance of the Holy Spirit in His final actions on earth before ascending to the Father:

> Jesus went to and endured the cross by the Spirit (see Hebrews 9:14)
>
> Jesus was resurrected by the Spirit (Romans 8:11; 1 Peter 3:18)
>
> Jesus preached to the spirits by the Spirit (1 Peter 3:19)
>
> Jesus gave commandments to His followers by the Spirit (Acts 1:2)
>
> Jesus breathed on His disciples and said, "Receive the Holy Spirit" (John 20:22)
>
> Jesus sent the Holy Spirit to His followers (John 16:7; Acts 2:33)

When Jesus was glorified (resurrected and ascended), a new dispensation was opened in the dealings of God. The glorified Jesus poured out His Spirit on His people so that the indwelling Spirit might both be a personal blessing and also flow out to others, like a current of water.

In the next chapter we will present Jesus' teaching on the Holy Spirit as a paraclete or helper. Then, in Part 2, we will discuss the wonderful promise that Jesus will baptize us with the Holy Spirit.

REVIEW QUESTIONS FOR CHAPTER 2

1. What are some of the ways that God calls people?
2. What Old Testament concept of the Holy Spirit impresses you most?
3. Can we overcome Satan as easily as Jesus seemed to do?
4. Was it easy for Him?
5. Did any one of Jesus' teachings on the Holy Spirit particularly appeal to you?

3

JESUS' PROMISE
THE HOLY SPIRIT WILL COME

IN THIS CHAPTER

- Consider the word *paraclete* (not parakeet!)
- Learn the deeper meaning of Comforter
- Find out why we are better off with Jesus "gone"
- Discover what Jesus really promised us

The disciples were given quite a shock at the Last Supper with Jesus in the Upper Room (see John 14–16). Two startling announcements were made:

- Jesus was about to leave them
- His replacement—the Holy Spirit!—would arrive shortly

These breaking news items, withheld until the very eve of the crucifixion, naturally caused surprise, concern and even consternation.

Jesus specifically assured them in John 14:18 that they would not be left as orphans (or, as F. F. Bruce says, "bereft of their natural supporter").[1] It was normal for disciples of a teacher to be called his children (see Galatians 4:19; 1 John 2:1; 3:18); so, if the father-teacher should leave, his followers would be like abandoned orphans.

John Rea points out that by using this terminology, Jesus was assuring them that He Himself would come back in the Person of the Holy Spirit. This meant that Christ was not excluded from their lives because of the Spirit's arrival; rather, Jesus' continuous presence and fellowship would be more real (see John 14:21–23).[2] "One of His [the Holy Spirit's] most lovable characteristics," wrote Catherine Marshall, "is that He deliberately submerges Himself in Jesus; He works at being inconspicuous."[3] The Spirit would care for them, comfort them, support them, help them and explain things to them. Jesus promised them that the Holy Spirit would come, and it would be as though Jesus Himself were present!

Jesus enthusiastically shared some amazing insights on His successor, all of which came from personal life experience. He knew firsthand the personality, the loving care and the helpfulness of this coming Friend. He had received ministry in the same way the disciples would be strengthened and supported. Jesus was such a great strength and help to the disciples because He had been helped in such excellent manner by the very One who would replace Him. His endorsement was without reservation!

INTRODUCTION OF A NEW TERM, *PARAKLETOS*

The Greek word *parakletos* (*paraclete* in English) is introduced four times in the Farewell Discourse (see John 14:16, 26; 15:26; 16:7) and means "someone who is called alongside to help."[4] When you need help and cannot help yourself, a paraclete is someone who can step in and do what is needed. The work *parakletos* emphasizes the unique ministry and future relationship of the Holy Spirit in a believer's life. Only John in the New Testament records this term, and then only in one other place, 1 John 2:1.

Catholic scholar George T. Montague suggests this basic meaning:

The English word Paraclete is a rendering of the Greek parakletos which in turn is derived from the verb para-kalein meaning literally "to call to one's side." Thus in the most radical sense of the word a paraclete is an advocate, a helper or spokesman or more precisely a lawyer who will plead on one's behalf. In Paul and in the Acts, the verb parakalein often means to exhort, encourage, less frequently to comfort.[5]

Wilbur Smith says "the Paraklete is one who comes to our side to help us, strengthen us, encourage us, to support us in moments of weakness, and counsel us in the difficulties of life."[6] C. F. D. Moule describes the Holy Spirit paraclete as "a champion or representative—an advocate."[7] Greek scholar Kenneth S. Wuest says the Spirit's "many-sided work can be summed up in the phrase 'one called in to stand by and give aid.'"[8] John Rea gives this interesting explanation: "A paraclete is like an intimate friend who acts as a personal adviser, such as an aide-de-camp, special consultant or private assistant to an emperor or a president."[9]

An Upgrade for Comforter

The word comforter is the well-known King James translation of *parakletos,* but it really needs updating in our day. William Barclay shares this helpful insight: "We often call the Holy Spirit the Comforter. That word goes back to Wycliffe; but in Wycliffe's day it had a different meaning. It comes from the Latin *fortis,* which means brave; and the Comforter is the one who fills men with courage and with strength."[10]

A. B. Simpson, founder of the Christian and Missionary Alliance, remarks how inadequate *Comforter* is. He feels that it

> is not a very happy translation. The Greek word . . . literally means "a God at hand, One by our side, One that we may call upon in every emergency." . . . [T]he Holy Spirit is represented to us as the present and all-sufficient God. Of course, there is comfort, infinite comfort in all this; but the primary idea is not so much spiritual enjoyment, as practical efficiency and sufficiency for every occasion and emergency that arises. . . . The Holy Spirit is—God for everything. God at hand under all circumstances and equal to all demands.[11]

English Words for Parakletos

The large number of usable, synonymous words (25 suggested below) need not frustrate us, for they greatly enhance our perception and appreciation of the Holy Spirit's many-faceted activity.

Here are various Bible translations definitions of *parakletos* (some Catholic versions not listed here use the term *Paraclete*): Comforter (KJV); Helper (NASB, NCV, NKJV, WILLIAMS); Counselor (RSV, NIV, NLT, WUEST); Advocate (NEB, JB); Friend (MESSAGE); Encourager (NLT margin); Comforting Counselor (JNT); Consoler (CON); Another to befriend you (KNOX); Comforter, Counselor, Helper, Advocate, Intercessor, Strengthener, Standby (AMPLIFIED).

J. I. Rodale's *Synonym Finder* provides additional insight into the English *paraclete,* all appropriate to describe the work of the Holy Spirit: defender, champion, vindicator, promoter, endorser, sponsor, proponent, favorer, maintainer, sustainer, upholder, supporter.

While teaching a Bible college class on this subject, I asked several of the students which title of the Holy Spirit they preferred. It soon became obvious that no one title would be a unanimous favorite. Each person's own experience with the Holy Spirit determined his or her preference. Albert Barnes is correct when he says that "no single word in our language expresses fully the sense of the original."[12]

Perhaps one title deserves special mention, however, if only because it is the consistent translation given by well-known Greek scholar Kenneth S. Wuest. He uses *Counselor* for the four occurrences in John,[13] a suggestion that has increasing appeal. When reflecting on how the Spirit gives practical counsel and guidance in daily things, one must conclude that considerable help comes through the impressions, directions and suggestions that come to the mind during times of serious prayer. We rely on the Holy Spirit to do miraculous things and provide protection, but the Spirit's help may be most evident and beneficial in the simple habit of the daily prayer exchange. This seems to have been a major factor in the success of Jesus' ministry.[14]

BETTER THERE THAN HERE

Jesus previously had called His followers disciples and addressed each by name. Now in this message, for the first time, Jesus called them friends.

Remarkably, in the same message He announced that He would be leaving them—without warning or satisfactory explanation! You can imagine the disciples' dismay.

And how could He possibly suggest that they would be better off if He left? What did He mean by these words found in John 16:7: "Nevertheless I tell you the truth. It is to your advantage that I go away; for if I do not go away, the Helper [parakletos] will not come to you; but if I depart, I will send Him to you"?

Catherine Marshall, in her delightful book *The Helper,* mused about how anything could be more wonderful than the physical presence of our Lord. She concluded that Jesus never spoke lightly or thoughtlessly, so this solemn word given at His Last Supper talk could only mean that "there is something better—His presence in the form of the Holy Spirit."[15]

Derek Prince, in his helpful booklet *The Holy Spirit in You,* explains: "We are better off with Jesus in heaven and the Holy Spirit on earth than we would be with Jesus on earth and the Holy Spirit in heaven."[16] Jesus intended that the disciples have more with this divine exchange than they had before.

How might they find themselves "better off"? Here are two key areas.

Jesus' Presence Would Be Made Universal

Jesus, in His earthly body, was limited physically just as we are. He could be in only one place at one time. In contrast, the infinite Spirit, being omnipresent and representing Jesus, could indwell simultaneously every believer in the whole world. One person praying in Africa, another in China and another in the United States can all be heard as though each is having a personal interview with Jesus Christ. Fulton J. Sheen says: "His continued presence on earth would have meant a localized presence; the descending of the Spirit would mean that He could be in the midst of all men who would be incorporated into Him."[17]

In addition, when Jesus spoke of His disciples doing "greater works" because of the Holy Spirit (John 14:12), He meant His own continuing works on a wider scale. In other words, Jesus' works on earth would now be accomplished not by His limited physical presence in only one setting but by His Spirit working in His followers worldwide (a universal presence).

Jesus was saying that the Spirit would take the place of His visible presence. And, the Spirit in the disciples would be as though Jesus Himself invisibly resided in each of them! In this sense, Michael Green says, "The Holy Spirit is 'another Jesus.'"[18] Sounding strange and mysterious at first, this insightfully reverent statement helps us realize that to have the Spirit is to have Jesus. In fact, because Jesus sent the Holy Spirit, the presence of Jesus is more real in our personal lives than ever before!

His Followers Would Now Have Two Advocates

The term *parakletos* is found also in 1 John 2:1 where the translation is usually "advocate" (the word for lawyer): "These things I write to you, that you may not sin. And if anyone sins, we have an Advocate with the Father, Jesus Christ the righteous."

Jesus is described as our heavenly attorney, appearing on our behalf, speaking in our defense and mediating our cases. Henry Swete describes Him in that capacity: "The first and most obvious of the functions of an advocate is to defend those whose cause he undertakes from the charges laid against them by their accusers."[19] When Jesus told His disciples of the coming paraclete who would dwell in them, He knew that He Himself would simultaneously act as their paraclete in heaven. His watchful eye would still be upon them!

Jesus is described as a *parakletos* in heaven in the forensic sense—that is, as an advocate before the throne of God. Here on earth, the Holy Spirit dwelling within us would take the place of Jesus as our Helper and plead the cause of God. We Christians are doubly blessed by having two Helper/Advocates: Jesus in heaven and the Holy Spirit in us. In a sense it is like having two high-powered attorneys that never lose a case taking care of our personal interests. Michael Green sums it up well: "Jesus is the one called to the Father's side to help us. . . . The Spirit is the one called from the Father's side to help us."[20]

Jesus' tenure on earth was short and temporary, only a few years. In contrast, the new paraclete would assume a permanent role in the Church. The disciples did not have to worry that this second advocate would leave them, for He would abide with them forever. Jesus left to assume His own permanent role as intercessor before the Father in heaven. Only He could qualify as our legal advocate in heaven, and only the Holy Spirit could function as the Church's worldwide advocate on earth helping us to pray and live as we ought. What a perfect combination!

The Farewell Discourse

Jesus' teaching on the Holy Spirit in the gospel of John can be divided into two parts:

- Part 1: John 3–7, The Giver of Life
- Part 2: John 14–20, The Paraclete[21]

In our last chapter we discussed the first part, John 3–7. Now we focus on the opening chapters of the second part, John 14–16, where five passages on the Holy Spirit are dispersed throughout the Farewell Discourse, Jesus' last sermon. Although Jesus made other references to the Holy Spirit in the gospel of John, this is His fullest teaching on the Person and ministry of the Holy Spirit. The various promises (mentioned elsewhere in the gospels) to send the Holy Spirit are listed in the endnotes for this chapter.[22]

These passages are sometimes treated as being detachable from the rest of the discourse, but they are actually an inseparable and consistent part of Jesus' message—and positioned strategically to keep the emphasis of the coming Spirit before the disciples. Most of all, these were living truths that vibrated with life experience and personal relationship; Jesus wanted them to experience what He Himself had joyfully experienced. I am sure that He smiled as He taught!

1. The Spirit Is Another Helper

"I will pray the Father, and He will give you another Helper [*parakletos*], that He may abide with you forever—the Spirit of truth, whom the world cannot receive, because it neither sees Him nor knows Him; but you know Him, for He dwells with you and will be in you."

John 14:16–17

Jesus' first action as heavenly paraclete was to ask the Father to give the Holy Spirit to the disciples. This was a priority in His mind, for His effectiveness as a paraclete in heaven would be reinforced and enhanced by the Holy Spirit as a paraclete in the Church on earth (see John 14:26; 15:26; 16:7). Peter on the Day of Pentecost described this scene from both heaven's and earth's viewpoints: "Therefore being exalted to the right hand of God, and having received from the Father the promise of the Holy Spirit, He poured out this which you now see and hear" (Acts 2:33).

Jesus prayed for His followers while on earth, and He now continues His intercession in heaven (see Romans 8:34; Hebrews 4:14–15; 7:25). Notice that the Upper Room discourse closes with a prayer, John 17, that is intimately connected with Jesus' message (like a minister ending his sermon with a prayer). The prayer shows us in many ways how Jesus now intercedes for us at the right hand of the Father.[23]

"Another Helper" is none other than "the Spirit of truth." In the opening of His discourse, Jesus proclaimed Himself as truth and the only way to God (see John 14:6). Here, Jesus called His replacement "the Spirit of truth," indicating there was none better to interpret and teach the ways of Jesus and His Kingdom.

The mention of "another paraclete" implies that one had already been with the disciples, and this, of course, was Jesus Himself. "Another" is the translation of *allos,* a word that indicates in this instance a difference in persons, but not a difference in kind (such as the word *heteros* would do). The Holy Spirit would be the same Helper that Jesus Himself had, and the disciples would be able to recognize the similarity of ministry. They would, however, find the Spirit no mere influence or copycat but rather a Person in His own right with recognizable characteristics.[24]

Various commentators have properly noted the parallelism between what John says about Jesus and what is promised of the Spirit.[25] This coming paraclete would be Jesus' successor, substitute and even His presence—and would, therefore, carry on the work Jesus initiated. Note these four similarities:

- Both were sent from the Father into the world (see John 3:16–17; 5:43; 14:26; 15:26; 16:7–8, 13, 27–28; 18:37)
- Both are called "holy" (see John 6:69; 14:26)
- Both are characterized by "the Truth" (see John 14:6, 17; 15:26; 16:13)
- Both are great teachers (see John 13:13–14; 14:26)
- Both were sent to convince and convict the world, but the world did not receive them (see John 1:11; 14:17; 15:18–26; 16:8–11, 20)

Max Turner of London Bible College makes a good suggestion. After also noting the above similarities, he emphasizes that the Holy Spirit was not just a replacement or substitute for Jesus. The Holy Spirit Himself came with a ministry. He would:

- Dwell in the disciples as the "Spirit of Truth," thereby continuing the revelatory wisdom they experienced from Jesus (John 14:17)
- Mediate the presence of the Father and of the glorified Son to the disciples (John 14:16–26)
- Come as Jesus' own emissary and executive power (John 14:26; 15:26; 16:7)[26]

"The world" (non-Christians focused on the secular and sinful things of this world—as opposed to the things of God) did not know Jesus or His Spirit then, nor does it now (see John 12:31; 1 Corinthians 1:21; 11:32; and 2 Corinthians 4:4). As Albert Barnes points out, "as the people of the world do not approve of or desire the aid of the Spirit, so it is said they cannot receive him."[27] There is a walk of sight and senses that wars against the spiritual walk of faith and makes it impossible for the Spirit to abide. The Spirit will indwell those who know and love Jesus. The disciples will joyfully recognize that the personality of the invisible second paraclete will be reminiscent of the visible first paraclete!

2. The Spirit Is a Teacher and Remembrancer

"These things have I spoken to you while being present with you. But the Helper, the Holy Spirit, whom the Father will send in My name ["as my representative," NLT], He will teach you all things, and bring to your remembrance [remind] all things that I said to you."

John 14:25–26

Jesus said and did many things during His earthly ministry. So much, in fact, that John said the world probably could not hold the books if those things were put in published form (see John 21:25). The disciples were constantly striving to understand Jesus and His ways (see John 2:22; 12:16; and 14:5, 8). Jesus, of course, was well aware of their lack of comprehension and retention, but He knew the coming Spirit would enable them to recall and understand. That is why Jesus said in John 13:7: "What I am doing you do not understand now, but you will know after this." Through the Spirit the disciples would be able to see the thrust and significance of Jesus' actions and sayings, and they would be taught all things that pertain to godly living.

John speaks of this in 1 John 2:20, 27:

> But you have an anointing from the Holy One, and you know all things. . . . But the anointing which you have received from Him abides in you, and you do not need that anyone teach you; but as the same anointing teaches you concerning all things, and is true, and is not a lie, and just as it has taught you, you will abide in Him.

Paul gives a similar thought in 1 Corinthians 2:13–16:

> These things we also speak, not in words which man's wisdom teaches but which the Holy Spirit teaches, comparing spiritual things with spiritual. But the natural man does not receive the things of the Spirit of God, for they are foolishness to him; nor can he know them, because they are spiritually discerned. But he who is spiritual judges all things, yet he himself is rightly judged by no one. For "who has known the mind of the LORD that he may instruct Him?" But we have the mind of Christ.

Comparing spiritual things with spiritual has been a difficult phrase to interpret. The Revised Standard Version says: "interpreting spiritual truths to those who possess the Spirit." The JNT says: "We explain things of the Spirit to people who have the Spirit." I like Michael Green's interpretation: "through the Spirit interpreting spiritual truths to men who possess the Spirit." He also makes this cogent summary: "It takes God to reveal God."[28]

Albert Barnes suggests that the Holy Spirit will aid our memories "in the same way as we remember a thing which would have been forgotten had not some friend recalled it to our recollection."[29] The Holy Spirit will be an interpreter and remembrancer and teacher, bringing understanding, aiding our memories and teaching us in all things that pertain to genuine discipleship.

Why do we need a teacher? I think Charles Spurgeon gave a good answer in his sermon "The Holy Spirit, the Great Teacher." He said, "The difficulty is that truth is not so easy to discover. We need a guide to conduct us into all truth."[30] This has been my experience, too. We simply cannot follow the winding paths of truth without a guide. Spurgeon used the illustration of a vast cave that can only be navigated with a guide who knows the way and holds a flaming torch of illumination.

3. The Spirit Is a Witness

But when the Helper comes, whom I shall send to you from the Father, the Spirit of truth who proceeds from the Father, He will testify of Me. And you also will bear witness, because you have been with Me from the beginning.

John 15:26–27

The coming of the Spirit is reaffirmed, as it is in each of these five statements. And once again the Helper is called the Spirit of truth. The fact that He proceeds from the Father indicates the divine nature of the Spirit. *Proceeds* is in a continuing, progressive tense. The JNT translates it: "who keeps going out."

Jesus said that not only the Spirit but also the Church would bear reliable witness of Him (Acts 1:8). *Testify* and *bear witness* are the same word. Just as the Spirit speaks forth in us what He knows of Jesus so we are to speak forth what we know of Jesus. The Spirit's witness within will be our great source of inspiration and supply of power for outward ministry.

4. The Spirit Is a Prosecutor

It is to your advantage that I go away; for if I do not go away, the Helper will not come to you; but if I depart, I will send Him to you. And when He has come, He will convict the world of sin, and of righteousness, and of judgment.

John 16:7–8

It seemed like an empty promise at the time, but we now see that Jesus had to depart and assume His position as heavenly advocate so that the Holy Spirit could come. Earlier in this chapter, we discussed why the Church is better off with Jesus in heaven rather than alive here on earth. When the Spirit came on the Day of Pentecost, the disciples knew without doubt that

Jesus was in heaven as their mediator and advocate. Jesus' promise to send the paraclete is much like the traveler who promises to send a postcard to some friends when he arrives in some distant land; the postmarked card does come, so his friends know he has arrived. When the Spirit came, the Church knew Jesus was in heaven!

Jesus said that the Spirit would act as a prosecutor in dealing with wayward, sinful mankind. He would convict of sin, righteousness and judgment—things the sinner is not anxious to discuss. The Spirit's challenge might be invisible and sometimes unwanted—coming through circumstances, people, the Bible—but the sinner's heart is convicted that he must be made right with God. If he responds with prayerful repentance, Jesus will claim the penitent sinner as His own—and make him a saint!

5. The Spirit Is a Revealer

However, when He, the Spirit of truth has come, He will guide you into all truth; for He will not speak on His own authority, but whatever He hears He will speak; and He will tell you things to come. He will glorify Me, for He will take of what is Mine and declare it to you. All things that the Father has are Mine. Therefore I said that He will take of Mine and declare it to you.

John 16:12–15

Again Jesus affirmed that the Spirit would come. Then He explained the prophetic ministry of the Spirit: He would guide into all truth, speak the words of the Father, tell things to come, glorify Christ and declare the things of Christ. The Holy Spirit is gifted to guide into all truth, since He is, in particular, the Spirit of truth (this seems to be Jesus' favorite title for the Spirit). To guide into truth means to explain it, to make it clear, understandable and, above all, practical in daily life.

The Spirit is particularly interpretive of spiritual realities as they apply to natural life. "The truth" Jesus refers to is, of course, theological, but it is also philosophical, practical and prophetic. Turner makes a good point when he describes the primary meaning:

"The Truth" into which the Spirit guides is principally the truth Jesus has incarnated and taught, or things in continuity with it. It clearly refers principally to things that Jesus would declare at their last meal together, if only the disciples could take it in (so 16:12). . . . [W]hat Jesus evidently wished to be able to explain was the fuller significance of his own ministry (in which they had shared), and especially his forthcoming death and glorification . . . to bring true comprehension of the significance of the historical revelation in Christ.[31]

The Spirit's primary task is guiding the disciples into lives of truth. Sometimes Christians are more interested in explaining finer points of theology than embracing the essentials of daily living. We would rather have a heated discussion on the "mark of the beast" in Revelation 13 than follow Jesus' teaching in the Beatitudes in Matthew 5 that emphasize qualities like humility, gentleness, mercy, peacemaking and bearing insults. Every gold miner seeks to find the mother lode where he can strike it rich; imagine having a guide who owns the richest vein and wants to give it to you! The Holy Spirit desires to bring every believer to the mother lode of truth—the ability to live out the basic life instructions of Jesus. This is the heart of "all truth."

We need more than textbook information. We need the Spirit helping us daily—literally guiding us in managing our thoughts and applying the principles of godly living that Jesus emphasized. The Spirit must work with us through a number of different situations before Jesus' lifestyle starts to emerge in our own. This requires sensitive prayer, renewed dependence on the Spirit and His personal, daily guidance.

The epistles of the New Testament abound in exhortation to live godly lives and allow the fruits of the Spirit to be evident. Paul and the other writers make this point but do not always give practical advice on how to do it. Our success is dependent on the Holy Spirit's personal help, guidance and incorporation of Scripture.

Jesus' reference to "all things" and "all truth" refer, I believe, to the same thing. The Holy Spirit will not speak on His own initiative; He will speak only what He hears from God. Everything that the Father has also belongs to Jesus Christ; therefore, all that God wills to be made known will be made known.

Summary of John 14–17

I would like to quote this summary of these four chapters from the *International Standard Bible Encyclopaedia:*

He is the Spirit of truth; He guides into all truth; He brings to memory
Christ's teachings; He shows things to come; He glorifies Christ; He speaks
not of Himself but of Christ; He, like believers, bears witness to Christ; He
enables Christians to do greater works than those of Christ; He convicts the
world of sin, of righteousness, and of judgment; He comes because Christ
goes away; He is "another Comforter"; He is to abide with the disciples
forever.

These teachings cover a very wide range of needs. The Holy Spirit is the
subject of the entire discourse. In a sense it is the counterpart of the Sermon
on the Mount. There the laws of the kingdom are expounded. Here the means
of realization of all the ends of that kingdom are presented. The kingdom
now becomes the kingdom of the Spirit. The historical revelation of truth in
the life, death, resurrection and glorification of Jesus being completed, the
Spirit of truth comes in fulness. The gospel as history is now to become the
gospel as experience. The Messiah as a fact is now to become the Messiah
as a life through the Spirit's action. All the elements of the Spirit's action are
embraced: the charismatic for mighty works; the intellectual for guidance
into truth; the moral and spiritual for producing holy lives. This discourse
transfers the kingdom, so to speak, from the shoulders of the Master to those
of the disciples, but the latter are empowered for their tasks by the might of
the indwelling and abiding Spirit.[32]

What a magnificent, heartfelt sermon! Although Jesus did startle the
disciples with His announcement of leaving and sending a replacement,
He nevertheless caught their attention with His glowing description of the
Holy Spirit. Jesus was extremely elated and happy that He would ascend to
the Father and that the heavenly counselor and paraclete would take His
place here. The disciples, although saddened, must have picked up Jesus'
infectious enthusiasm. Later, when the Spirit had come, they remembered
with affection this warm, wonderful promise that Jesus had made—and
was now a reality in their lives.

REVIEW QUESTIONS FOR CHAPTER 3

1. Which of the paraclete terms do you like best? Why?
2. Are you comfortable with "Comforter"?
3. Have you experienced interaction with the "other" Paraclete?
4. What do "all things" and "all truth" mean to you?

PART 2

A Glorious Disturbance Interrupts Pentecostal Festivities

Howling Wind, Blazing Fire and Supernatural Tongues

4

THE MIRACLE OF PENTECOST
GOD'S GIFT ARRIVES

IN THIS CHAPTER

- Review the setting for the Day of Pentecost
- Explore the Temple of Herod
- Analyze the opening verses of the most read chapter in the Bible
- Read about three miracles: howling wind, blazing fire, miracle tongues

The momentous day dawned in Jerusalem as had many warm festival days before it. Little wind was stirring, a fact of minor significance at the moment, yet one that provided stark contrast to that which was about to happen. The swollen city groaned with excited visitors joining their friends and relatives—all gathering together to worship the living God.

Unknown to the thousands of pilgrims or the thousands of city residents, the God of Israel was about to invade history again. Jerusalem was the chosen city and this particular religious holiday was the chosen time; the place would, in retrospect, seem the ideal location—for this occasion was the fulfillment of prophecy to Israel and to the world. No Jew present that day had the slightest inkling of the glorious disturbance that was about to break upon the beloved city.

It was Pentecost, the great harvest festival, when the firstfruits of the wheat harvest and certain produce crops were presented to the Lord. This second great feast of the Jewish year was taking place at the beginning of June (in the approximate year of A.D. 33). Improved weather conditions afforded Jews from far-flung places the safest opportunity for travel to Zion, so this was possibly the best attended of Israel's festivals. "In the spring time the sea was troubled violently, and in the winter almost impassable," Joseph Parker comments, "but in the quiet solemn harvest time everybody seemed to be more at liberty than at any other period of the year, and the sea and the land seemed rather to invite than to repel the traveller."[1]

The previous day, new arrivals had poured into the city, filling it to overflowing. Jerusalem never witnessed a more international crowd than at this happy time. The pilgrims came in a grand parade of colors, costumes and customs—accompanied by the babble of distinctive languages and dialects spoken in their native lands. These travelers represented the Diaspora, or dispersion, of Jews who had been flung out into the nations. Now they returned, proudly displaying their various national characteristics, yet anxious to bond in spirit with ethnic kinsmen in the worship of their God.[2]

A large portion of those gathered were, of course, native Jews, bringing their homegrown offerings to the house of the Lord, for only fruits grown in the soil of the Holy Land, the earth flowing with milk and honey, could be presented. Sholem Asch, acclaimed Jewish historical novelist, gives this colorful description:

> Every province sent the fruits and vegetables which ripened earliest within its borders. There was a rivalry of long standing between the patricians of Jericho, great landowners in the rich Jordan valley, and the poorer Galileans of the north, as to who should bring to Jerusalem the first figs ripened in advance of the season, or a new variety of vegetable, a thornless artichoke, a stringless bean, or some other novelty springing in sacred soil. . . . [A]ccording to the custom, the shopkeepers and artisans of Jerusalem waited in the streets for the deputations from their native provinces; and when these approached, carrying their baskets of first fruits, the cry of welcome rose:

"Ho, you, brothers of such and such a village, come in peace!" Every group came marching in to the sound of flutes and timbrels; an ox, the sacrificial offering, led the way, its horns adorned according to the means and social status of the deputation, with costly ribbons or with a wreath of olive leaves. The farmers of the neighboring village of Modiin carried the fresh vegetables which were considered such a delicacy in Jerusalem; those that came from remoter areas brought such fruits as would retain their freshness over a longer journey. In the procession of gifts were to be seen yellow sheaves of early wheat from the rich fields of Benjamin, while here and there, from among the sea of rough-woven baskets resting on the broad shoulders of peasants, flashed a fine-wrought golden tray heaped with figs and held aloft in the jeweled hands of a patrician.[3]

The great Temple of Herod, already 46 years in construction (see John 2:20), was easily the central attraction. Every Jewish heart burst with pride for this magnificent place—the great religious hub of Judaism. J. W. Shepard, author of *The Christ of the Gospels,* says the vast building "could accommodate within its area 210,000 persons. It was a mass of snowy marble and glittering gold, standing out from the common level of the city, like an island from the surrounding billows of the sea."[4]

None in the throng knew that in fewer than forty years (A.D. 70, shortly after completion) the Romans would obliterate Herod's masterpiece. Jesus alone perceived the destiny of the Temple whose God was forsaken (see Matthew 23:38). The immediate events were merely God's token use of the building before its fiery demise.

THE DISCIPLES' FRAME OF MIND

An insignificant group of Galilean folk, all sincere followers of Jesus, the rabbi of Nazareth, found themselves in Jerusalem at this momentous time. Swallowed by the great tide of humanity engulfing the city, they reached the close of prayerful days, waiting.

For them, Judea's capital was not a friendly place—their beloved leader was crucified there as a criminal a scant fifty days before. Concerned about safety and their future, they stubbornly hung on to an awesome promise that countermanded fear or apprehension. Jesus had made a pledge to them, and they awaited the fulfillment.

The "breaking news announcement" at His Farewell Discourse had actually caught the apostles by surprise. Jesus had given notice that He would return to the Father and send a personal replacement to help and care for them. Deliberately using the vivid word *parakletos* (*paraclete* in English), He had pinpointed the ministry of the Holy Spirit as one of assisting, aiding, comforting, befriending, helping and strengthening (see John 14–17, Greek text; as explained in chapter 3). Naturally, the astonished disciples wondered how, when and where the heavenly replacement would arrive.

For forty days after His resurrection, Jesus amazed them by appearing and giving further directions: The Spirit would come in Jerusalem! As in a game of "Treasure Hunt," the clues were leading to the reward. They were to stay in Jerusalem and wait for the arrival of the Holy Spirit (see Acts 1:4–8). Jesus both urged and assured them: "Behold, I send the Promise of My Father upon you; but tarry in the city of Jerusalem until you are endued with power from on high" (Luke 24:49).

Following this dramatic announcement, Jesus ascended bodily to God in heaven. The awestruck disciples stared at the sight—and the bell-toned words rang in their ears: "John truly baptized with water, but you shall be baptized with the Holy Spirit not many days from now" (Acts 1:5).

Then, Luke says, they returned to Jerusalem "with great joy" (Luke 24:52; see also Acts 1:12). Ordinarily they would have scattered to their own interests, but now, under mandate, they went quickly to the city. There, they spent the remaining days between an upper room and the Temple courts. It was time to seek the Lord, for the time was short. Jesus had said "not many days from now."

WAITING AND PRAYING

A possible five hundred disciples heard Jesus' directive, so a strong group departed for Jerusalem (see 1 Corinthians 15:6). During the ten-day prayer marathon, wonderful expectancy seized those who persevered. Although total attendance apparently decreased to one hundred and twenty, the fervency and determination of those who remained increased! How else can we explain Luke's statement that they "were continually in the temple praising and blessing God" (Luke 24:53)?

These praying disciples had been born again and justified by faith in Christ. They had experienced what we might call New Testament salvation.

The disciples were regenerated, or born again, when Jesus breathed on them
and said, "Receive the Holy Spirit" (John 20:19–22).

On that Easter Sunday, they received the inbreathed Spirit of the resurrected Christ; now they awaited the outpoured Spirit of the glorified
Christ. Begotten by the Spirit, they sought the baptism of the Spirit. They
followed the pattern of Jesus Himself, who, as the divine Son conceived
of the Spirit, was later (at age thirty) baptized with the Holy Spirit. Their
own baptism with the Holy Spirit would be the climax of Jesus' promised
ministry to them.

When would the Spirit come? Since Jesus had been crucified, buried
and resurrected during Passover festivities, it would not be illogical
for the disciples to think the Spirit might come on Pentecost. It was,
after all, the first major festival since those critical days. And two of Jesus'
clues had already taken place: They had returned to Jerusalem and several
days had passed.

But where would the Spirit come, and how? We will discuss both of these
questions in the course of this chapter. The manner in which the Spirit
came, though astonishing, is clear from the biblical record. The question
of where the disciples and followers of Jesus were gathered is, however, a
matter of some debate. Many Bible readers, accustomed to the "Upper
Room" idea, may be surprised to learn that other options are possible. I
will discuss this in more depth later in this chapter, but consider for now
that the location was a usual gathering place for the disciples, one in which
thousands of people would have been witnesses, and one that they might
have anticipated: the Temple.

THE TEMPLE OF HEROD

The magnificent Temple of Herod was an architectural wonder of that
world. Conceived more for political influence than spiritual benefit, it was
Herod's pride, Judaism's religious shrine—and a thorn in the flesh to the
Roman government. Jesus spent much time ministering there, so every
reader of the gospels is aware of the important place the structure occupied
in His ministry.

Since little is usually known of its grandeur and layout, it is worthwhile
to pause and consider its construction. Numerous attempts have been made
to reproduce this great building in model form. A recent book by Alec

Garrard, *The Splendor of the Temple,* shows colorful pictures of his carefully documented model. He says that "the temple was a vast building for its period, covering some thirty-five acres (fourteen hectares)—about one fifth of the area of the city of Jerusalem—with huge retaining walls built around its periphery to support the flat platform on which it was built."[5]

The early Church was to be birthed there in a spectacular way, as we shall see in a few moments.

Jerusalem was situated and construction undertaken in a series of increasingly higher levels that climaxed in the Most Holy Sanctuary. This progression was meant to symbolize ascending degrees of holiness, starting with the land of Israel itself, then the city of Jerusalem, then the great Temple structure with its courtyards. The spirit of this ascent is captured in Isaiah 2:3: "Come, and let us go up to the mountain of the LORD, to the house of the God of Jacob; He will teach us His ways, and we shall walk in His paths." I have diagrammed it as follows.[6]

> 10. The Most Holy
> 9. The Temple
> 8. Court of the Priests
> 7. Court of Israel
> 6. Court of the Women
> 5. Court of the Gentiles
> 4. The Temple Mount
> 3. City of Jerusalem
> 2. Walled Cities in Palestine
> 1. The Land of Israel

Both Jews and Goyim (Gentiles) could enter the Court of the Gentiles, a huge open area paved with the finest variegated marble. Located mainly in the southern sector, surrounded by covered porches or colonnades, this great courtyard was as big (some estimate) as twenty football fields put together. This area housed the noisy market where oxen, sheep and doves (selected as fit for sacrifices) were sold; here also were located the tables of the devious money changers who drew the angry displeasure of Jesus (see Matthew 21:12; John 2:14).

The next level was the Court of the Women, so called because this was as far as women could progress into the Temple. This court was closed to Gentiles. A balustrade (some say it was a simple four-foot fence, others a more substantial wall) guarded this level; priests stood at the openings and ominous signs forbade the entrance of any Gentile on the penalty of death. It was sometimes called the Court of Prayer because that was a primary function for Jewish men and women.

Then followed the Court of Israel. Climbing the fifteen Steps of Ascent on the western side of the enclosed Court of the Women, a Jewish man could then pass through the main gate into the smaller Court of Israel. This was another open area surrounded by walls, and it led to the Court of the Priests, which housed the great stone altar of sacrifice. Finally, beyond the altar, stood the massive doors that opened to the Sanctuary, which in turn was divided by a great veil or curtain into two parts, Holy and Most Holy (see Matthew 27:51). This building was the tallest structure in the complex.

I want to return for a moment to the Court of the Women, since it occupied a particular position of importance. It was a large, open area, more than two hundred feet square. The stone pavement and surrounding walls gave a sense of privacy. It was here that people gave their monetary offerings (as did the widow in Mark 12:42) and presented their animal sacrifices. Joseph and Mary brought the baby Jesus to this court for His dedication (see Luke 2:27).

As in the other courts, a portico (or porch) ran around the perimeter of the Court of the Women, and benches or seats were placed there for the convenience of worshipers. Balconies were built on three sides of the court so that women could worship above and men below, as they were to be segregated during worship.[7] In each corner of the court stood a massive brass candelabra 85 feet tall. A Levite had to climb a ladder to add oil to the burning lamps.

The followers of Jesus, this author believes, made the Court of the Women their principal place of prayer. (It was this court, at a later date, that Peter and John entered through the Beautiful Gate where the lame man lay, as described in Acts 3.) Although smaller in size than the Court of the Gentiles, it still was very large, appropriately secluded and open to Solomon's Porch. Consecrated women were welcome there, but they could proceed no farther. The fact that this court was (1) a place dedicated to prayer, (2) the innermost place where both men and women could pray and (3) forbidden to Gentiles (so Gentile languages were not customarily spoken there) presented a most appropriate setting for what was about to happen on this festival day!

ON THE DAY OF PENTECOST

Jesus' followers, along with thousands of other pilgrims, arrived early at the Temple (before nine o'clock). Some pilgrims, in fact, had prayed through the night in the eerie light of the great lampstands of the women's court. Some possibly slept in prescribed areas of the Temple,[8] while others came at sunrise. Everywhere under the ornate, wooden roofs of the great porticos people prayed, some sitting, some walking, highlighted now and then by blocks of sunlight streaming through windows cut high in the massive outer walls. Majestic, granite pillars cast early morning shadows across the great polished marble floor and on many pilgrims quietly performing their duties.[9]

The huge concourse of people from every quarter of the Diaspora, scattered throughout the various courts, porticos and terraces, was not expecting anything miraculous to interrupt their usual prayer, conversations and Temple rituals. They were present, as was their custom, to blend with and absorb from the spiritual atmosphere of the brilliant ceremonies. Levites blew on the sacred, silver trumpets and sang verses from the Psalms accompanied by their harps. In the inner court, white-robed priests stood barefoot and offered the festival sacrifices, while family groups watched from the balconies. In the great courtyard, amid the colorfully costumed pilgrims, devout souls fell emotionally and unashamedly on their faces in worship. Crowds of people continued to push their way through the streets and into the Temple.

THE DESCENT OF THE SPIRIT

Suddenly the atmosphere grew electric with heavenly presence—the Holy Spirit arrived in glorious manner! Paraclete power interrupted Pentecostal pageantry! No more glorious arrival was ever staged by potentate, king or president. The lowly Nazarene's replacement made His grand entrance!

The Spirit's descent through the sky came on wind-driven fire—similar to Elijah's blazing chariot ascent to heaven. It was quite like God's splendid arrival at the dedication of Solomon's Temple (see 1 Kings 8:10–11; 2 Chronicles 7:1–3), but there was one important difference. In that ancient building, the overwhelmed priests were rendered unable to minister. In contrast, the Pentecostal Spirit descended not into a place but into the people of God themselves! His people became His newly appointed habitation. Rather than struck silent like the ancient priests, these priests of the new covenant broke forth in miracle languages that declared the greatness of God.

What a moment—mere disciples transformed into the Temple of God, the Church of Jesus Christ! It was the dawning of the great and glorious day of the Lord.

Pentecost was the commencement of the "last days" outpouring of the Spirit—the new era of the Holy Spirit—promised by God, the time when the gift of the Spirit was made available for all of the Lord's people. G. Campbell Morgan gives this description:

> This was the beginning of a new departure in the economy of God; not a new departure rendered necessary by the failure of the past, but a new departure rendered necessary by the accomplishments of the past. Everything in the economy of God had been preparatory to this. This never could have been until this hour. But the hour had come; everything was accomplished; all the preparatory work was over, and there broke upon human history a new dawning; there began a new economy in the enterprises of God.[10]

WHY PENTECOST? WHAT HAPPENED? AND WHERE?

Why did God choose the Day of Pentecost for this new dawning? Let's begin to answer the question with a statement of the key text, Acts 2:1–8.

> When the Day of Pentecost had fully come [seven weeks after Jesus' resurrection], they [the believers] were all with one accord in one [the same] place. And suddenly there came a sound from heaven [in the skies above them], as of [like] a rushing mighty wind [the roaring of a mighty windstorm], and it filled [was heard throughout] the whole house where they were sitting. Then there appeared to them [the 120-plus disciples] divided [dividing from a single source] tongues [flames], as of [like] fire, and one [flame of fire] sat [settled] upon each of them [the 120 disciples]. And they were all filled with the Holy Spirit and began to speak with other [foreign] tongues [languages], as the Spirit gave [enabled, prompted] them utterance [this ability to make these bold proclamations].

And there were dwelling in Jerusalem Jews, devout [godly] men, from every nation under heaven [the known world of that day]. And when this sound [made by the disciples] occurred, the multitude came [running] together, and were confused [bewildered], because everyone heard them speak in his own language [dialektos]. Then they were all amazed [astonished] and marveled [beside themselves with wonder], saying to one another, "Look, are not all these who speak Galileans? And how is it that we hear [keep hearing], each in our own language [dialektos] in which we were born?"

"Fully Come"

Three great religious feasts or festivals were held in the Jewish year: Passover, Pentecost and Tabernacles. Every devout Jew, if at all possible, would celebrate these festivals in Jerusalem; in fact, every male Jew living within twenty miles of Jerusalem was legally obligated to come.

The events of Acts 2 occurred on the second great feast of the year. It was actually a harvest festival, when the firstfruits of the wheat harvest were presented to the Lord. It was called the "Feast of Weeks" because it was celebrated on the day following the passage of seven Sabbaths, a week of weeks, after Passover. It was called "Pentecost" (Greek, *pentekostos,* "fiftieth") because it occurred "on the fiftieth day after the presentation of the first sheaf to be reaped of the barley harvest, that is, the fiftieth day from the first Sunday after Passover."[11]

The words noting that the Day of Pentecost *had fully come* can be translated as "was in process of being fulfilled" (Wuest's translation). Each of the three feasts was actually prophetically predictive, anticipating some future spiritual fulfillment (although the average Jew had no conception of the Christian application). The Feast of Passover, for instance, was fulfilled at Calvary: "For indeed Christ, our Passover, was sacrificed for us" (1 Corinthians 5:7). Pentecost was fulfilled with the Spirit's coming, as seen in three particular areas of significance.

The first is *agricultural.* During this feast the Jews thanked God for the harvest. On this particular day the ancient symbolism of Pentecost found dramatic realization: It marked forever for the Church the beginning of the long-awaited spiritual harvest. In other words, the disciples tarried to receive power to tackle the huge challenge of world evangelization. This empowerment, says Wagner, was "needed for carrying the gospel across all conceivable barriers."[12] Later that day, at the conclusion of Peter's sermon, three thousand converts became the actual firstfruits. It is estimated that

within a few short days the ranks of Jesus' followers had swollen to thirty
thousand!

The second area of significance is *historical.* Pentecost also celebrated the
giving of the Law on Sinai, a feast of covenant renewal. Edersheim says:
"According to unanimous Jewish tradition, which was universally received
at the time of Christ, the day of Pentecost was the anniversary of the giving
of the Law on Mount Sinai, which the Feast of Weeks was intended to com-
memorate."[13] The custom of reading Exodus 19 at the Feast of Pentecost
was probably already established in the century before Christ. Scripture is
not specific but does indicate that the Law was given on Sinai fifty days
after the first Passover in Egypt (see Exodus 12:51; 19:1).

Both the book of James and the epistles of Paul point out that the Holy
Spirit came to write "the perfect law of liberty, the law of the Spirit of life"
on tablets of the heart not on stone.[14] This clearly contrasts the Law at
Sinai with the Spirit at Pentecost. Also, note the similarity between Israel's
deliverance (the first Passover) being completed in the giving of the Law
and Jesus' crucifixion (the final Passover) being completed in the outpouring of the Holy Spirit at Pentecost.

The third area of significance is *practical.* The Spirit came on Pentecost
simply because it was the time that the greatest multitude of Jewish worshipers would be assembled at Jerusalem. The Law demanded attendance and
that no servile work be done, so all men were there for religious purpose
and rest. The crowds on the street and in the Temple were at maximum.

H. B. Swete, in his well-known book on the Holy Spirit, comments:
"If the coming of the Spirit was to be made known through the Jewish
world, the Pentecost offered the next opportunity."[15] These people would
spread the startling news of this new Pentecost everywhere. And as James
D. G. Dunn suggests, waiting any longer might have adversely affected the
corporate structure of the believers: "With any longer interval the cohesion
of the disciples would have been greatly strained. Pentecost was the next
great pilgrim feast when followers of Jesus were likely anyway to gather
in Jerusalem in hopes of some further confirmation of their new faith in
Jesus as risen."[16]

"With One Accord"

One hundred and twenty of the disciples were assembled (see Acts
1:15)—the eleven apostles, the newly appointed Matthias, Mary, the

mother of Jesus, other women, the brothers of Jesus, as well as others un-named. They prayed and thought "with one accord," that is, "with one intent" (ROTHERHAM). Called to evangelize the world, they faced possible martyrdom (which many later did in noble fashion)—a fact that would only add fuel to their fervency.

"These all continued with one accord in prayer and supplication . . ." (Acts 1:14). It seems that the disciples did not pray with ever increasing fervor until they reached a spiritual apex, at which moment the Spirit was given. Instead they assumed a posture of ongoing, fervent, unified prayer, and then He came.

"In One Place"

They were together in one place when the Spirit came. The Bible gives two locations for their times of prayer together: an upper room (see Acts 1:13) and the Temple of Herod (see Luke 24:53). As I suggested earlier, the more likely place is the Temple. An upper room in a private home (which could hold one hundred and twenty people and be accessible to the public) is not realistic in light of the construction of that day. And, actually, several places in Herod's Temple could be called an "upper room" (Acts 1:13) and a "house" (2:2). Here are four possibilities, all in Herod's Temple:

- The open raised gallery in the Court of the Women
- The upper floor between the Court of the Women and of Israel
- The Royal Porch and possibly its second story
- The Court of the Gentiles (the covered eastern section known as Solomon's Porch) and possibly its open second floor

R. C. H. Lenski, a popular Lutheran commentator, suggests this in-terpretation of the Upper Room: ". . . it was the room where the apostles gathered after they heard the news of the resurrection, John 20:19, 26."[17] G. Campbell Morgan comments: ". . . the upper room was merely a place of tarrying for some of the fellowship; but their meeting-place day by day was in the Temple."[18] Our key reference is Luke 24:53: "[They] were continually in the temple praising and blessing God." We do not know for sure, but the disciples possibly spent their nights in an upper room or in homes and came unobtrusively into Solomon's Porch (or other place in the Temple) day by day to continue in their united prayer vigil. Some possibly slept at the Temple.[19]

Although commentators have various opinions about an upper room, all agree that eventually the disciples ended up in one of the Temple's large courts. So, why complicate the interpretation? If we place the hundred and twenty in the "house" or Temple on the early morning of Pentecost, the whole picture easily comes together. For my past sixty years of Bible reading, this is the only interpretation that has made sense to me.[20]

Verse 2 says that the sound "filled the whole house where they were sitting." The "house" (Greek, *oikos*) to any Jew would easily mean the Temple.[21] The disciples were sitting, I believe, in the Court of the Women, most likely on the stone pavement or on benches in the porticos. They were in prayer. Customarily people sat on the pavement when they listened to the learned rabbis (who would sit on benches); this could have been the posture of the praying disciples awaiting the arrival of their new teacher.[22]

Let us note here in our analysis of the text that three miracles marked the Spirit's advent:

- "a sound from heaven, as of a rushing mighty wind"
- "divided tongues, as of fire"
- disciples speaking "with other tongues, as the Spirit gave them utterance"

All are significant because they show continuity between the Hebrew prophets and Holy Spirit activity in the New Testament. This is, after all, the beginning of the prophetic era when all of God's people may prophesy. Peter calls the happenings "what was spoken by the prophet Joel: '. . . Your sons and your daughters shall prophesy . . . I will pour out My Spirit in those days; and they shall prophesy'" (Acts 2:16–18).

The Hebrew prophets received their messages and direction in four ways: (1) audible voice, (2) mental picture/vision, (3) immediate unction and (4) ecstatic experience.[23] The Pentecostal happenings parallel this Old Testament pattern: (1) a tremendous sound like rushing wind: something heard, (2) the appearance of what appeared to be fire: something seen, (3) speaking in languages not previously learned: an immediate personal unction and (4) an ecstatic inward experience of God's presence—which looked to observers like drunkenness!

"A Rushing Mighty Wind"

This was the startling, dramatic appearance of a friend, but unexpected at this exact moment. The benevolent intruder was none other than the promised Holy Spirit of God making glorious entrance through sight and sound. Suddenly He was there! This word "suddenly," according to David Ewert, "is another way of saying that when God's time comes, he acts and nothing can stop him."[24]

The sound was similar to that of ("as of") a rushing mighty wind, a violent, gale-force wind ("an echoing sound out of heaven as of a wind borne along violently," Wuest's translation) that blew into the house of God and filled it with heavenly presence. The voluminous sound could only connote vast, supernatural power. Only one thought would register in Jewish minds: the *ruah,* Hebrew for breath, Spirit, wind. The Breath of God promised by Jesus had arrived![25] Note, it was sound alone, and not an actual wind; a literal wind of such force would have blown the city and people to pieces.

The sound "filled the whole house," which means that it must have been heard by everyone in the Temple. It was like a trumpet call alerting and summoning the people. "Rushing," says Herbert Lockyer, "suggests the approach, the irresistible action of the Spirit."[26] The description of the violent wind-sound expresses empowerment rather than relationship. It is meant, I believe, to show strong contrast between the light, gentle breath of the Spirit in regeneration that brings new life and a mighty blast of the Holy Spirit that imparts power.

The way of the Holy Spirit is likened to that of the wind. Jesus said to Nicodemus: "The wind blows where it wishes, and you hear the sound of it, but cannot tell where it comes from and where it goes. So is everyone who is born of the Spirit" (John 3:8). Ezekiel, in his vision, prophetically called for the wind, the breath of God, to blow over the dead bones of Israel, an action that transformed them into a vast standing army of rejuvenated people (see Ezekiel 37).

"Divided Tongues, as of Fire"

Immediately following the audible manifestation, a sheet of fire descended over the disciples. Abruptly, this mass broke up (divided) into individual tongues of fire (like a chunk of meat on a butcher's block "cloven" into smaller pieces by a cleaver; hence the King James Version says "cloven tongues"). These small flames then scattered out, dancing through the air, with each tongue finally finding and coming to rest on the head of some disciple present.

It was not said to be fire but rather *as of fire*, or in other words to be similar in appearance to fire. Luke's record does not actually say that all the pilgrims present in the Temple courtyard saw the fire. It does say "there appeared unto *them*," referring to the disciples. My conclusion is that the fire was prophetic and visionary and only witnessed by the early believers, but we cannot be sure of this.

The mass of fire was a spectacular manifestation of God's presence or glory, known to the Jews as the Shekinah. It was given to the disciples just as the burning bush was to Moses; and just as the flaming fire continued burning without consuming the bush, so the flames of Pentecost burned without hurting anyone, only inspiring awe and reverence.

That which previously had been unapproachable and unendurable now became the experience of the waiting disciples. God impressively and effectively showed that His presence would inhabit not only heaven but His people as well. He would share Himself with every believer and become a personal God to each one.

The tongues of fire gradually faded from view, apparently absorbed into the believers. The fire disappeared into the Church! The disciples no doubt assumed that this was the fulfillment of John's promise that Jesus would baptize them with the Holy Spirit and fire (see Matthew 3:11; Luke 3:16).

How Many Tongues of Fire?

Some say there were only twelve tongues of fire, one over each of the twelve apostles, and that they alone spoke miraculously in tongues. This supposedly confirmed them as the authorized ambassadors of Jesus.[27] A more broadminded explanation, however, does seem warranted by the text and is believed by a majority of commentators. The words *they were all* in verse 1 seem most clearly to refer to the one hundred and twenty men and women present, not just the twelve men.[28] Since Joel predicted that "sons and daughters" would prophesy, we are compelled to believe that tongues of fire lit on all the disciples present. All of them received the promised Spirit to show that all of us can likewise be endowed by the same Spirit.

Such an interpretation allows for the orderly manifestation of more than twelve languages spoken to the crowd. Consider the impact of a hundred and twenty Spirit-filled disciples scattering out, excitedly declaring the great works of God in the various languages of the Diaspora!

A Prophetic and Visionary Experience

The signs of wind and fire were momentary, heavenly phenomena—prophetic and visionary, experienced by the disciples and possibly observed by others. I do not believe that an actual flame of fire was visible on Peter's head as he preached. Although the sound of wind was spectacular and attention getting, it was the declaration of God's greatness by the disciples in many languages that drew the crowd and created readiness for the Gospel message.

The scene is similar to Jesus' water baptism. As Jesus came up from the water, the Holy Spirit descended in the shape of a dove and rested upon Him. The gospel accounts only say that John the Baptist and Jesus actually saw the Spirit descend (see Matthew 3:16; Mark 1:10; Luke 3:22; John 1:32–33). The main purpose of the dove's appearance was to confirm Jesus' true identity to John. This was, I believe, another prophetic, visionary experience.[29]

The dove was not a literal bird, but rather an easily recognized prophetic symbol to give visual authenticity to the Spirit's presence. Since the dove is such a universal symbol of the Holy Spirit, it may come as a shock to realize that, as Bishop Fulton Sheen has pointed out, the Spirit of God is never represented as such anywhere else in the Bible. Sheen adds this significant insight: "The dove was the symbol of gentleness and peacefulness, but above all it was the type of sacrifice possible to the lowliest people. . . . Therefore, the Spirit descending upon Our Lord was for them a symbol of submission to sacrifice."[30] As Jesus began His ministry as the Spirit-anointed Son of man, He simultaneously began the course that would bring Him as the Son of God to His crucifixion on Calvary—to die as the Lamb of God slain for mankind.

In Jesus' baptism of the Holy Spirit, the Spirit descended like a dove, alighting upon Him. In the disciples' baptism of the Holy Spirit, the Spirit descended like a tongue of fire and "sat on each of them." The symbols are not identical, but both refer to the same Holy Spirit. The fire was a sign to the gathered disciples of the power, presence, cleansing and confirmation of God; the dove was a sign to John the Baptist that Jesus was God's sacrifice to redeem the world.

Biblical Fulfillment

The disciples' baptism fulfills in a remarkable way the prophecy of Psalm 104:4 (quoted in Hebrews 1:7): "Who makes His angels spirits and His ministers a flame of fire."[31] The tongues of fire illustrated the way in which God's word would be proclaimed: human languages imbued with God's presence.

Because this expression *and fire* appears in Matthew and Luke, and the immediate context refers to judgment, some commentators feel that the baptism of fire signified a coming judgment. We will discuss this further in the next chapter.

"And They Were All Filled with the Holy Spirit"

This "filling" was the great miracle. The outward signs of wind-sound, visible fire and unlearned tongues merely attested to the Spirit's presence. Emptiness was transformed into overflowing blessing! "Filled with" or "full of" the Holy Spirit (Acts 2:4; 4:8, 31; 6:3, 5; 9:17; 11:24; 13:9, 52) is one of many descriptions of the Holy Spirit's activity (see chapter 7). Did the disciples already have the Spirit before they were filled with the Spirit; that is, were they already Christians? And how was this "baptism of the Holy Spirit" different from Jesus' breathing on them when He said "receive the Holy Spirit"? We will consider these interesting questions later.

"They Spoke with Other Tongues, as the Spirit Gave Utterance"

An immediate result of the Spirit's filling was that the disciples had an amazing unction to speak forth the praises of God in languages they had never learned! The Holy Spirit gave "this ability" (NLT) or "enabled them" (NIV). The Greek word translated "gave them utterance" *(apophthengesthai)* is a seldom-used word, but here describes an enthusiastic declaration that is suggestive of prophetic activity (and later describes Peter's Spirit-inspired preaching).[32] This was similar to some types of prophecy; however, the disciples did not speak in languages that were native to them!

These were uneducated Galileans, conversant in the Galilean Aramaic dialect, familiar with Hebrew, knowing some common words in Greek and Latin. Later when Peter and John were brought before the Sanhedrin, their guttural speech branded them as cultural hillbillies (see Acts 4:13). The miraculous "tongues" spoken by the disciples employed words beyond their conscious knowledge, languages that, in normal circumstances, they could not speak. Greek scholar A. T. Robertson describes these supernatural tongues as "Other than their native tongues . . . a language that had not been acquired and yet was a real language, and understood by those from various lands familiar with them. It was not jargon, but intelligible language."[33]

What were the disciples saying in the miracle languages? Luke gives a simple answer in Acts 2:11: "the greatnesses of God" or "the mighty deeds of God" (Greek, *ta megalia tou theou*). The tongues of existing languages served as a wondrous living metaphor of the various ethnic groups of the world boldly declaring the glory of God. This was not the preaching of the Gospel but rather the enthusiastic worship of God. G. Campbell Morgan makes this delightful comment:

> That phrase is a very arresting one; and indeed, is found in only one other place in the New Testament, and that is in the Magnificat of Mary, as given to us in the Gospel of Luke. That is how she in her singing described the activities of God. This then is what these disciples were doing. They were not preaching . . . they were not attempting to interpret . . . but in the full consciousness created by the fullness of the Spirit, with eyes open to see as they had never seen, and ears attuned to hear as they had never heard, with all their being stirred to its depths by the inrush of this life of God through Christ, they were uttering words of ecstatic joy as they celebrated the mighty works of God.[34]

After the display of languages, Peter preached the Gospel and harvested three thousand souls! The people's hearts had been awesomely prepared.

"Jews . . . from Every Nation"

More than a dozen languages are listed in Acts 2:8–11. Herod Agrippa confirmed the vast disbursement of the Jewish Diaspora when he said: "There is no people upon the habitable earth which have not some portion of you [Jews] among them."[35] During the first century A.D. some one hundred and fifty Jewish colonies were established throughout the Roman Empire in major population areas.[36] These people had acclimated to their non-Jewish environments, and many of them were now more conversant in the language of their locale than their mother tongue. The map following shows where the places mentioned in Scripture were located. These nations sketch a great, rough circle around the Holy Land, and Jerusalem appears like the hub of a wheel with spokes going out in all directions to the places named by Luke.

"When This Sound Occurred"

The "sound" (Greek, *phone*) that drew the crowd together is not specified, but most likely it is the aftermath noise generated by more than a hundred people spreading out among the crowd and praising God enthusiastically in languages they had not learned. The wind-sound (a different Greek word, *echos,* verse 2) may have alerted the populace, but it was the miracle languages that focused and drew the crowd's attention and attendance.

"The Multitude Came Together"

The great crowd that quickly assembled was made up of Jerusalem Jews, foreign-born Jews from many nations (see verse 5) and proselytes (see verse 10). William Barclay comments on this last term: "Proselytes were Gentiles

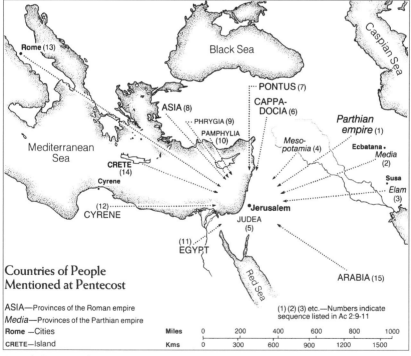

Countries of People Mentioned at Pentecost

ASIA—Provinces of the Roman empire
Media—Provinces of the Parthian empire
Rome —Cities
CRETE—Island

(1) (2) (3) etc.—Numbers indicate sequence listed in Ac 2:9-11

Miles	0	200	400	600	800	1000
Kms	0	300	600	900	1200	1500

who had grown tired of the multitude of heathen gods, and who had grown weary of heathen immorality and laxity had come to the synagogues to learn of the one true God and the clean way of life, and who had accepted the Jewish religion and the Jewish way of life."[37]

"Each in Our Own Language"

The crowd of pilgrims stood stunned as "each one" heard the unlearned Galileans speak like expert linguists in the diverse languages and dialects of the Diaspora. Verses 6 and 8 use the Greek word for *dialects—dialektos—*which means known and understood ethnic languages. Verse 8 indicates these were the languages of the listeners' home countries.

What a powerful beginning for the Church of Jesus Christ! Jesus Himself was the prototype Spirit-filled man. He was followed by the first-century Spirit-filled Church.

Today, our churches may also have the Holy Spirit's active presence. It is the privilege of all, not just the prerogative of a few. Let us never lose sight of our heritage, remembering Paul's admonition that the Church, begun by the Spirit, must continue its progress in the power of that Spirit (see Galatians 3:3).

More about the fire and Spirit in the next three chapters. Why did God choose the sign of speaking with tongues? Seven solid reasons are given! The chapters that follow will introduce the heart of our discussion: the baptism with the Holy Spirit and fire. Can and should today's Christian speak in tongues? Often debated, this topic should not and need not be such a divisive issue, especially since it was so carefully explained by the apostle Paul and has proven to produce such beneficial results when properly handled.

REVIEW QUESTIONS FOR CHAPTER 4

1. Does Jesus' announcement at His Farewell Discourse relate to you?
2. Have you found it profitable to "tarry" on the Lord as the disciples did?
3. If the Spirit came to the Court of the Women, what message does that send us?
4. How many spoke in tongues in Acts 2? What does that say to us today?

5

GREAT BALLS OF FIRE!
"WHOA! ME ON FIRE?!"

IN THIS CHAPTER

- Discover the meaning of being "on fire for God"
- Review the examples of divine fire in the Hebrew Scriptures
- Find out the three main houses of God that have been "set on fire"
- Decide: Would you boldly agree with Spurgeon's plea for fire?

How would you describe a person who exhibits these characteristics: having intense zeal, excited, animated, filled with ardent desire, inflamed, stirred up, fervent, passionate, enthusiastic, eager, inspired with strong passion, energetically active? We often use these words to describe someone who is "on fire" for something. For many Christians, even those who have never considered the coming of the Holy Spirit, the term of being "on fire for God" is a familiar—and positive—one.

This suggests excitement and fervor—important aspects of the Christian witness. Yet, is this what is meant by the fire at Pentecost? When fervent believers in every age pray for "God to send the fire" in the Church, do they know what they are asking for? As we will learn in this chapter, probably not! Divine fire is not the same as human success or enthusiasm. Also, Scripture uses fire in various, impressive ways: literal, spiritual and symbolic. The fire of God cannot be easily categorized for it can be all three at the same time!

We have discussed when the Spirit came, and where. In this chapter we will look at one aspect of how He came: on wind-driven fire. Was this fire literal or spiritual? Does the baptism with the Holy Spirit always include fire? Was this the fire that John the Baptist spoke of, or is that prophecy yet to be fulfilled? Let's start there.

HAS THE COMING OF FIRE BEEN FULFILLED?

John the Baptist declared that he baptized with water unto repentance, but that the Coming One, Jesus, who was mightier and much more important, would baptize with the Holy Spirit and fire (see Matthew 3:11; Luke 3:16). Other references mention this baptism (see Mark 1:8; John 1:33; Acts 1:5; 11:16), but they do not mention "fire."[1]

Since John the Baptist mentions coming judgment in connection with the "baptism with the Holy Spirit and fire" (see Matthew 3:10–12; Luke 3:7–18), some commentators believe that there yet remains a future fulfillment of "fire." Although this is a compatible interpretation for the context of the passage,[2] Jesus' clear reference to the Spirit and fire (as mentioned by Matthew and Luke) indicates strongly an immediate fulfillment.

Four possible interpretations of what "baptism with the Holy Spirit and fire" means are outlined by George E. Ladd in *A Theology of the New Testament:*[3]

- John announced only a baptism of fire ("an imminent judgment of purging fire," which makes the idea of Spirit-baptism a spurious Christian addition).
- The baptism of *pneuma* is not the Holy Spirit but the fiery breath or wind of divine judgment.

- John announced a single baptism with two concurrent elements (purifying the righteous and punishing the wicked).
- The Coming One will baptize the righteous with the Holy Spirit and the wicked with fire.

There is also a possible fifth meaning: John announced a single baptism that involved two elements (an outpouring of the Holy Spirit and also a baptism of fire) that occurred at two different times, once at the beginning of the Spirit age and then again at the end of the age.

Many, including myself, believe this last suggestion, that the baptism of Spirit and fire had a fulfillment on the Day of Pentecost and yet will also find fulfillment at the end of the age. I feel this approach is more direct and less abusive to the text than some interpretations. Consider these thoughts.

Fulfilled at Pentecost

To understand how the baptism was fulfilled in the outpouring of the Holy Spirit, we need, first, to allow John the option of prophetic innovation; after all, he was the last of the old order and the announcer of the new! His was an original idea, inspired by God. No precedent was necessary! There had never been such a baptism before. God sent him to baptize in water to dramatize the baptism of Spirit and fire that the Messiah would bring.

Second, it would be hard to persuade Peter and the other disciples on the Day of Pentecost (with flames dancing on their heads!) that their experience did not fulfill the prediction of John. This thought should be given serious consideration; we should attempt to interpret John's words as the apostles understood their fulfillment. Fire certainly could indicate judgment and cleansing (purging), but in this case—linked with the Holy Spirit and various statements in the Acts—it is justifiable to signify empowerment as well. Human tongues anointed by the fire of heaven made "His ministers a flame of fire" (Hebrews 1:7; see also Psalm 104:4).

Third, in the Greek text the two nouns *Spirit* and *fire* are coupled with one preposition, which can indicate grammatically that the two words refer to the same baptism. Greek scholars call this *hendiadys,* meaning that two words are used, but one thing is meant.[4] This could be the way in which Jesus and His followers explained the baptism of "Spirit and fire." On the Day of Pentecost the fire was a manifestation of the Holy Spirit with symbolic meaning. Just as the dove on Jesus was the Holy Spirit, so also the fire on the disciples was the Holy Spirit.

Fulfilled at a Future Time

At the same time, we cannot ignore "the fire of judgment" emphasis. The context of John the Baptist's prophecy of the baptism with the Holy Spirit and fire was his warning of "the wrath to come" (Matthew 3:7). Harold Horton points out that "John fails to distinguish [because he just did not know] between the time of the baptism in the Holy Spirit and the baptism in fire." Jesus did distinguish. He told His disciples just before His ascension: "For John truly baptized with water, but you shall be baptized with the Holy Spirit not many days from now" (Acts 1:5). Horton adds: "Thus he [Jesus] identified the baptism in the Spirit with the outpouring that took place at Pentecost. But he recognized the fire of judgment would be at the end, as does Paul (2 Thessalonians 1:8)."[5]

Some commentators look so closely at the context, which talks of judgment and fire, that they will not concede any baptism with the Spirit being fulfilled on the Day of Pentecost. This approach, of course, seems shortsighted. As G. E. Ladd has said: "The great messianic outpouring of the Spirit is about to take place. Against this background of prophetic expectation there is no valid reason to insist that John announced only a baptism of judgment."[6]

A Logical Solution

The balanced approach seems to be a twofold fulfillment of one baptism.

The first was at the beginning of (and continuing through) this age: an outpouring of the Spirit geared to individuals with the purpose of enduing each of God's people with personal power and the cleansing, spiritual fire of the Spirit that will burn up the chaff of life (see Matthew 3:11–12). It is, therefore, a baptism with the Holy Spirit and fire.

The second is a baptism of judgment at the end of the age: a climactic outpouring of the fullness of the Spirit to be released on the whole world. Its purpose will be to receive God's people in glory to Himself and to bring simultaneously a universal baptism of fire to judge the ungodly. Paul describes it like this in 2 Thessalonians 1:7–8: "when the Lord Jesus is revealed from heaven with His mighty angels, in flaming fire taking vengeance on those who do not know God, and on those who do not obey the gospel of our Lord Jesus Christ." Jude gives this description of the same judgment at the Second Coming of Christ: "to execute judgment on all, to convict all who are ungodly among them of all their ungodly deeds which they have committed in an ungodly way, and of all the harsh things which ungodly sinners have spoken against Him" (Jude 15). This, too, will be a baptism with the Holy Spirit and fire.

Two important Scriptures reinforce this idea of a twofold fulfillment of prophecy, and they seem to bear directly on our discussion. First, when Jesus was reading from Isaiah 61 in the synagogue, He stopped abruptly after saying, "To proclaim the acceptable year of the LORD" (Luke 4:19). He closed the scroll before reading the next line: "And the day of vengeance of our God" (Isaiah 61:2). First the Gospel of grace; the time of judgment would follow later.

Also, Peter's famous quotation of Joel 2:28–32 in his Pentecostal sermon (see Acts 2:17–21) has two distinct parts. The quote refers first to the gracious outpouring of God's Spirit upon His people, but then speaks of a "last days" time of judgment.

It is not unusual for Hebrew prophecies to outline a distant mountain range of truth. Upon closer examination, however, we see that skyline is actually two ranges melded together in view with a considerable distance (time gap) in between them.

TODAY'S HOLY SPIRIT FIRE

What does this mean for us living the Spirit-filled life today? The Christian is "on fire" when the Holy Spirit brings inspiration and vision; when the Spirit quickens the things of God; when burning, cleansing conviction comes; and when He empowers to do God's will. A Christian responding in obedience, confidence and faith experiences "fire"! As we noted at the beginning of this chapter, this is different from a psychologically induced fervor. Holy Spirit fire is more than natural feeling; it is the unction of God's Spirit. It is an actual, literal presence and impartation that comes directly from God and is the true source of immediate help and continuing zeal. It is being "filled with the Spirit." *Enthusiasm* means basically "to be filled with God." This is the biblical meaning of "being on fire" for God or being filled with the Spirit. To experience the power and intensity of the Holy Spirit is to have the fire or divine presence. Put simply:

> Holy Spirit Power = The Fire of God = Enthusiasm (being filled with God)

Remember Paul's admonition to the Romans: "Be . . . not lagging in diligence, [but be] fervent in spirit [burning, boiling in the Spirit]" (12:10–11); and also to the Thessalonians (4:19): "Do not quench [put out the fire of] the Spirit" (1 Thessalonians 5:19).

One of the great preachers of London in the 1880s was Joseph Parker of The City Temple. He ties in the above characteristics beautifully with that special spiritual quality or presence of the Holy Spirit:

> We see also how unmistakable fire is. Who can mistake fire? The difference between one man and another is a difference of heat. Heat, or fire, is the secret of all things. God is fire. It is so in all things. The difference between one reader and another is a difference of fire; the difference between one musician and another is that one man is all fire, and the other man all ice. The difference between one preacher and another is a difference of fire. Who can mistake the gift? Did not our hearts burn within us while he opened unto us the Scriptures? So with a true revival: we shall find it manifesting and vindicating itself, not in an accession of intellectual cleverness, but in that burning glowing fervour which purifies whatever it touches, consuming the dross and leaving the fine gold for the king's using.[7]

Examples of Divine Fire

The God of the Bible is known as a God of fire: "For our God is a consuming fire" (Hebrews 12:29; see also Deuteronomy 4:24). Fire often accompanied the revelation of God or His will: David called to the Lord "and He answered him from heaven by fire on the altar of burnt offering" (1 Chronicles 21:26; see also Exodus 13:21; 19:18). God's throne is likened to a "fiery flame, its wheels a burning fire" (Daniel 7:9). Elijah declared that "the God who answers by fire, He is God" (1 Kings 18:24). "The sight of the glory of the LORD was like a consuming fire on the top of the mountain in the eyes of the children of Israel" (Exodus 24:17).

God's fire sometimes consumes objects (as with the camp of Israel, see Numbers 11:1; 16:35), or it can appear without affecting objects (as with the burning bush, see Exodus 3:2). Elijah's prayer for vindication was answered dramatically with fire that issued forth from God (see 1 Kings 18:38). This was more than a flash of lightning; it was miraculous fire with unlimited capability. It consumed the sacrifice and the wood piled upon the altar. But that was not enough! It burned up the altar stones, the earth piled up to form a trench—and then licked up the water in the trench!

These references illustrate graphically the intensity and purity of God's nature; they do not, of course, reduce God to an earthly element. God displays spiritual reality through things familiar to the human mind. He may appear as fire, but the actual being of God is incomparable, immeasurable and not understandable by mere earthly standards (see 1 Timothy 1:17). That is why the fire of Acts 2 is said to be "as of fire," which means "like fire."

I like F. B. Meyer's summary of the ancient appearances of divine fire:

> Every Israelite could recall many an occasion in the glorious past when Jehovah had answered by fire. It burnt in the acacia-bush, which was its own fuel; it shone like a beacon-light in the van of the desert march; it gleamed on the brow of Sinai; it smote the murmuring crowds; it fell upon the sacrifices which awaited it on the brazen altar. It was the emblem of Jehovah, and the sign of his acceptance of his people's service.[8]

FIRE WITH SYMBOLIC SIGNIFICANCE

Fire symbolized the divine presence and also judgment (see Psalm 50:3; 97:3; Isaiah 6:6–7; 2 Thessalonians 1:8). Notice that of the eight judgments that the prophet Amos pronounced upon various nations, seven stated, "I will send fire" (Amos 1:4, 7, 10, 12, 14; 2:2, 5). Fire as God's divine presence is shown most notably in the filling of His habitations.

Fire on the Houses of God

The three main houses or habitations of God mentioned in Scripture are:

- The Tabernacle of Moses
- The Temple of Solomon
- The Church of Jesus Christ

Fire from heaven showed God's acceptance of the worship and confirmation of His pleasure in each sanctuary. Fire descended on the sacrifice at the Tabernacle (see Leviticus 9:24), and fire came and consumed the sacrifice at Solomon's Temple (see 2 Chronicles 7:1). The falling fire was not repeated at either place. (Note: The structures built by Zerubbabel and by Herod were reconstructions of Solomon's Temple; hence, no fire.)

The third sanctuary was the Church. This time, however, fire fell on the people rather than a structure—and they were not harmed! God's Spirit bypassed Herod's beautiful building of stone and gold and came instead upon the believers there. Herod's Temple was later destroyed by Roman fire, but God's greatest Temple—the Church of Jesus—remained, overcoming even the flaming torches of Nero, which consumed her martyrs' bodies.

Visible fire accompanied the baptism with the Spirit only on its initial occurrence, when God confirmed the Church as His new sanctuary. Such outward fire was not meant to accompany every succeeding infilling of the Holy Spirit. Once lighted (as in Tabernacle and Temple), the fire of the Spirit was to be kept burning perpetually on the altar of the people's hearts. On occasion godly people throughout the Church's history have seen visions of fire, but the fire of Pentecost was not meant to be repeated visually with every succeeding baptism with the Spirit. This becomes obvious from the pattern recorded in Acts in which no more visible fire was seen or mentioned.

The Lighting of the Lamps

John, the apostle, saw in a vision seven golden lampstands (see Revelation 4:5) and Jesus standing in the midst (see Revelation 1:13). The seven lamps of flame, called "the seven Spirits of God," are another way of visualizing the fullness and perfection of the Holy Spirit in the whole Church.

The candelabra used in the Tabernacle and later in the Temple were actually lampstands with seven branches. A lamp with oil and wick was placed on the platform top of each branch of the stand. Once lighted, the flames were not to be extinguished. Each day the priest filled each lamp with oil and trimmed the wicks. The lampstand was prophetic: The seven branches depicted the fullness of the Christian Church, the seven flaming lamps spoke of the Spirit-inspired message or light of each church and the oil, of course, portrayed the Holy Spirit.

The Pentecostal tongues of fire resting on the disciples confirmed the presence of the Holy Spirit. They proclaimed the lighting of the global Church with the illumination of the Holy Spirit. When Jesus told us to be the lights in the world (see Matthew 5:14), it naturally implied the presence of fire. Without electricity, the ancient peoples relied on fire. With fire there was light. This is still true for us today and so is Psalm 18:28: "For You will light my lamp; the LORD my God will enlighten my darkness."

Zechariah's Vision

Zechariah prophesied to Zerubbabel: "'Not by might nor by power, but by My Spirit,' says the LORD of hosts" (Zechariah 4:6). The accompanying vision pictured the familiar lampstand with a peculiar addition. Two olive trees poured oil into a heavenly bowl, which then drained through individual pipes (tubes) directly into each lamp. The trees, I am sure, had a meaning for that time, probably representing the two anointed prophets, Haggai and Zechariah, pouring their spiritual encouragement into the rebuilding of God's house in that day.

For the Church, however, the flowing oil depicts these last days when God is pouring out His Spirit. His people no longer need manual filling with oil (spiritual strength) by religious rites, traditions and authorities to meet spiritual needs. Instead, the Holy Spirit flows directly to each of us (see 1 John 2:20, 27). The days of manual, ritualistic filling are over!

SPURGEON'S EMPHASIS ON FIRE

The Holy Spirit is portrayed in the Bible as an actual entity—a Person of the Godhead. What better visual aid than fire? The figure of fire expresses the intensity and power of God—and also the force of the baptism of the Holy Spirit. A person cannot experience the power of the Spirit without being set on fire!

Few have understood the need of the Holy Spirit's fire more than the legendary Charles Spurgeon. In 1861, when he preached his first Sunday sermon in the large, newly constructed Metropolitan Tabernacle of London, he used 2 Chronicles 5:13–14 as his text. He fervently emphasized the necessity of "fire":

> Let God send the fire of His Spirit here, and the minister will be more and more lost in his Master. You will come to think less of the speaker and more of the truth spoken; the individual will be swamped, the words uttered will rise above everything. When you have the cloud, the man is forgotten; when you have the fire, the man is lost, and you only see his Master. Suppose the fire should come here, and the Master be seen more than the minister, what then? . . . It is easy enough for God to double our numbers, vast though they are even now. We shall have the lecture and we shall see in this place young men devoting themselves to God; we shall find ministers raised up and trained and sent forth to carry the sacred fire to other parts of the globe . . . heralds of the Cross who have here had their tongues touched with the divine flame. . . . Let God but send down the fire and the biggest sinners in the neighbourhood will be converted; those who live in dens of infamy will be changed; the drunkard will forsake his cups, the swearer will repent of his blasphemy, the debauched will leave their lusts.[9]

Such burning oratory should inspire us all to beseech the Lord: "Send the fire!"

Some well-meaning religious folk wince at the thought of an actual spiritual manifestation. To use the term *fire* in connection with their Christianity seems absurd to them. To those of us, however, who have experienced the wonderful power and demonstration of the Holy Spirit, the discussion of the Holy Spirit's presence as "fire" seems perfectly logical.

The Bible describes the Spirit with symbols that people understand: water, wind, fire and dove. Our conclusion is that the fervency and intensity of natural fire is an apt and accurate illustration of Holy Spirit activity.

Pray with me this prayer of Dr. Paul S. Rees. Make it your own. "Lord, end our lukewarm, mumbling religion. Lord, set us on fire. Put the divine fire in us before the atomic fire destroys us. Take away our small, selfish thoughts and make us big. Make us as big as the world's needs. Take away our weakness and fill us with Thy Power. Keep Thy promise, Lord, and baptize us with the Holy Ghost and with fire."[10]

REVIEW QUESTIONS FOR CHAPTER 5

1. Which of the Old Testament illustrations of divine fire impress you the most?
2. Do you think it is appropriate to say we are "on fire for God"?
3. Do you think the tongues of fire that settled on the disciples should be interpreted as the baptism of the Holy Spirit and fire?
4. How do you react to Parker's statement and Spurgeon's prayer? Are they just a little melodramatic?

6

SPEAKING IN TONGUES
IS THIS REALLY NECESSARY?

IN THIS CHAPTER

- Here's a miracle for you: Deaf mutes can speak in tongues!
- Discover seven good reasons for speaking in tongues
- Find the connection between tongues and praying in the Spirit
- Be surprised at how God uses this unusual manifestation

At Pentecost, when the disciples declared the greatness of God in languages they had never learned, a remarkable, life-changing experience was initiated. The invisible Spirit, our personal Helper, expressed Himself through the disciples in a special, dynamic way that bonded the disciples to God and each other—and made the awareness of Jesus dynamically real. This miracle of tongues was more than a visible sign or confirmation; in a marvelous way it combined both the initiatory act of

Holy Spirit baptism with the participation of people. More on this later in this chapter.

Also later, in chapter 9, we will look closely at how speaking in spiritual languages is associated with present-day Holy Spirit baptism and is theologically justified. Now, since we have just talked about Pentecost and the attendant wind and fire, it seems appropriate to discuss in this chapter and the next the reasons for this unusual manifestation of speaking in tongues.

To introduce our discussion, I would like to recall the advice of the Reverend David du Plessis, the man known affectionately as Mr. Pentecost. His wise counsel opened the door of blessing to thousands of people. He emphasized a shift of emphasis from "seeking an experience" of tongues to seeking "an encounter with Christ." This is excellent advice, and these chapters will promote such an encounter with Jesus Christ, the mighty baptizer with the Holy Spirit. Sinners need an encounter with Jesus the Savior. The sick need to encounter Jesus the healer. And, every disciple needs to encounter Jesus, the baptizer with the Holy Spirit.

WHAT IS SPEAKING IN TONGUES?

This phenomenon is not meant to be just a token illustration of supernatural power. Instead, it is to be a dynamic, exciting, spiritual tool in the believer's life that is enlightening, transforming—and an ongoing, daily experience. Speaking in tongues is not meant to replace normal Christian responsibilities or minimize the importance of the Bible, but it will enhance and enliven all the good things of God already in your life.

Speaking in tongues is the ability through the inspiration of the Holy Spirit to speak a language not learned through natural means. Sometimes the words are recognized as a specific language. Particularly, it is a spiritual language for devotional relationship with God through prayer, and one whose use needs the enabling of the Holy Spirit.[1]

There are generally four ways that God uses Christian glossolalia. It happens as:

- An immediate, spontaneous evidence of the indwelling Holy Spirit
- An ongoing "prayer language" that enables you to pray in the Spirit

- A gift coupled with interpretation that God uses to communicate to His assembled people
- The gift-ability, in a missionary situation, to speak to people in their languages

The Greek word *glossa* means "tongue" or "a language spoken." In the New Testament sense (as used by Jesus in Mark, by Luke in Acts and by Paul in Corinthians), it is "the supernatural gift of speaking in another language without its having been learnt" (W. E. Vine).[2] "[T]he technical term *glossolalia* derives from *glossais lalein,* a Greek phrase used in the NT meaning literally 'to speak in' [or 'with' or 'by'] tongues" (Spittler).[3]

This phenomenon is variously called: glossolalia, glossolalic utterance, praying in the Spirit, spiritual language, heavenly language, tongues, devotional tongues, speaking in tongues, tongues-speech, ecstatic speech and automatic language.

The New Testament refers to "new tongues" (Mark 16:17), "other tongues" (Acts 2:4), "different kinds of tongues" (1 Corinthians 12:10) and "a tongue" (1 Corinthians 14:2). There is no essential difference in any of these four expressions.

Some Bible versions give potentially misleading translations in the expressions used for tongues. A few are: "unknown tongue" (KJV), "strange tongues" (TEV), "a strange language" (BECK), "language of ecstasy" (NEB) and "languages that others don't know" (cev). The Greek word *glossa* simply refers to a language, and in this context to a language "you haven't learned" (LB) or "another language" (NIV footnote).

ARE "TONGUES" LITERAL LANGUAGES?

Happily for modern study, the New King James Version has dropped the word *unknown* used in the old Authorized Version. There are five occurrences in the Authorized Version of 1 Corinthians 14 where the translation is "an *unknown* tongue" (verses 2, 4, 14, 19, 27). The word is italicized, indicating that it was not part of the original meaning but that the translators felt it added clarification; it conveyed that the tongues mentioned were not known to the speaker. Casual readers have overlooked this significant point. Because *tongues* has an archaic ring and an unfortunate reputation, Jack Hayford suggests calling it "spiritual language"[4]—a term I like very much.

It is regrettable that readers have assumed through the years that the tongues were unknown in the sense that no one could understand them because no one had heard them spoken as actual languages. The use of *glossa* in Greek—or *language* and *tongue* in English—suggests by definition that the words spoken are understandable somewhere. There are some thirty "home languages" in the world, each of which has more than forty million speakers. For instance, Mandarin Chinese, at the top of the list, is spoken by more than 865 million people. English is second with more than 334 million people. A bona fide language is one that is used and understood by a community of people.

The "tongues" miraculously spoken past and present in the Christian Church are not gibberish, irrational or garbled speech, nonsensical jabbering or gobbledygook.[5] I believe, with many others, that spiritual language can be either one of the six thousand actual languages of the world or else angelic language, based on 1 Corinthians 13:1: "Though I speak with the tongues of men and of angels. . . ."[6]

Jack Hayford makes this comment:

> I wish to submit that the languages spoken by people today who employ spiritual language under the enabling power of the Holy Spirit are all actual languages. I'm aware that a few instances of linguistic analysis conducted by experts who have scrutinized tapes of speakers in tongues have made such judgments as "gibberish," or "This does not contain the usual structures of recognizable speech." But my own experience and that of many other Pentecostals and charismatics I have met strongly argue against this laboratorial judgment.[7]

Spiritual languages often prove to have human interpretation. As a teenager, having newly experienced this phenomenon (described in the Introduction), I marveled at the beauty of the experience and wondered at its authenticity as words of various languages were articulated clearly out of my mouth. Later, I was startled and amazed to hear veteran missionary W. W. Patterson tell of the Holy Spirit's activities in Indonesia. A great visitation of God occurred in that Southeast Asian archipelago in the early 1900s when many of the nationals were filled with the Holy Spirit and spoke in tongues. Some of those speaking in tongues, the missionaries reported, were speaking pure, proper English, in which they had had no training. The natives believed that what they spoke (English) was actually tongues, unknown to them. So it was!

A similar story is told of Carlton Spencer, president of Elim Bible Institute in New York State, visiting East Africa in the early 1950s. "What a glorious time it was," writes biographer Marion Meloon, "a veritable tidal wave of the Spirit. Carlton was privileged to behold the unusual sight of an African woman lost in worship and speaking in a language unknown to her—English! She sat with her babe at her breast, oblivious to all about her, even the babe's sucking and then slumber, as she worshiped on and on in English. Similar Baptisms swept through the crowds gathered, beyond numbering."[8]

Dennis J. Bennett gives several illustrations. Here is one of them:

> I have encountered many examples of someone speaking in known languages, but unknown to himself. At our Thursday communion service not long ago, an elderly lady presented herself at the altar rail for healing prayer. I had never seen her before and I have not seen her since. I didn't know her needs. Laying my hands on her head, I said the liturgical prayers for healing, and then added some of my own. Then realizing that although I did not know her needs the Holy Spirit did, I prayed quietly in words the Holy Spirit gave me to utter. I did not recognize the language that came to me, and I'm sure the woman did not either. Soon, feeling that my prayer had been completed, I moved along to pray for others. The next day a friend called: "Did you realize that Gloria S. was kneeling next to that woman yesterday, and she says you prayed in Japanese?"
>
> Gloria S. is an old acquaintance, the daughter of a well-known family in the diocese who were occasional attendants at St. Luke's. She and her husband had just returned from four years in Japan, where he had been with the State Department. I called Gloria. "Oh, yes," she said. "You prayed in Japanese." She proceeded to tell me some of the phrases of the prayer in Japanese and then in English. She had not heard the whole prayer but had picked up phrases. "Your conclusion was, 'Because you have asked this thing,'" she said, giving it to me in Japanese and English. "By the way, your accent is perfect."[9]

I once demonstrated speaking in tongues in an Oregon church (to show the people the ease of speaking in a devotional prayer language without excessive behavior), and I was surprised to have a couple who had served in China as missionaries tell me that I had spoken in Mandarin Chinese. David Sell, one of our elders who now pastors in Pleasanton, California, prayed once in Spanish at a prayer meeting in our San Jose church, and once in Portuguese. David did not know either language, but some in the congregation did and they confirmed hearing these languages.[10]

I recently heard Pastor David Walker of Las Vegas tell of a Pentecostal meeting a few years ago in which a Chinese man was present in the service. A woman spoke in tongues and the interpretation was given. The Chinese man was visibly impressed, and after the service asked the pastor about the woman who had spoken in Chinese. The pastor was mystified, since no one to his knowledge in the church spoke Chinese. The visitor assured him that the woman had actually spoken in Chinese.

C. Peter Wagner tells of another episode:

> On a recent visit to England . . . I learned of an incident where a monolingual British pastor was ministering to a multilingual Arab who happened to be serving as the principal translator in England for the OPEC oil cartel. The pastor sensed that God wanted him to pray about a certain physical ailment that the Muslim was suffering, and as he did so, he prayed some in tongues, as was his custom. The Arab was amazed just as were the unbelievers on Pentecost. The pastor had first prayed in fluent Iranian, then later in fluent Ugaritic, an obsolete language! The meaning of the prayers in the two different languages was identical. In this case, the Arab acknowledged it as a miracle of God, was born again, and is now a strong witness among fellow Muslims.[11]

Seven Reasons for Speaking in Tongues

Research and experience show that there are specific reasons for the use of a spiritual language. (Some of these parallel the four uses given above.) They demonstrate seven underlying, marvelous spiritual truths:

- Personal Evidence
- A Declaration of Praise
- A Prophetic Call
- A Uniform Experience
- Spirit-Inspired Prayer

- Spiritual Release
- Continuity

Consider with me these appealing reasons to speak in tongues.

Personal Evidence: It Signifies His Presence

During the Old Testament era, the nation of Israel constituted the people of God. They spoke their own language, and when God wished to communicate with them, He spoke through prophets in that language. This prophetic manifestation was the predominant evidence that the Holy Spirit had come upon a person.

With the coming of the Holy Spirit at Pentecost, the Lord graciously chose to introduce speaking in tongues as the immediate, uncontestable proof that a person is filled with the Spirit. Such evidence is valuable, for it lets the person involved, and others as well, know beyond question that God has indeed done a miraculous act. Peter and his Jewish companions knew that the Gentile household of Cornelius was filled with the Spirit, "For they heard them speak with tongues and magnify God" (Acts 10:46). Glossolalia was "a supernatural sign that God was in the midst of these believers" (Christenson).[12] As C. S. Lovett observes: "Every case of tongues in the book of Acts was a sign that the Holy Spirit was indwelling the believer."[13]

The Spirit, of course, also manifests Himself in believers' lives in the "fruit of the Spirit" (see Galatians 5:22–23), which, as we all know, takes time for development (like natural fruit ripening on a tree). This is a slow, although highly esteemed and significant, way for the Holy Spirit to show His presence in a person's life. Both of these proofs are valuable for the believer: immediate manifestation triggered by faith and mature fruit produced by spiritual growth. Tongues will come instantly, but patience will take a little longer! Both are a dynamic work of the Holy Spirit.

Speaking in tongues is quite a remarkable idea when you consider the physical process. God gives evidence of the inner presence of the Spirit by using the body member most dependent on volitional, human intelligence: the tongue! "No man can tame the tongue. It is an unruly evil, full of deadly poison" (James 3:8). God controls the most rebellious member of the human body (and by implication, all the others). Bypassing the mind, the Spirit uses the tongue to glorify God in words unknown to the person's brain and, thus, not corrupted by any self-serving motivation. Speaking in tongues allows an individual to pray words undefiled, because it is the Spirit Himself who directs the utterance.

A Declaration of Praise: It Expresses Inspired Worship

When the disciples spoke in tongues at Pentecost, the Bible says that they were not preaching the Gospel to the gathered Jews but were joyfully magnifying almighty God: "We hear them speaking in our own tongues the wonderful works of God" (Acts 2:11). Prayer in a spiritual tongue is one of the highest forms of inspired worship.

Such worship is called inspired because, as we noted earlier, the words spoken originate with the Holy Spirit: "And they were all filled with the Holy Spirit and began to speak with other tongues, *as the Spirit gave them utterance*" (Acts 2:4, emphasis added). One of the chief characteristics of the Holy Spirit is that He glorifies Jesus. Jesus said, "He will glorify Me, for He will take of what is Mine and declare it to you" (John 16:14). The Holy Spirit delights in inspiring us to speak the praise of Jesus and the Father.

A good application of this point is found in Isaiah 57:19: God creates the fruit of the lips—a promise given to both Jews and Gentiles. Notice the wording in the Amplified Bible (and how it is used of worship in the Hebrews verse):

> Peace, peace to him who is far off [both Jew and Gentile], and to him that is near! says the Lord; I create the fruit of his lips and I will heal him—make his lips blossom anew with speech [in thankful praise]. [Acts 2:39; Ephesians 2:13–17, 18; Hebrews 13:15.]

It is also one of the greatest enhancers of a person's prayer life. I have discovered that sometimes in prayer, the Lord will empower me to pray in a language that I have never experienced before. The freshness and inspiration of that kind of quickening of the Holy Spirit causes the heart to soar in worship! It is truly a declaration of praise!

A Prophetic Call: It Reaffirms the Great Commission

God loves all nations! Pentecostal tongues reaffirmed for the disciples that they must take the Good News to every nation, for Jesus had said: "Go therefore and make disciples of all the nations, baptizing them in the name of the Father and of the Son and of the Holy Spirit" (Matthew 28:19). F. Dale Bruner comments that

> nothing more aptly expressed the will of God for the world mission of the church than proclaiming the great deeds of God in the world's languages. This is what gives the Pentecost story its beauty and meaning. To be filled with the Holy Spirit is to want others to know God's deeds in Christ. The Holy Spirit moves men to praise the "mighty works of God" (v. 11).[14]

The Hebrew prophets often emphasized God's desire for salvation for all nations and gave universal calls to worship. This is beautifully evident in the Psalms. "Praise the LORD, all you Gentiles! Laud Him, all you peoples!" (Psalm 117:1, quoted by Paul in Romans 15:11). Psalm 96 captures this thought magnificently: "Oh, sing to the LORD a new song! Sing to the LORD all the earth. . . . Declare His glory among the nations, His wonders among all peoples. . . . Say among the nations, 'The LORD reigns.'" This is the song of the Pentecostal believer!

Praying in a spiritual language reminds us that Jesus' message is to be proclaimed without racial, social, ethnic or linguistic barriers or filters. His religion will be more than a Jewish religion—one that will embrace every kindred, tribe and nation. Henceforth, the divine message will go to all nations in their own heart languages and on their own turf! Gentile converts would no longer be required to meet the outward standards of Hebrew tradition; they can be saved, yet remain Gentiles: "For from the rising of the sun, even to its going down, My name shall be great among the Gentiles" (Malachi 1:11). The Gospel will transform and redeem lives, not destroy culture. Only when culture promotes immorality and idolatry must it change.

I have already proposed that the Pentecostal outpouring actually happened in the Court of the Women in the Temple. If this is true, then Gentile languages spoken in a place where no Gentile could come speaks dramatically to the fact that God had opened the doors of the true Temple to the nations. As C. Peter Wagner states: "All people groups, not just the Jews, could now have direct access to God through Jesus the Messiah."[15]

In addition, since this court was the farthest place in the Temple that a devout Jewish woman could go, the choice of location speaks as well to the inclusion of women. The Church was now truly global!

As Peter explained what was happening on the Day of Pentecost, he referred to the tongues spoken by the disciples as prophecy—quoting the prophet Joel as saying that God would pour out His Spirit and people would prophesy (see Acts 2:17–18). This evidence of the Holy Spirit's presence was prophecy in the sense that these groups heard the worship of God in their own languages—prophetic expressions of joy and praise. The new element, however, was that the speakers did not know the languages they spoke—they simply spoke under divine inspiration.

Now, instead of only a few people prophesying in Hebrew (their mother tongue) on infrequent occasions to special audiences, the door was open for *anyone* to experience the Holy Spirit's anointing through this special enabling. In other words, prophecy served as evidence of Holy Spirit empowerment when the people of God were national; now that the people of God—the Church—are international, both tongues and prophecy are evidence of Holy Spirit empowerment. Tongues, however, serve as a personal, immediate sign to each believer. This is a new spiritual gift, a unique sign of a new age, which signifies that God comes into His people in a new prophetic dimension.

Actually, Pentecost was not the first time that the Lord intervened in human history regarding languages on an international scale. You will recall that the descendants of Noah spoke the same language until they rebelled against divine authority and began construction of a great tower (see Genesis 11:1–6). God then separated them by destroying their communication—causing them to speak in new languages and forget their original languages! He then "scattered them abroad from there over the face of all the earth" (verse 8). At Pentecost, the curse of spiritual separation was broken. The Holy Spirit began drawing from every ethnic group those who would serve the Lord and accept His salvation. This international group—retaining ethnic identities and languages—became the authentic, unified people who make up the Body or Church of Jesus Christ, the true messianic community.

The Spirit of Pentecost was, and is, the one force that can override human differences and bring people together. Miracle-tongues demonstrated this and continue to remind us of the foundational truth that the door is open to all. When praying in tongues, we connect—on a sort of spiritual Internet—with the Holy Spirit and the worldwide Church whose members also pray in the Spirit. Speaking in tongues reaffirms our missionary witness to all nations and reminds us that all believing people are welcome in His Church.

The promise of the Holy Spirit is for all peoples, in every generation, throughout this entire age. Each time a person speaks in tongues, that person is linked both to the original Church at Pentecost as well as today's global Church (see Romans 10:12; Galatians 3:26–28; Colossians 3:11). As Peter said in his sermon: "The promise is to you and to your children, and to all who are afar off, as many as the Lord our God will call" (Acts 2:39).

A Uniform Experience: It Is the Same for All

Speaking in tongues provides uniform evidence that authenticates the experience of all believers everywhere and in every generation. Carl Brumback, who some years ago wrote a comprehensive work on tongues in the Pentecostal movement, produced his own list of "reasons why God chose tongues." He made an interesting point of the fact that it was a "uniform experience." I would like to borrow that thought to include in my own list:

> It is only natural to expect the differences in temperament and capacity to cause different reactions to the gift of the Spirit. While all will greatly value the privilege of being filled with the Spirit, yet each one will react according to his own peculiar disposition. Thus, it would be impossible to establish the mental, emotional, or spiritual behavior of any single individual as a requisite in all. This reveals the need for a uniform evidence by which the experience of all, whether educated or uneducated, emotional or unemotional, mature or immature, could be authenticated.[16]

George Canty, another pioneer Pentecostal, makes this interesting comment about tongues in the Pentecostal movement:

> Progress in true Pentecostal revival world-wide only broke out when the Baptism with the Spirit attested by tongues became the standard basis of thousands of new churches. We shall lose the secret of the global revival if we adopt again the unclear theology of the 1890s [the Wesleyan-Holiness Movement], and bypass what happened in 1901 [the beginning of the Pentecostal movement].[17]

This footnote in Brumback's book gives an unusual confirmation of believers' bonding through the experience:

> Pentecostal workers among the mutes inform us that these silent saints, when being filled with the Spirit, speak in tongues just like anybody else! Even if the divine economy had dictated an exceptional policy for these friends, should this have made void the necessity for tongues as an evidence of the infilling of normal believers? No more than their inability to confess with their mouth the Lord Jesus (Rom. 10:9, 10) makes such a confession less binding on us who have the powers of speech.[18]

A young mother called our pastor the other day so excited that she could hardly make herself understood. While she was having a devotional time with her two boys (ages six and eight), she explained to them the possibility of speaking in tongues when they prayed. As they prayed, each of them began to pray in the language of the Spirit! The tongues were an instant verification to the mother and boys (just as it was to the apostles) that the Holy Spirit was indeed active in their lives. They had been blessed with a new exciting awareness of Jesus but also with the recognizable, uniform sign of the experience shared by people around the world and of every age.

Spirit-Inspired Prayer: It Actuates a New Dimension of Prayer

Prayer is speaking or conversing with God. We do this consciously with words and thoughts that express our needs or desires or praises. Faith must be exercised to believe that God actually hears us. Many wonderful Bible verses affirm this general mode of prayer (such as 1 John 5:14).

Paul's suggestion that we can also utter unlearned spiritual language and know that we are speaking to God, speaking mysteries, edifying ourselves and giving thanks well is quite revolutionary! William G. MacDonald, minister in the Assemblies of God, says: "Prayer may now be made 'in the Spirit' as well as in the ordinary manner. This new edifying manner is not limited by the constrictions of the believer's knowledge and oral competence."[19]

As a supernatural happening, praying in the Spirit defies human ability to explain, but so many of us can testify that it works. An amazing confidence occurs as your mind focuses upon God, the Holy Spirit gives you miraculous expression and you encounter the reality of Jesus in a wonderful new way. Praying fluently for several minutes under the inspiration of the Spirit is truly uplifting!

Don Basham put it this way: "Speaking or praying in tongues is a form of prayer in which the Christian yields himself to the Holy Spirit and receives from the Spirit a supernatural language with which to praise God."[20] Such prayer should then become an ongoing work of the Spirit, practiced daily. The first, visibly miraculous evidence of the Spirit-filled life thrusts your prayer into a glorious new dimension (thus showing the priority of spiritual prayer). You are actuated, moved to action, in a new level of spiritual prayer. You are introduced to the realities of the spiritual realm in spectacular fashion. Suddenly there is new meaning to Jude 20–21: "But you, beloved, building yourselves up on your most holy faith, praying in the Holy Spirit, keep yourselves in the love of God." This experience of praying in the Spirit will prove to be one of your greatest sources of inspiration and power, a key to unlock the operation of the various gifts of the Spirit and a marvelous way to enhance the presence of Jesus in your life.

In Paul's famous discussion about the spiritual armor of God, he wrote the following: ". . . and [take] the sword of the Spirit, which is the word of God; praying always with all prayer and supplication in the Spirit" (Ephesians 6:17–18). Gordon Fee, one of the premier New Testament scholars of our day, says this about Paul's intent in the words "praying in/by the Spirit":

> There is every good reason to think that Paul intends this phrase precisely as he has used it elsewhere—especially in 1 Cor 14:14–15 (cf. Rom 8:26–27)—to refer specifically to that form of prayer in which the Spirit assumes a special role in praying, especially, though probably not exclusively, praying in tongues. In that passage Paul distinguishes between two forms of prayer: one he will do "with the mind" and in the public assembly; the other he will do "in/by the Spirit" and in the privacy of his own life of devotion before God. If that catches some of us off guard because it is so little a part of the prayer life of most people in the church, we probably ought not to read our experience of church back into the life of Paul. What Paul says about this kind of praying in 1 Cor 14:1–5 and 14–19 demonstrates that he engaged in it regularly, and that he urged the believers in Corinth to do so as well.[21]

Let me add that this spiritual activity is not (in my estimation) a gift; this is rather an operation of the Spirit who Himself is our gift. This thought surprises some people, who assume that speaking in tongues is the spiritual gift mentioned in 1 Corinthians 12:10: ". . . to another different kinds of tongues." Some will find that they specifically have a gift of languages, which enables them to minister in foreign languages in the church (as described in 1 Corinthians 14) or in a missionary situation. But I suggest that all Christians can experience prayer in devotional tongues as a regular part of Christian living, even praying in a different language each day!

Praying in the Spirit should not be considered just the operation of a spiritual gift; it is, in a grander sense, the Holy Spirit Himself enabling you to pray more effectively. We expect Christians to do certain things because they are Christians, not because they are gifted. It is a role in which we function more than a gift in operation. We should all witness for Christ, for instance, even if we are not all evangelists. We all exercise faith, although we all do not have the gift of faith. We should all give tithes and offerings, even if we all do not have a gift of bountiful giving. We Christians do these things because they are a part of our role—what we do regularly—in being an active Christian.[22] It is the same with praying in a prayer language.

Some feel that every Spirit-baptized believer should speak in tongues at least once to validate the experience. This would be just a brief, token experience and would certainly prove inadequate and unsatisfactory. This unfortunate approach is very substandard for Spirit-filled believers! The initial experience of speaking in tongues should be followed by a lifestyle involving daily, flowing, anointed prayer in heavenly language. Evidently, that was Paul's conviction, for he said: "I thank my God I speak with tongues more than you all" (1 Corinthians 14:18). Gordon Fee says this of Paul's life in the Spirit: "We know from all the letters that he was a man of prayer, joy, and thanksgiving; what we learn here is that his 'spirituality' included a continual life of praying and singing in the Spirit—in this case, with glossolalia."[23]

Dennis Bennett, the Episcopal rector whose experience launched the present-day charismatic renewal, says this:

> Speaking in tongues is not the baptism in the Holy Spirit but it is what happens when and as you are baptized in the Spirit and it becomes an important resource to help you continue, as Paul says, to "be being (or keep on being) filled with the Holy Spirit."[24]

Spiritual Release: It Enhances the Spiritual Life

Speaking in tongues releases new avenues of spiritual expression that greatly enhance your spiritual life. From 1 Corinthians 14 we learn why Paul spoke in tongues so much and why he advocates this practice. Because a person:

- Speaks to God (verses 2 and 14): speaks or communes with God by the Spirit
- Speaks mysteries (verse 2): utters things outside natural understanding
- Edifies himself (verse 4): receives personal edification through private prayer and praise
- Is able to sing with the Spirit (verse 15): truly a song of the Lord
- Gives thanks well (verse 17): a case of divine enabling

These points are sometimes swept aside as unimportant because Paul's primary objective is missed. Actually, his emphasis is the appropriate use of both prophecy and tongues—not the depreciating of one in favor of the other!

Paul was not a novice in using these marvelous tools of the Holy Spirit to empower spiritual life; he taught from the context of life experience. That is why he made this significant statement in verse 18: "I thank my God I speak with tongues more than you all." The importance is often lost because of the special emphasis in the rest of the sentence (verse 19): "Yet in the church I would rather speak five words with my understanding, that I may teach others also." Paul wishes all to prophesy but also wishes everyone to experience glossolalia (see verse 5). In no way does he wish to eliminate or downplay tongues, for he says plainly, "Do not forbid to speak with tongues" (verse 39). In other words, Paul condemns unbridled use of tongues in a public service, but he stresses the blessing of a personal prayer language.[25]

We all would like to know the secret of Paul's great success. Could it possibly have been his personal devotional life of praying in a spiritual language? You will find that a regular habit of praying in the Spirit will be like a key that unlocks the charismatic gifts and ministries to you.

Continuity: It Declares His Continuing Presence among Us

Speaking in tongues gives evidence of the continuing, abiding presence of the Holy Spirit in both the individual and the Church.

Initiated at Pentecost, miraculous tongues continue as a convincing witness, evidence of the Spirit wherever the Gospel is preached: "And these signs will follow those who believe: . . . they will speak with new tongues" (Mark 16:17).[26] Tongues with interpretation has continued as a sign-gift in many Christian worship services to confirm the presence of the blessed Holy Spirit.

Today, charismatic believers throughout the world attest to the validity of the experience of speaking in tongues. Vinson Synan, church historian, gives this recent report of the Pentecostal/charismatic proliferation:

> [It is] the most important religious movement of the entire twentieth century. . . . Christians around the world have experienced a renewal of the gifts of the Spirit. . . . This movement, which now constitutes the second largest family of Christians in the world (after the Roman Catholic Church), is found in practically every nation and ethnic group in the world. By the end of the century, over 500,000,000 people were involved in this revival which continues its massive growth into the new millennium.[27]

IS SPEAKING IN TONGUES NECESSARY?

If you are an authentic Christian—that is, truly born again by the Holy Spirit—you will not be refused entrance to heaven if you do not speak in tongues. We are saved by God's grace and by putting our faith in Jesus Christ. Tongues are a separate issue.

Speaking in tongues is a wonderful experience that first occurs when the born again believer is baptized with the Holy Spirit. This is meant to be an ongoing experience that will greatly empower and facilitate your Christian life—and make your service for and relationship with Jesus Christ more wonderful than it otherwise would be. Please do not ignore, disbelieve or treat lightly something so emphasized in the Bible and experienced by multiplied thousands of believers.

So, a person can live without speaking in tongues, but why would anyone want to do so when the promise is so grand and the results so beneficial? If you are still somewhat hesitant about personally praying in the Spirit, please make your focus that of being filled with the Holy Spirit and drawing closer to Jesus. Let your loving worship be given unreservedly to Jesus and you will delightedly find yourself speaking in tongues!

REVIEW QUESTIONS FOR CHAPTER 6

1. Explain how tongues could mean an invitation to all nations.
2. How do you respond to the concept of God using our "unruly member" for the miraculous?
3. Does it seem logical to you to have evidence for the baptism with the Holy Spirit that is consistently alike for all those filled with the Spirit?
4. Do Gordon Fee's thoughts about Ephesians 6:17–18 make sense to you?
5. How would you answer the question, Is speaking in tongues really necessary?

7

ANSWERS TO PESKY QUESTIONS
REASONS PEOPLE GIVE

IN THIS CHAPTER

- Analyze thirteen objections people voice about tongues
- Learn which teaching makes it most difficult for a person to pursue tongues
- Discover if it is necessary for everyone to speak in tongues
- Learn whether or not a person must be "emotional" to speak in tongues
- Find out: Did the church at Ephesus speak in tongues?

If the early Church believed and practiced speaking in tongues, wouldn't you think that all Christians today would be open to the possibility of personally praying in the Spirit? Not necessarily. This chapter lists thirteen reasons that people give for hesitancy toward speaking in tongues—or not accepting this phenomenal spiritual gift as authentic in our day.

123

"IT'S UP TO GOD"

Perhaps you have heard someone say, "If God wants me to have the gift of speaking in tongues, then He will give it to me." That individual might be surprised to learn that this is not God's style. The Lord makes His gifts available. He then encourages us to "ask . . . seek . . . knock" (Luke 11:9). In fact, He even commands us through His Word to "desire spiritual gifts" (1 Corinthians 14:1). God, however, does not force His spiritual gifts upon us—they will only come in response to one's own desire, responsive heart and faith. If a person does not want to speak in tongues, or does not see the need to, God will not thrust it upon him or her. Instead, He patiently waits for His children to ask. "If you then, being evil, know how to give good gifts to your children, how much more will your heavenly Father give the Holy Spirit to those who ask Him!" (Luke 11:13).

When our hearts are open, the Spirit can bring His gifts into our lives. It is unfortunate when people do not want or need manifestations of the Holy Spirit. I say unfortunate because they are, in the case of tongues, shrinking back from clear teaching in the Bible about spiritual manifestations.

"I DON'T APPRECIATE BEING TOLD WHAT TO DO OR NOT DO"

Some Christians understandably resist being told they "must" speak in tongues. But, if this is an improper demand, then it seems appropriate to ask, Why *not* speak in tongues? Especially since it is a Bible-based teaching. Remember, Paul admonishes: "Do not forbid to speak with tongues" (1 Corinthians 14:39).

Does a person have to speak in tongues when he receives the baptism with the Holy Spirit? There is actually no statement in the Bible that says someone has to speak in tongues. Luke, the recorder of the book of Acts, does not make a single theological statement or lay down any requirement. Instead, we are given a pattern to follow. As Larry Christenson says, "God tells us how others knew and did His will, so that we, by looking at their lives, may not only know His will but see how to do it, too."[1]

The Word of God is given so that we may know those things that are to be a part of our Christian heritage and experience. Read the Acts of the Apostles and also 1 Corinthians 12–14 and see how the Bible advocates that speaking a spiritual language is important for our well-being. This fact alone should cause us to desire it.

You are "fearfully and wonderfully made" (Psalm 139:14). God knows exactly what is needed in your life to bring you to highest fulfillment. He presents you with a marvelous gift that ensures your best possible success. If you feel resistant at the suggestion of speaking in tongues, try not to see it as a human directive but a blessing from your loving Father. Once you experience the edifying benefits of a spiritual language, you will see why the Bible advocates this wonderful practice. That reality cannot be comprehended before it happens. Your faith in responding to God's invitation opens the door to a marvelous experience.

"IT'S TOO EMOTIONAL"

Human beings are emotional beings. Almost everyone can be highly emotional in certain settings—which usually does not mean church! Look at the Christians who are extremely demonstrative at an athletic event or a rock concert or a political rally but sit unmoved in a religious setting. The Bible (particularly in Psalms) teaches God's people to be full of feeling and even exuberant in worshiping Him—and indicates that our emotional nature finds its greatest satisfaction in God.

Having said that, let us remember that speaking in tongues is not initiated by human emotion but by the Holy Spirit moving upon an individual. Acts 2:4 says that the disciples on the Day of Pentecost "began to speak with other tongues, as the Spirit gave them utterance." Speaking in tongues raises your emotional nature to its finest form. Paul said: "He who speaks in a tongue edifies himself" (1 Corinthians 14:4). This means "builds you up, strengthens you," so it is not something of which to be fearful but rather grateful. Our emotions find their highest fulfillment in the worship and service of almighty God—and responding to His Holy Spirit.

People all react differently to different situations—for example, people reacting to a football game, a symphony orchestra, a comedian's funny antics. To watch such a crowd when you are not part of it would cause you to be outside the flow of activity. On the Day of Pentecost, some watching the disciples thought they were "drunk." Peter quickly explained that they were experiencing the outpouring of the Spirit. Everyone who experiences the Holy Spirit will be emotional in the sense that deep feelings will occur and a renewed appreciation of and dedication to God will occur. But this is not some strange, scary "out of mind" experience that is destructive. As I explained in the Introduction, when I first spoke in tongues I was one excited fourteen-year-old boy, but one of the marvelous things that I noticed was that my mind was sharper and clearer than it had ever been—so much so, that I began articulating every prayer I could think of since I knew that this wonderful experience of the Holy Spirit had brought me directly into God's presence.

It is important to realize that Christians often receive the Spirit-baptism in a quiet, outwardly unemotional manner. The main thing is openness of heart and faith to believe. The emotional level does not determine the effectiveness of the Spirit's work.

"SPEAKING IN TONGUES IS OF THE DEVIL"

Biblical tongues are the work of the Holy Spirit and not the devil. Jesus Himself says that believers "will speak with new tongues" (Mark 16:17). Paul's great concern about tongues in the church (see 1 Corinthians 14) was not their source. Rather, Paul was attempting to help the believers cooperate with the Holy Spirit and each other in the proper exercise of a spiritual gift.

The gift of tongues is not to be confused with the ecstatic "tongues" spoken in some cults and by shamans and witch doctors. These are indeed activities of the devil, done by those who do not profess Jesus as Lord. Note 1 John 3:10: "In this the children of God and the children of the devil are manifest: Whoever does not practice righteousness is not of God." The fact that some people practice unrighteousness does not mean that we must eliminate biblical activities such as speaking in tongues, prophesying, praying for the sick, casting out devils, receiving offerings or lifting our hands in praise. Do we lay aside the good merely because these activities might be counterfeited by other groups? We are to be guided by the Bible and judge any activity by its adherence to biblical teaching.

A Spirit-filled Christian need not worry about receiving tongues under the adversary's influence. Counterfeits are easy to recognize—very obvious, but infrequent in our culture. Every Christian has spiritual sensitivity and discernment that kicks in at a moment like that.

If you have been taught all your life that speaking in tongues is of the devil, you might have difficulty yielding to the Holy Spirit. In fact, this objection of all the thirteen may cause the biggest barrier to receiving the gift. Empty your mind of religious prejudice, and instead open your mind to what the Bible says. You will be so happy when you do!

"Speaking in Tongues Is Practiced by Hypocrites"

There will always be hypocrites and people with poor testimonies in the church. It is utterly regrettable that people become excited about supernatural gifts and neglect godly living. The epistles teach the importance of righteous behavior, and Acts teaches the demonstration of the Spirit. Both are essential and needed in the church. This argument clearly shows the need for solid, moral teaching in our churches—and the pastoral boldness to confront people who attempt to manifest the supernatural without living a life of holiness to back it up.

Faith triggers spiritual gifts, and this can be done by people not living as righteously as they should. Such people, however, will soon lose their effectiveness, their consciousness of God—and their spiritual walks. Churches should take a strong stand on maintaining balance.

"It's Discouraging to Seek and Not Receive"

Sometimes people have not had appropriate teaching on the subject of faith, and it leaves them trying to function in neutral when they should be shifting into gear. Just as we "prophesy in proportion to our faith" (Romans 12:6), so we exercise faith to activate tongues.

It is good for us to seek the Lord and search our own souls to know our degree of sincerity and readiness. A person who prays for an hour seeking to be filled with the Spirit has no reason to be discouraged. This is not wasted time! But be sure to seek the Lord for who He is, not for what you can receive from Him, and believe that He has heard you.

Present yourself to God with audible worship and abandon yourself to His adoration. Ask sincerely for spiritual empowerment. You will soon be conscious of the Spirit's presence coming upon you, and as you continue to speak you will be enabled to speak in tongues by the Spirit's ability.

Jeremiah 29:13 says: "You will seek Me and find Me, when you search for Me with all your heart."

"The Spirit Cannot Be Divided into Two Experiences"

This is an awkward and confusing statement, but I have heard it repeated by those who feel that if they have the Spirit they will only need to have one experience with the Holy Spirit. People sometimes become very comfortable with their spiritual conditions and resist hearing that the Lord might have something more for them. Actually, the Christian life is much like natural life; there are periods of growth that provide us with new learning experiences and relationships.

Even before we become Christians, the Spirit is working upon our minds and hearts. It is His magnetism that draws us to Christ. Then, as we repent and accept Christ, the Spirit causes spiritual birth to take place—we are, as Jesus said, born of the Spirit. New Christians have Jesus living in their hearts by the power of the Holy Spirit. Even Jesus, as explained in chapter 1, grew in the things of the Spirit as pertaining to His personal relationship with God and character development.

But then Jesus was baptized by John and received a new work, a second blessing, a special baptism or empowering of the Holy Spirit. The Christians of Bible days (as explained in the closing chapters of this book) had conversion experiences produced by the Holy Spirit, but then they also realized that the same Spirit would also empower or baptize them with the Holy Spirit.

It is not that the Spirit is divided up, but rather that the same Spirit comes upon a person at various intervals, to the degree of his or her readiness, expectation and faith. Whenever we sense that we are being challenged by God to take a step of faith in our personal lives, we should do our best to respond. Sometimes it is sensing the need of the Holy Spirit's renewal to help us in a given situation.

The early apostles found that although they were baptized with the Spirit, they still from time to time needed a fresh "filling." Note this verse: "And when they had prayed, the place where they were assembled together was shaken; and they were all filled with the Holy Spirit, and they spoke the word of God with boldness" (Acts 4:31). This refers to believers who had previously experienced the miraculous infilling at Pentecost. We also need to be "refilled" with His Spirit. God has created us so that we must remain humble and dependent on Him. Just as a car must return to the gas station for a refill of gas, we too must be drawn to our source of supply. Our discernment, strength and boldness need a daily endowment of power.

Thus, we can truthfully say that the Christian life is a series of renewals or "empowerments" of the Spirit: one Spirit, but many ongoing, maturing experiences. The one Holy Spirit is referred to in Revelation as "the seven [seven-fold] Spirits of God" (Revelation 1:4; 4:5; 5:6), which verifies that the Spirit is not divided up but rather multiple and profuse in His manifestation.

"WHY, THEN, ARE TONGUES NOT TAUGHT IN THE EPISTLES?"[2]

This question is usually raised because of the perception that the epistles discuss the Holy Spirit extensively without mentioning tongues. While teaching on tongues is given in the epistles, specifically in 1 Corinthians 12–14, it is debatable that the Holy Spirit is written about extensively in these books. Four epistles have no mention of the Spirit; one epistle gives one verse; four have two verses; three have four verses; two have eight verses; one has nine verses. Five of the epistles give more attention to the subject of the Holy Spirit: Romans (27 verses), 1 Corinthians (31 verses), 2 Corinthians (13 verses), Galatians (14 verses) and Ephesians (15 verses).

Each New Testament book and chapter has a divine purpose for its inclusion in the Bible. Actually a great deal is said about tongues in the epistles, but it is localized in 1 Corinthians 12–14; that is the subject under discussion in an epistle that says much about Holy Spirit activity. This does not mean that the other churches receiving epistles did not speak in tongues; the text is simply discussing other aspects of the Spirit's work in Christian lives.

The comment is made: "Paul did not mention the gift [of tongues] in Galatia and Ephesus, where he spoke much about the Spirit."[3] Actually, Ephesians has only fifteen verses out of 155 that mention the Holy Spirit, and it is true that the subject of tongues is not included. Paul's theme was the liberty we have in the Spirit through faith (as opposed to the Law and circumcision). He was emphasizing another aspect of the Holy Spirit, and tongues were not relevant to the discussion. Paul's comments about praying in the Spirit (Ephesians 6:18), however, are easily connected with his teaching in 1 Corinthians 14.[4]

When the church first started in Ephesus, the record does state that some of the early converts in that city spoke in tongues and prophesied in Paul's presence (see Acts 19:6)!

Only four verses in Colossians (out of 95) mention the Holy Spirit, and it is obvious that the nature of Paul's presentation did not lend itself to an extended discussion of the Holy Spirit, let alone the subject of tongues.

Some feel that Corinth was a very carnal church and Ephesus a very spiritual one. The implication is sometimes drawn, therefore, that tongues are associated with carnal churches while spiritual churches like Ephesus were not bothered with such things. Later, however, the Spirit indicted Ephesus for leaving its first love (see Revelation 2:1–11). The whole teaching of the New Testament was for the whole Church—both then and now—and this includes spiritual manifestations.[5] Paul's teaching on the Holy Spirit to the Corinthians and Ephesians was both theological and practical, but the subject of glossolalia happens not to have been a discussion in the epistle to the Ephesians.

It is important to remember that the apostolic epistles were passed around among the churches, so the same information was being received by a large number of Christians. Paul closes Colossians, for instance, by saying: "Now when this epistle is read among you, see that it is read also in the church of the Laodiceans and that you likewise read the epistle from Laodicea." Also, see 1 Thessalonians 5:27; 2 Thessalonians 3:14. The apostle Peter comments on the circulation of Paul's epistles in 2 Peter 3:15–16: "As also our beloved brother Paul, according to the wisdom given to him, has written to you, as also in all his epistles, speaking in them of these things. . . ." This means, of course, that Paul's discussion on tongues was reaching more than one church!

"TONGUES WERE ONLY FOR THE 'INFANT STAGE' OF THE CHURCH"

I respectfully disagree with Charles Stanley when he says: "I believe the practice of prophecy, words of knowledge, and tongues were associated with the infant stages of the new church. Paul knew that a day would come when the church would reach a level of maturity where it could put away the things of childhood."[6]

My response is that the same foundation and structure of the early Church is also that of today's Church. The doctrinal teaching and the spiritual activity of the early Church—as given in the New Testament—are to be that of the ongoing Church. We need miracles and spiritual gifts today as much as they did in Bible days! Every generation needs the theological undergirding of the written Word but also the practical application and expression.

That foundation and structure must be carefully tended by each succeeding generation. There must be constant evaluation by the Church to see that the faith that began the Church is the faith that perpetuates it. As Jude 3 says: "Contend earnestly for the faith which was once for all delivered to the saints." Nothing in the epistles or Acts indicates or teaches that the miraculous signs were relegated to the opening stages of the Church.

The underlying concept behind this criticism is this: "I believe maturity has been achieved in the Church because of the completeness of the Word of God available to us so that sign-gifts are no longer necessary."

Thank God we do have a complete Word of God; there is no need for additional chapters to be added! It is one thing, however, to have a mature, completed text of the Word and another to have a Church that can maturely appropriate all that that Word teaches. The gifts of the Spirit are part of that mature corpus of Scripture; can we cut out those sections and still maintain that we have maturity?

There were sign-gifts in the early Church. Ronald A. N. Kydd has made a scholarly research of this in his book *Charismatic Gifts in the Early Church*. He makes this interesting observation:

[T]he Church prior to A.D. 200 was charismatic. . . . These three centuries [the first three of this era] saw dramatic changes in the Christian Church. In the midst of all this, the gifts of the Spirit vanished. There came a point around A.D. 260 at which they no longer fitted in the highly organized, well-educated, wealthy, socially-powerful Christian communities. The Church did not lose its soul, but it did lose these special moments when God broke into the lives of men and women.[7]

The gifts ceased, not because God wanted them to cease, but because of the Church's unbelief, a less charismatic leadership and tightening institutionalism (which left no room for spiritual manifestation).

There is absolutely no indication that the apostles expected the Church to exist without the supernatural! The Church does not follow a linear time line that makes it more mature spiritually simply because more time has passed. The Church of every generation must stay vigilant. It must evaluate its immediate spiritual condition and make any adjustments necessary to realign with the apostolic principles laid down in Scripture.

Scripture is mature and needs no additions. That is the foundation of both the early Church and today's Church. This does not mean that new generations in the Church attain spiritual maturity automatically because they believe in the apostolic foundation. The truths have been laid, but each generation must pursue and appropriate their fulfillment.

"SOME PEOPLE MAKE TONGUES A SUBSTITUTE FOR THE CROSS"

It is sad but true: "A person can speak in tongues and not have victory over sin and be crucified with Christ."[8]

Paul and the other writers contended consistently for both supernatural manifestations and responsible human behavior that is victorious over sin because of Christ and His cross. The reason that the New Testament is so full of admonitions about godly living is that God knew our propensity to live in the flesh, even if we have been filled with the Spirit!

It is true that Christians can speak in tongues and not be living victoriously, but that is not God's wish or the teaching of the Bible. It is equally true, of course, that Christians who do not speak in tongues might not be living victoriously. The criticism is valid, but it applies to all churches and whatever aspect of teaching has gotten in the way of the cross. Tongues and the spiritual gifts will enable a Christian to live a better life, but this will not happen without human responsibility and a living faith in Christ.

"TONGUES PROMOTE AN INVISIBLE 'CASTE SYSTEM' IN THE CHURCH"[9]

It is deplorable when speaking in a spiritual language is categorized as a status symbol or the qualifier for some initiation rite. Devoted believers who have not spoken in tongues are easily turned off by such a cultish and unscriptural teaching. We should do everything we can to eliminate such an attitude.

Howard M. Ervin, professor at Oral Roberts University, comments:

> The Pentecostal baptism in the Spirit is for power-in-mission. It is not instant maturity—contrary to the assumptions of an anti-Pentecostal rhetoric. Paul makes it clear that the Corinthians are carnal and spiritually immature because of their schismatic spirit (1 Cor. 1:11f., 3:11f.), while at the same time acknowledging that they did not lack any spiritual gift (1 Cor. 1:6). The manifestations of the Spirit's charisms are neither evidence of, nor contingent upon, spiritual maturity.[10]

We must also honestly face the fact that as long as the Word of God is proclaimed in a church, there will be those who respond and those who choose not to follow the Lord as closely as they should. Some will exercise faith for tithing, for example, but others will not. Should there be no teaching on tithing for fear that some nontithers will have their feelings hurt? Every subject, every challenge, will cause some to respond and others to reject. Jesus Himself faced the same situation with a message that often turned His hearers away, and we know His objective was not to make second-class citizens but rather to create incentives for people to continue growing in their faith.

Having said that, it is appropriate to say that those in a church who are responding to God's will should not flaunt their spirituality or obedience but rather show the reality of His work in their lives by love, patience and kindness. Teaching regarding tongues also should be diplomatic and loving while dedicated to the clarity of God's Word and will. Such a loving environment will encourage rather than alienate the church attendee or visitor.

"IT IS NOT CALLED A 'PRAYER LANGUAGE' IN THE BIBLE"[11]

True, speaking in tongues is not called a "prayer language." The use of the terminology is much like the word *millennium,* which also is not in the Bible; however, since the meaning of the word is "a thousand years," Bible teachers do not hesitate to refer to the six times that "a thousand years" is mentioned in Revelation 20 as the millennium. The same is true of *trinity*, yet it is commonly used because of its obvious meaning.

When the charismatic renewal began in the 1960s, many Christians in the historic denominations adopted the term "prayer language" because of the great delight they were finding in praying in tongues. This is, of course, scriptural. Paul in 1 Corinthians 14 makes it clear that when we speak in tongues we speak to God and speak the mysteries of God. On that basis, the terminology is justified.

"Tongues Was a Lesser Sign-Gift in the Early Church"

Charles Stanley states: "I believe the position of tongues in the church was the position of the lesser sign gift." He feels that "the Bible teaches prophecy was the greatest sign gift."[12]

For public communication Paul did teach the importance of prophecy over tongues (unless those tongues were interpreted). The main theme of 1 Corinthians 14 is the importance, in public meetings, of bringing the Word of God in a clear, understandable language. For this reason, prophecy is a better sign-gift in a church service.[13] For personal edification, however, the prayer language of tongues is a marvelous sign of the miraculous to the individual believer—and certainly more beneficial than prophesying to yourself.

Summary

We have now completed Parts 1 and 2. Part 1 stressed Jesus' dependence on the ministry of the Holy Spirit. Jesus had personally experienced the concerned assistance of the Spirit, so He naturally was delighted that His disciples would be given the same help. Part 2 emphasized "The Glorious Disturbance" on the Day of Pentecost that brought howling wind, blazing fire and supernatural tongues to the praying disciples. Two chapters were devoted to the miraculous "speaking in tongues" because it is not always understood by today's reader.

The next chapter opens Part 3 where "The Peter Pattern," a prescription for every believer's success, is carefully outlined. You will see how the Spirit works in our conversions, water baptisms and Spirit-baptisms. The last chapters of the book, Part 4, will trace the glorious sweep of the Spirit through the days of early Christianity, and we will glean principles that apply to our churches today.

REVIEW QUESTIONS FOR CHAPTER 7

1. Do you feel we have any responsibility in manifesting spiritual gifts?
2. Are you emotional in your seeking of God?
3. What benefits do you see in speaking in tongues?
4. How do you feel about tongues being mentioned specifically in only one of the epistles (1 Corinthians)?

PART 3

THE BAPTISM WITH THE HOLY SPIRIT

A MARVELOUS GIFT FOR ALL

8

THE PETER PATTERN
A PRESCRIPTION FOR SUCCESS

IN THIS CHAPTER

- Read the amazing proclamation of Peter that directly affects you!
- Say! Do you know how many New Testament baptisms there are?
- Search out the amazing terms that describe your life in Christ
- Learn why 1 Corinthians 12:13 is such a controversial verse

In this chapter and the next, we will see how conversion, water baptism and Spirit-baptism work together to form an apostolic paradigm. I call it the Peter Pattern because the concept was first articulated by the apostle Peter in Acts 2:38–39:

> "Repent, and let every one of you be baptized in the name of Jesus Christ for the remission of sins; and you shall receive the gift of the Holy Spirit. For the promise [of the Holy Spirit] is to you and to your children, and to all who are afar off [the Gentiles], as many as the Lord our God will call."

Let's begin our study of this pattern with the threefold breakdown of verse 38. Peter told his listeners that they must:

- "Repent,
- "and let every one of you be baptized in the name of Jesus Christ for the remission of sins;
- "and you shall receive the gift of the Holy Spirit."

The new believers were eager for others to experience a full, personal encounter with Jesus Christ and the Holy Spirit. Thus, Peter outlined, from the apostles' own experience, the ideal way to start! These three events made up the induction package for active life in the New Testament Church, the Body of Christ. We might describe them further as follows:

- Conversion: Acceptance of Jesus Christ as Savior and Lord through volitional choice, sincere repentance and personal belief that His shed blood covers our sins
- Water baptism: A sacred rite symbolizing purification from sin and a personal dedication to Christ and His teaching
- Baptism with the Holy Spirit: Reception of the Holy Spirit just as happened in Bible days, attended by speaking with other tongues[1]

All three events are introductory; they initiate a life of ongoing sanctification and service. A person is not launched into immediate spiritual maturity; rather, the elements of the Peter Pattern continue to feed our ongoing spiritual growth. This will happen through the ministry of our Paraclete-friend, the Holy Spirit. Remember also, the Peter Pattern is one followed by Jesus Himself; He was born of the Spirit, baptized in water and baptized with the Holy Spirit. (Note: Later in the book we will address the meaning of *filled with the Spirit* and other terminology as it relates to the above three experiences.)

Here is a scriptural overview of some of the key thoughts that relate to the threefold Peter Pattern and its elements of conversion, water baptism and baptism with the Holy Spirit. The chart that follows encapsulates those ideas.

SCRIPTURAL OVERVIEW OF THE PETER PATTERN

	Born again through the Holy Spirit by faith in the Lord Jesus Christ	Baptized by water into the Lord Jesus Christ	Baptized with the Holy Spirit
1. Objective	Salvation	Sanctification	Service
2. Identified with Christ in . . .	The cross: Death 1 Cor. 15:3–4	The tomb: Burial and resurrection Matt. 12:40; Rom. 6:3–5	The throne: Ascension and pouring out of Holy Spirit Acts 2.33; Eph. 1:3; 2:6; Rev. 3:21
3. Terms used	Regeneration, born again, adopted, new creation Rom. 8:15; 2 Cor. 5:17; Titus 3:5; 1 John 5:1, 4	Water baptism; "buried with Him" Rom. 6:4	Baptism in/with the Holy Spirit Matt. 3:11; Mark 1:8; Luke 3:16; John 1:33; Acts 11:16
4. What is imparted	Life to human spirit John 3:1–5; Eph. 2:1	Remission of sins Acts 2:38; 22:16	Power to regenerated spirit John 1:33; Acts 1:8
5. What you receive	Christ as Savior John 1:12; Rom. 8:9	Circumcision of heart Rom. 2:29; Col. 2:11	Holy Spirit power John 7:39; Acts 19:2; Eph. 1:13
6. Purpose	Develop Christlike character John 14:20; 15:4–5; Eph. 3:14, 19	Burial of "old man" Rom. 6:3–14; Col. 3:9–10	Receive power of Christ for service Mark 16:15–18; Acts 6:8; 8:5–8
7. Immediate evidence	Inward witness Rom. 8:15–16; 1 John 5:10	Clear conscience 1 Peter 3:21	Speaking in tongues Acts 2:4; 10:44–46
8. Long-term evidence	Nine fruit: to demonstrate nature and life of Christ John 15:1–5; Gal. 5:22–23	Ongoing sanctification Rom. 13:14; 1 Thess. 5:23; Titus 3:5	Nine gifts: to show the power of Christ 1 Cor. 12:1–9, 31; 14:1
9. The gift	Eternal life from God John 4:10–14; Rom. 6:23	To bear His name Gal. 3:27	Holy Spirit from Christ Acts 2:38–39; 10:45
10. Relationship	With you and in you John 14:17	United with Christ in His death and resurrection Rom. 6:5	Shall come upon you Acts 2:1–4

A PIVOTAL VERSE

To call a verse "pivotal" may seem a bit extreme, especially if we remember the word means "decisive, crucial, critical, vital, determining and climactic."

Although Paul probably did not intend for his casual statement—made in the rush of his excited discussion about the Body of Christ—to be elevated to such importance, it nevertheless has become a key player in the discussion on Holy Spirit baptism.

The verse is 1 Corinthians 12:13: "For by one Spirit we were all baptized into one body—whether Jews or Greeks, whether slaves or free—and have all been made to drink into one Spirit." In the next section we will discuss the interpretation of the verse in depth, but first it is appropriate to review the broader meaning of baptism in the New Testament.

This is relevant to our overall discussion since a key element of the Peter Pattern is the idea of baptism. Water baptism and baptism with the Holy Spirit are two uses of this word, but conversion is also a form of baptism. Consider that when the sinner repents, he or she has a whelming or washing over of the sinful soul by the precious blood of Christ (see 1 John 1:9). Note my endnote number 5 for other references.

Why Use Baptism?

In the Greek language of Bible days, the word *baptizo* was an ideal word to incorporate into Christian use, and from it has come our English word *baptize*. Various lexicons give the basic meaning as "to submerge or immerse." The Greeks used the word to describe the drawing of water by dipping a vessel into another and even to describe the dyeing of a garment. Several sources refer to a sunken vessel submerged in water or a person overwhelmed with calamities.

Paul used the word dramatically in describing water baptism as a dynamic *burial service:* "Therefore we were buried with Him through baptism into death" (Romans 6:4) and "In Him you were . . . buried with Him in baptism" (Colossians 2:11–12).

John the Baptist, busily engaged in water baptizing hundreds of repentant Jews, used the word to describe graphically how the coming Messiah would baptize people with the Holy Spirit (as in Mark 1:8).

The Seven New Testament Baptisms

In fact, it does not take long to realize that the word *baptism* is used in the New Testament several ways with different meanings. It does not always refer to water baptism, as many assume. There are actually seven baptisms and they are itemized in the chart below. Keep in mind that each one has the following five aspects:

- the actual baptism (the happening, the experience)
- the agent (the baptizer) who administers the baptism
- the candidate (the baptized) who undergoes the baptism
- the element with or in (*en,* Greek) which the candidate is baptized
- the objective (purpose) for which the baptism takes place[2]

SUMMARY OF NEW TESTAMENT BAPTISMS

Experience	Agent	Candidate	Element	Objective
1. Baptism of suffering[3]	Jews and Gentiles	Jesus and His disciples	The cross, difficult situations	Humiliation
2. Baptism of John[4]	John the Baptist	Israel and Jesus	Jordan River	Repentance
3. Conversion[5]	Father	Unregenerate sinner	Blood of Christ	Salvation
4. Water baptism	Church (minister)	New convert	Water	Sanctification
5. Baptism with the Holy Spirit	Jesus	New convert	The Holy Spirit	Service
6. Baptism with fire[6]	Jesus	The Church, the world	Divine fire	Purification, judgment
7. Baptism into one Body 1 Cor. 12:13 (also called "one baptism") Eph. 4:5	The Holy Spirit	The initiated believer	The Body of Christ	Metamorphical illustration drawn from Israel's being "baptized into Moses"

A CLOSER LOOK

Now, with that background in mind, let us return to the "pivotal verse," 1 Corinthians 12:13: "For by one Spirit we were all baptized into one body . . . and have all been made to drink into one Spirit." Our reason for focusing so much attention on this verse is twofold: first, because the way it is interpreted has a strong bearing on whether or not we can expect an experience of Spirit-baptism after conversion, and, second, it provides an excellent way to summarize the importance of the Peter Pattern.

"Into One Body"

The apostle Paul made an interesting comparison between Israel becoming a nation and the Church becoming the Body of Christ. He used the word *baptism* as an overarching expression to indicate this process. Israel was "baptized into Moses" (1 Corinthians 10:2), and those in the Church "were all baptized into one body" (12:13).

Look at the remarkable similarities. Israel's exodus from Egypt involved:

Saved from death by the blood of the Passover lamb[7]

Separated from Egypt by going through the Red Sea

Living as God's people under the cloud of His presence

Now, in similar fashion, we Christians are:

Saved through the blood of Christ

Separated from the world by water baptism

Living to serve by the presence of the Holy Spirit

These steps follow precisely the Peter Pattern, as shown in the diagram below.

THE THREEFOLD PATTERN

	Blood	Water	Spirit
Israel: Baptized into Moses	Passover blood of the lamb	The Red Sea	The cloud of His presence
The Church: Baptized into one Body	Born of the Spirit by the blood of Christ	Water baptism	Baptism with the Holy Spirit
The Peter Pattern	Conversion	Water baptism	Baptism with the Holy Spirit

The Israelites followed the directives for the Exodus: marking their doors with the Passover blood of lambs, following Moses through walls of seawater and finally entering the covering of the cloud. Israel was thereby "baptized into Moses." This was obviously metaphorical (figurative or analogical) language. Paul's phrase "baptized into one body" was a parallel expression that used Israel's experience to illustrate our relationship to the Body of

Christ. In both cases "baptized into" refers to God's action of separating for Himself a people and bringing them into a covenant relationship.

It was only natural for Paul to say "into Moses," because Moses was the leader who delivered Israel and represented God. "To baptize into Moses means to immerse in Moses, i. e., to bring in close relationship with Moses. . . . The Israelites, by following Moses' leadership and by passing behind Moses through the Sea which separates them forever from Egypt, have thus been joined to him forever and are compelled to follow him from henceforth" (Grosheide).[8]

When the Israelites followed Moses through the Passover, the sea and the cloud, they declared their acceptance of his divine commission and authority. They were now more than a wandering crowd—they had become a nation and a community.

Similarly, today's believer is baptized into one Body (the Church). Israel became a nation with Moses as its leader; we become a part of the Church with Christ as our leader. We too are now identified as the people of God, separated from "Egypt" (the world) and under God's protection and guidance as one Body.

The early Church moved people quickly through the basic steps of conversion, water baptism and Holy Spirit baptism. Today, in contrast, it is not hard to find twenty-year church members who have never been water baptized or who lack even a basic understanding of the Person of the Holy Spirit. Many believers are Christians in name only because they have no personal, present, conscious awareness of and union with Jesus Christ and the Holy Spirit. Tragically, we are fogged in by centuries of misunderstanding, unbelief, disagreement and absence of charismatic appreciation. It is time for the fog to lift! Let the Church return to the simplicity of the Gospel and "contend earnestly for the faith which was once for all delivered to the saints" (Jude 3).

This is happening to an amazing degree in some parts of the Body. One of the most fruitful approaches in modern Christianity is being practiced by fast-growing churches in South America. Weekend "intensives" gather the new converts for concentrated Bible training, teaching on water baptism, prayer, confession, renouncing witchcraft, casting out demons, etc., which is followed by public water baptism. The baptism with the Holy Spirit is the crowning experience! This accelerated method is producing fervent, evangelistic Christians.

"By" or "In" One Spirit?

It is interesting that 1 Corinthians 12:13 has become something of an academic storm center in the discussion of Holy Spirit baptism. The words *For by one Spirit we were all baptized into one body* seem to have been written almost as an aside in Paul's fervent plea for unity of the Body. Yet they are vitally important to our study because the interpretation affects whether or not we expect and seek the experience of Holy Spirit baptism after conversion. Paul would probably be surprised at the diverse views on this statement.

Several interpretations are available, and this verse is considered to be crucial in support of each one! The three big questions are:

1. Who does the baptizing?
2. Into what are we baptized?
3. When does this baptism take place?

The answers to these questions are determined by the two ways in which the Greek text is translated. One states that we are baptized "by" the Holy Spirit: "For by one Spirit we were all baptized into one body—whether Jews or Greeks, whether slaves or free—and have all been made to drink into one Spirit." (The words *by one Spirit* are also used in the AMPLIFIED, BECK, GNB, JNT, KJV, MLB, NASB, NCV, NIV, NLT, RSV and WILLIAMS translations.)

The other translation states that we are baptized "in" the Spirit: "In the one Spirit we were all baptized, Jews as well as Greeks, slaves as well as citizens, and one Spirit was given to us all to drink" (JB). (The word *in* is also used by ABUV, NAB, NEB, NJB, NRSV and ROTHERHAM.)

What did Paul have in mind when he wrote that all of us are baptized by/in one Spirit? To aid our discussion, I would like to quote two paragraphs from Simon J. Kistemaker's commentary:

> The Greek text has the preposition *en* that can be translated either "by" or "in." Most translators have adopted the reading *by* to reveal means or agency. They think that this interpretation is the better of the two, for it avoids the awkwardness of having two quite similar prepositional phrases in the same clause: "*in* one Spirit . . . *into* one body." I prefer the translation *by*.
>
> Conversely, other translators believe that the Greek preposition *en* denotes sphere or place and thus translate it "in." They point out that in the New Testament, the Holy Spirit is never described as the baptizer. Rather, the

Spirit is the sphere into which the baptismal candidate enters. The Gospels declare that Jesus baptizes his followers with the Holy Spirit (Matt. 3:11; Mark 1:8).[9]

So we are faced with two choices: Either the Spirit is the one who does the baptizing (the baptizer) or the Spirit is the "element" into which a person is baptized. As you can see from the last chart, I believe that the context of 1 Corinthians 12:13 shows that the Spirit is the baptizer and the Body of Christ is the element.

Before continuing let me pause to say that I believe that the three parts of the Peter Pattern give the ideal, composite picture of "Baptism into one Body." The early Church, according to Acts, desired this full experience for all of her members. I would like to see the Church today make this same emphasis. I readily confess, however, that everyone who is truly born again is a member of the Body of Christ—and is certainly saved by the grace of God. Such a person would, I believe, go into the presence of God if he or she should die before being baptized in water or the Spirit. Our challenge here is to awaken every living believer to continue on in the very apparent path of obedience laid down by Jesus and the apostles. A child is born into a family—is considered a family member—but the child must still continue maturing to assume full family member status.

Now, back to our discussion. We face two choices in our controversial text: Either the Spirit does the baptizing, or the Spirit is the element of baptism. My approach is that the Spirit is the baptizer and the Body of Christ is the element. Not everyone agrees with this, of course. Those who oppose this idea generally state that the Spirit cannot be the baptizer in this text because the expression in the Greek text is identical to six other passages in which the same preposition *(en)* is used and Jesus is clearly the baptizer.[10] They say that Paul's reference here to baptism is just the same as those other references in which Jesus is the baptizer and the Holy Spirit is the element into which one is baptized (more on this in the next chapter). This line of reasoning discounts the idea of two Holy Spirit baptisms.

In other words, some believe that since seven passages all use "in" (from *en*) they all mean the same thing. The seven verses referred to are: Matthew 3:11; Mark 1:8; Luke 3:16; John 1:33; Acts 1:5; 11:16; 1 Corinthians 12:13. At first it appears that if the word has one meaning in six verses, the seventh simply follows suit. Paul's emphasis here is that it is the one Spirit whose activity brings the believer into living relationship with the rest of the Church. Paul's statement is not meant to say that there can be no baptism with the Spirit after conversion. Jesus is always the baptizer, not the Spirit. Thus, there can be no baptism with the Spirit after conversion, because conversion is when it all happens.

Does the Corinthian passage stand alongside the six other verses? According to Howard M. Ervin that is not a correct alignment. He says: "Such a methodology is, however, fallacious since the six non-Pauline references are all directly related to the one utterance of John the Baptist. The comparison is, therefore, in the nature of a one to one ratio."[11]

With this clarification we can see that it is possible to use *by* in this case instead of *in* without feeling that the interpretation is strained or out of line linguistically. Ervin also argues that in the 1 Corinthians 12 context, the preposition *en* appears thrice with *Spirit* in verses 3 and 9 where *by* best serves the meaning of the passage, so the interpretation of verse 13 follows consistently.

When Paul spoke in 1 Corinthians 12:13 of how we "have been made to drink into one Spirit," he described, I believe, the ongoing activity of the Holy Spirit, the norm for Christian living. Ervin connects this phrase with Ephesians 5:18, "be filled with the Spirit," which is translated in the Centenary Translation: "Do not be drunk with wine . . . but drink deep in the Spirit." The Spirit is essential to our beginning and to our continuing on in the things of God.

First Corinthians 12 deals with the heart of Pauline theology: how the Church has been made into one Body by a lavish experience of the Holy Spirit. We are born of the Spirit, immersed in the Spirit and, by the action of that same Spirit, we become the unified Church of Jesus Christ.

Just as happened with early believers, the events that define the Peter Pattern often happen close together. Each one, however, is significant, specific, unique and important. In the remainder of this chapter, we will examine conversion and water baptism (steps 1 and 2 of the Peter Pattern). The baptism with the Holy Spirit will be defined and discussed in the next chapter.

The jeweler cuts the diamond so the many facets may better reflect the glory of the whole stone. So it is with the descriptive biblical terms we will study. Each sparkles with some wonderful aspect of our glorious salvation. It is essential that we Christians know and appreciate all that the Holy Spirit has accomplished in our lives.

Prayerfully appropriate these meaningful terms into your personal experience in Christ. The Spirit, without question, is the dynamic One who makes Jesus Christ real in our lives. His great desire is to guide you into spiritual maturity.

CONVERSION

Following are thirteen terms that give insight to our basic conversion-salvation experience. We will discover the work of the Spirit in making us spiritually alive.

A New Beginning

Four terms emphasize our spiritual new beginning.

1. Conversion: We Turn to the Better Way

We must simultaneously turn toward Christ and away from worldly sin. We must repent, that is, renounce sin, and also exercise faith or acceptance of Christ, and this is done through the help of the Holy Spirit. Jesus said: "No one can come to Me unless the Father who sent Me draws him" (John 6:44). Note Luke 22:32; Acts 3:19; James 5:20. The conviction to turn to God comes from the Spirit (see John 16:8).

2. Regeneration: We Are "Born Again" into the New Life of the Spirit

Spiritual regeneration causes our spirits, dead in trespasses and sins, to be born again (or from above). New life is created in us when we repent and believe in Christ. This birth is the work of the Word and the Holy Spirit. Physical birth is a work of God's creation; regeneration is the beginning of life that is spiritual, a work of the Holy Spirit. The experience can also be described by *quickening* (see 1 Corinthians 15:45). Other terms include: *born of the Spirit* (John 3:5–6, 8); *the washing of regeneration and renewing of the Holy Spirit* (Titus 3:5); *you received the Spirit of adoption* (Romans 8:15; see also Galatians 4:5–6). As Conner says, "The repentant and believing are changed from the old creation in Adam to being a new creation in Christ. They receive and become partakers of a new nature as the new creation race" (Conner).[12]

3. Incarnation: We Receive Christ Within

Conversion is more than being remade. It is also the glorious presence of Christ Himself in us, reliving His life in us: "Christ in you, the hope of glory" (Colossians 1:27; see also John 14:15–23; Ephesians 3:16–17).

4. Resurrection: We Are Raised from Spiritual Death to Life

Those of us who die while holding active faith in Christ will have our bodies brought to life again at His Second Coming (see 1 Corinthians 15; 1 Thessalonians 4). Those who participate in that physical miracle of resurrection life are those who have already had a spiritual inner resurrection: "The last Adam became a life-giving spirit" (1 Corinthians 15:45).

Personal Transformation

Five terms emphasize the transformation that occurs.

1. Bearing Witness: We Hear the Confirming Inner Voice

The inner witness of the Spirit is similar to the steady beating of our hearts that assures us all is well. The Holy Spirit brings a convincing awareness or consciousness that the grace of God's forgiveness has come. Our own spirits are brought to life, which is a witness within, but Scripture indicates that the Holy Spirit Himself comes alongside with a confirming witness to authenticate and strengthen our own conviction: "The Spirit Himself bears witness with our spirit" (Romans 8:16; see also Romans 9:1).

2. Cleansing: We Are Loosed from Sinful Defilement

It is like a mechanic who cleanses his hands of filthy oil and dirt by washing with a strong soap. When we repent and believe in Christ, the worldly defilement of the old sinful life is washed away by the blood of Christ. Revelation 7:14 gives us this picture: They "washed their robes and made them white in the blood of the Lamb." The blood of Christ, water baptism and the baptism with the Holy Spirit accomplish a wonderful miracle. "You were washed . . . in the name of the Lord Jesus and by the Spirit of our God" (1 Corinthians 6:11); "the washing of regeneration and renewing of the Holy Spirit" (Titus 3:5; see also John 3:3–6; Acts 22:16; Ephesians 5:26).

3. Renewal: We Are Made New, Restored Back to God's Image

We fell in Adam; we are renewed in Christ. (See Romans 8:26–28; 12:2; Ephesians 4:23; Colossians 3:10.)

4. Translation: We Are Transposed from Darkness into Light

We are picked up out of Satan's kingdom and placed into the Kingdom of Jesus Christ. Formerly, we abode in a place of sin, sickness and death, but now we abide with Christ where there is life, health, peace and righteousness. (See John 3:1–5; Acts 26:18; Galatians 6:15; Ephesians 1:3–6; Colossians 1:13–14.)

5. Transplanting: We Have a New Heart to Replace a Heart of Stone

As sinners our hearts were spiritually hard—like stones. But as Jeremiah promised, we have had those old hearts exchanged for hearts of flesh upon which the laws of God can be written. First Corinthians 6:19 states: ". . . the Holy Spirit who is in you, whom you have from God." (See Jeremiah 17:9; 31:31–34; Ezekiel 36:26; Mark 7:21–23; Hebrews 8:8–13.)

A State of Grace

Four terms emphasize our present spiritual status.

1. Salvation: We Are Saved by the Grace of God

Salvation means that we are delivered, preserved, healed and made whole. David Shibley explains it like this: "The incarnation made possible our reconciliation and our salvation. The sin that was ours was laid on Christ, and the righteousness, which is His, is imputed to us: 'He made Him who knew no sin to be sin for us, that we might become the righteousness of God in Him' (2 Corinthians 5:21). Now we have right standing with God. We have been saved from our sins. What a glorious exchange!"[13] (See Mark 16:16; John 3:17; 10:9; Romans 10:9–13; Acts 2:21, 47; 11:14; 16:30–31; Revelation 21:24.)

2. Justification: Our Debts Are Canceled

It is like being notified that a wealthy benefactor has paid our debts in full and has secured our total pardon for unlawful deeds done. We will not be punished for our mistakes. "You were justified . . . by the Spirit of our God" (1 Corinthians 6:11).

3. Adoption: We Are Made Part of the Family of God

We can be compared to the poor beggar boy who is accepted unconditionally and without apparent reason into the home of a rich patron who grants him equal status with his own children. God welcomes the estranged sinner into His family to enjoy the relationship and benefits of being His child. "The term connotes positive favor, as contrasted with mere forgiveness and remission of sins" (Erickson).[14] It "signifies the place and condition of a son given to one to whom it does not naturally belong" (Vine).[15] We are given this high privilege simply by the grace of God. The Holy Spirit Himself gives constant assurance in our hearts that we are truly a part of the family of God. "You received the Spirit of adoption" (Romans 8:15; see also Galatians 4:5; Ephesians 1:5).

4. Marriage: We Are Joined to Christ

Like a wife, we bear the name of our beloved husband. He is our heavenly bridegroom (see Romans 7:4; Ephesians 5:23–32; Revelation 19:7–9).

WATER BAPTISM

In conversion, a person is saved by the grace of God. We do not merit this wonderful gift of eternal life. The Holy Spirit is the life source of our new birth when we accept Christ. He initiates our conversion by loving entreaty, culminating with bestowal of undeserved grace and acceptance.

In water baptism, the reverse is true. We give rather than receive. We dedicate ourselves to Him. The process of sanctification or being set apart for His glory begins.

Converts who have not experienced this outward sign of an inner work should be urged to participate in water baptism immediately. John the Baptist had no hesitancy in calling for repentance and water baptism. Jesus had no reservations about advocating water baptism: "He who believes and is baptized will be saved" (Mark 16:16); "Go therefore and make disciples of all the nations, baptizing them in the name of the Father and of the Son and of the Holy Spirit" (Matthew 28:19). The Holy Spirit is very present at water baptism, coming alongside the believer as Paraclete-friend to help and strengthen in walking with Christ. The apostles diligently pursued this same bold course of action. Peter said: "Repent, and let every one of you be baptized" (Acts 2:38). Ananias urged Saul to be baptized (see Acts 22:16).

It may come as a surprise to learn that people, on occasion, do come out of water baptism filled with the Spirit and speaking in tongues. When new converts are taught to expect these things, they happen. Romans 10:17 states: "So then faith comes by hearing, and hearing by the word of God." This has been a routine approach in my ministry, and I can testify to the wonderment of seeing newly baptized converts coming out of the baptismal water speaking in tongues, filled with the Spirit!

The following seven expressions of baptism give us a well-rounded picture of its significance and God's purposes.

1. Death, Burial and Resurrection: Removal of the Old Life

Water baptism is the physical action that identifies us with the death, burial and resurrection of Jesus Christ. What was true of Jesus is now true of us. "When He died we died; when He was buried, we were buried; when He arose, we arose. Identification is declaration of the reality of the work of the cross in our lives. The epistle to the Romans explains the work of the cross in the believer and exhorts us to live as though dead to sin. The old man (who we were before salvation) is dead and we demonstrate this by being buried with Christ in baptism."[16]

> Therefore we were buried with Him through baptism into death, that just as Christ was raised from the dead by the glory of the Father, even so we also should walk in newness of life. For if we have been united together in the likeness of His death, certainly we also shall be in the likeness of His resurrection.
>
> Romans 6:4–5

This newness of life is only possible through the work of the Holy Spirit. Burial is followed by resurrection through the Spirit!

2. Clear Conscience: Free of Condemnation

Hebrews 9:14 tells us that the blood of Christ will "purge your conscience from dead works to serve the living God." First Peter 3:21 states: ". . . the water of immersion, which is not the removal of dirt from the body, but one's pledge to keep a good conscience toward God" (JNT). Graham Truscott explains: "If your sinful conscience has been washed in the blood of Christ and purified, you no longer feel guilty and ashamed to come into the presence of God. Your conscience is clean. Therefore in baptism you are pledging to God that your conscience has been purified by the blood of Christ and is now clear. Praise the Lord!"[17]

3. Circumcision of Heart: Sign of the New Covenant

Under the Abrahamic covenant, circumcision in Israel removed flesh from every male in every generation as a sign of God's agreement made with Abraham (see Genesis 17). Physical circumcision is no longer necessary to please God. Instead, New Testament circumcision is of the heart, in both male and female. Water baptism is the outward sign of the New Covenant of Jesus Christ. Colossians 2:11–12 states: "In Him you were also circumcised with the circumcision made without hands, by putting off the body of the sins of the flesh, by the circumcision of Christ, buried with Him in baptism" (see also Romans 2:28–29; Philippians 3:3, 9–10).

4. Remission of Sins: Cancelation of Past Offenses

In baptism we publicly renounce our former lifestyles, thereby authorizing God to cancel and remove all past offenses. True repentance grants us forgiveness of sins, and water baptism brings meaningful closure to the old life. (See Acts 2:38; 22:16.)

5. Sanctification: Set Apart for His Glory

Sanctification is the dedication of body, soul and spirit to God for the purposes of Christ's holiness in us. It is the setting aside of our lives for the glory of God. It is a progressive work that starts with water baptism with the ultimate goal that the believer is able to love the Lord with all his/her heart, soul and mind (see Romans 13:14; 1 Thessalonians 5:23; Titus 3:5).

6. "In the Name of . . .": Coming Under the Authority of God

To be baptized "in the Name of the Father, and of the Son, and of the Holy Spirit" is both to come under God's authority and ownership and also to be clothed with or enshrouded in the power of that name. It is interesting to note, therefore, that *Father, Son* and *Holy Spirit* are not actually names; they are titles! Add to this another perplexing thought. Baptismal rites use Jesus' words from Matthew 28:19: "Go therefore and make disciples of all the nations, baptizing them in the name of the Father and of the Son and of the Holy Spirit." Actually, we have no record of the apostles using these titles (although I am sure they did and that they used Jesus' words to teach the tri-unity of God). Luke indicates they baptized in the name of the Lord Jesus Christ or some form of that expression. They understood that this was fulfillment of Jesus' intended meaning.[18]

- *Jesus Christ* (Acts 2:38; 8:12; also 10:48 in some versions)
- *Lord Jesus* (Acts 8:16; 9:5; 19:5, which is *Christ Jesus* or *Jesus* in various versions)
- *Lord* (Acts 10:48, or *Jesus Christ* in some versions)
- *Christ Jesus* (Romans 6:3, most versions)

7. Personal Testimony: Public Declaration

Although the Bible does not specifically say that a person must be baptized publicly as a community testimony, this has been an important traditional belief in the Church from the very beginning (as in Acts 16:33). It is an open, bold testimony before others. This is particularly powerful in heathen communities where idolatry is practiced. In these instances baptism is often accompanied by burning magical books and destroying idols that had belonged to the candidate for baptism. Like Israel going through the Red Sea, the new convert severs himself/herself from idolatry and worldly living. Although this is a personal commitment, the Holy Spirit is present to strengthen and encourage—He is the great Helper. Whenever a new convert is baptized and confesses faith in Jesus Christ, it is a powerful, public testimony of Christ's resurrection and also of that person's personal intent to follow Christ's teachings.[19]

REVIEW QUESTIONS FOR CHAPTER 8

1. Do you feel it is reasonable to make the Peter Pattern out of Acts 2:38?

2. What three conversion terms would be the most meaningful to you?
3. Were significant words spoken over you when you were baptized?
4. How do you interpret 1 Corinthians 12:13?

9

THE BAPTISM WITH THE HOLY SPIRIT
EVERY BELIEVER LINKED TO PENTECOST

IN THIS CHAPTER

- Discover a marvelous experience that can be yours!
- Find out what the immediate evidence is
- Consider whether or not certain requirements need to be fulfilled
- Learn fourteen descriptions of the indwelling Spirit

Now we come to the third part of the Peter Pattern and the main emphasis of this book: the baptism with the Holy Spirit. Six areas will be considered:

- Definition
- A Distinct Experience

- Subsequence
- Initial Evidence
- Fourteen Descriptive Terms
- How to Receive Spirit-Baptism

DEFINITION

The baptism with the Holy Spirit is a wonderful experience that happens in the lives of those who have accepted Jesus Christ as personal Savior and Lord. At conversion, as we have noted, Jesus comes to live in the believer's heart by the power of the Holy Spirit. The baptism with the Holy Spirit is a separate and distinct infilling. (We will talk more about this baptism as a second or additional Holy Spirit experience later.) It could happen immediately upon conversion, unexpectedly at a later time or in direct response to serious prayer and seeking God. A person could be alone or with others, praying or not, or receiving prayer with the biblical example of laying on of hands. Various examples are given in the Bible.

As God's Spirit moves upon the individual, his heart and mind are awakened to a new awareness of God's presence and love. As he responds in worship and thankfulness to God, the Holy Spirit introduces him to an exciting new dimension of prayer, "praying in the Spirit." Suddenly he finds himself praying or glorifying God in a language that he has never learned! It is a miracle! He begins "speaking in tongues"—a new language—as the Spirit gives him the ability to do so.

The exact expression "baptism with the Holy Spirit" is not found in Scripture but is based on the following six references:

> "I [John the Baptist] indeed baptize you with water unto repentance, but He who is coming after me is mightier than I. . . . He will baptize you with the Holy Spirit and fire."
>
> Matthew 3:11

> "I indeed baptized you with water, but He will baptize you with the Holy Spirit."
>
> Mark 1:8

John answered, saying to all, "I indeed baptize you with water; but One mightier than I is coming. . . . He will baptize you with the Holy Spirit and with fire."

Luke 3:16

[John said,] "He [God] who sent me to baptize with water said to me, 'Upon whom you see the Spirit descending, and remaining on Him, this is He who baptizes with the Holy Spirit.'"

John 1:33

[Jesus said,] "For John truly baptized with water, but you shall be baptized with the Holy Spirit not many days from now."

Acts 1:5

"Then I [Peter] remembered the word of the Lord, how He said, 'John indeed baptized with water, but you shall be baptized with the Holy Spirit.'"

Acts 11:16

God commissioned John the Baptist to immerse Israelites in a baptism of repentance to prepare their hearts for the coming Messiah. By this action He was depicting what would later happen when the Messiah Himself would pour out the Holy Spirit on believers—filling them, immersing them fully—for empowerment.[1]

Joyce Meyer, in her characteristic down-to-earth style, gives an illustration that beautifully captures the intended meaning of *baptism:*

We could say it means to engulf, which may cause whatever is baptized to be filled with something. For example, if we took an empty drinking glass and submerged it in water, it would become engulfed and filled with that water. We could say that glass had been baptized in water or baptized with water. That is a simple explanation of what I believe takes place when we receive the baptism of the Holy Spirit—we become completely engulfed and filled with all the power and presence of God, which means we don't have to go through life trying to do everything on our own anymore.[2]

I choose to use the phrasing baptism *with* the Holy Spirit because that is the wording in many translations (KJV, NKJ, NASB, NIV, LB, NLB, NEB, RSV, NCV, CEV, TEV, PHILLIPS) and it conveys the original intent quite adequately.

Sometimes I use the shorter term *Spirit-baptism,* but this does not imply any change in meaning. Scholars agree that the Greek *en* can mean "in," "of," "by" and "with." The key thought is that Jesus is the baptizer as Acts 2:32–33 confirms:

> This Jesus God has raised up, of which we are all witnesses. Therefore being exalted to the right hand of God, and having received from the Father the promise of the Holy Spirit, He poured out this which you now see and hear.

Some prefer baptism *in* the Holy Spirit, and I agree that this is a good and accurate use. H. I. Lederle comments: "Pentecostals like the late David du Plessis underscore that Jesus is the Baptizer, the agent in Spirit-baptism. A consequence of this focus has been the preference [by some] for the preposition *in* as a translation of the Greek *en* in the phrase 'baptized *in* the Holy Spirit,' rather than the instrumental alternative *by.*"[3]

A DISTINCT EXPERIENCE

Anyone who believes in the authority of Scripture cannot ignore this emphasis: God is real, tangible and knowable. It is this quality of the Bible that is daunting to the scientific mind. Yet without the reality of the supernatural and miraculous, the Bible loses its reason for existence and Judaism and Christianity have no foundations. The Acts of the Apostles is sometimes challenged as an authoritative norm for today's Church because of the abundant supernatural episodes recorded—but that is the way it was!

The Church age began with Pentecost—admittedly a "glorious disturbance" in the lives and religion of the people of that day—and it has continued with the repetition of that glorious reality. Church people sometimes tend toward quiet, personal disciplines, a kind of "ascetic model" of Christianity. The apostolic Church certainly practiced these spiritual disciplines, but they combined and balanced those things with the "Pentecostal model," which promoted experiential union with Christ and the Spirit. Gradually, however, as the Church age progressed (and the Church neglected Paul's admonition in Galatians 6:2–3, 5, to continue in the Spirit), the reality was lost by neglect.

It seems apparent that Luke's record of Acts is intended to guide the Church in continuous Holy Spirit activity. Pentecost, the first mention of Holy Spirit baptism, prescribes the importance of a life-changing encounter with God; it "gives us an historic pattern to go by" (Basham).[4] We can receive the Spirit in such a dynamic way that it impacts us for the rest of our lives—a connection with God so alive that it makes Christian living powerful. This is not just an educational transfer of Pentecost (i.e., theological or historical teaching); people are enabled to say with Peter, "This [experience that I have] is what was spoken by the prophet Joel" (Acts 2:16).

The Immediate Effects

It is as though you are projected back in time among the disciples at Pentecost when they received the outpouring of the Holy Spirit. The believer now finds himself bonded by the same Spirit to the same Church that was birthed on the day of Pentecost—and more deeply in love with the Christ of that Church. The believer senses that he or she is in continuity with and the extension of the same foundational truths and experiences of the newly birthed apostolic Church.

Specific evidence assures the believer that this miraculous event has truly occurred, a distinct experience, "a deep revitalizing of one's faith" (Christenson).[5] The following six effects, abbreviated from an article by William G. MacDonald, exemplify "what classical Pentecostals teach relative to the effects of a filling with Christ's Spirit. . . . The first four are internal and the last two are external in terms of visible results."[6] I instantly identified with his list, because these very things were dramatically evident in my own life.

1. The reality of Jesus
2. Spiritual sensitivity
3. The illumination of God's Word
4. Prayer "in the Spirit"
5. The process of sanctification
6. Dynamic testimony

Long-Range Effects

If a person will then "walk in the Spirit," that is, live a lifestyle that fosters the things of the Holy Spirit, that person will find his or her life blessed with a new joyfulness, a deepened reverence, a more active love for Christ, His Word and the lost. There will be a growing sensitivity to the gifts of the Spirit, and like Miracle-Gro to a plant, the Spirit-baptism will enhance spiritual fruit development. Along with a new sensitivity to divine leading, there will be new awareness of satanic activity. The baptism with the Holy Spirit particularly enhances one's relationship with Jesus Christ and empowers one's service for Him.

Four Pentecostal Beliefs

Pentecostalism is an established part of the evangelical Christian community worldwide, both as a general movement that touches all denominations and as specific denominations that have formed on their own. As John Osteen said in 1960, however, "Pentecost is not a denomination, it is an experience."[7]

Spirit-baptism as summarized below is "the distinctive teaching" that makes Pentecostalism unique among various Protestant and Catholic groups.

First, the experience first recorded in Acts 2 is to continue in the life of the Christian Church.

Second, this experience is distinct from regeneration (conversion) and subsequent to it (although sometimes occurring immediately or shortly thereafter).

Third, this experience is called "the baptism of/in/with the Holy Spirit," and it is accompanied by the outward sign of speaking in other tongues.

Fourth, this is the normal experience to be expected in every believer.[8]

SUBSEQUENCE

I want to dwell for a moment on the second teaching of Pentecostalism given above, the topic of "subsequence." This refers to the fact that the baptism with the Holy Spirit occurs after a person is converted and thus is a second or separate experience. Water baptism can either precede or follow Spirit-baptism, but the baptism with the Holy Spirit is an empowerment experience for someone who is already a believer in Christ. It is not necessary to have Spirit-baptism to go to heaven—accepting Christ assures us of our salvation—but to live an empowered life in the Spirit, a person does need this additional experience.

If we could be projected back into the setting of Acts, we would be surprised at how little debate existed on the subject. Not hindered by centuries of theological wrangling, early Christians would be joyfully promoting the Peter Pattern—bringing people to faith in Christ, baptizing them in water and praying for them to be baptized with the Holy Spirit. None of the three events was neglected or postponed.

The idea that there is an experience in the Holy Spirit that is distinct from and subsequent to the new birth, according to Gordon Fee, "is not unique to Pentecostalism." He says: "Rather, it reflects a classical view of many pietistic groups, reaching at least as far back as early Methodism, and found subsequently in various holiness and deeper life movements, namely that there is for all believers a 'baptism in the Holy Spirit,' which is separate in form and sequential to the initial experience of conversion."[9]

Background Concept

The Pentecostal movement is sometimes called a "restorationist movement," and this expression seems an accurate way to assess the spiritual longing for the vitality and miracles of New Testament Christianity. "These early Pentecostals were experiential primitivists in the sense that they consciously hailed back to the dynamic, Spirit-filled, Spirit-led first-century church—especially that of the Day of Pentecost and the church at Corinth."[10]

Whenever the established church becomes entrenched within its institutions and forms, the dynamic of the Spirit is usually pushed into the background. Invariably there will be those in the church unwilling to accept any toned-down version of biblical Christianity. The result will be a schism in the established church, with a new group formed of revivalistic people. This desire for a deeper experience and the power of the Holy Spirit has been present throughout the Church age, but it seemed to find particular expression in the 1800s. This prepared the way for the Pentecostal-charismatic movements of the 1900s.

A persistent thought during these past two centuries has been that God poured out His Spirit as "the early rain" on the early Church and now God wants to do the same again as "the latter rain" at the end of history. This concept was a spiritual application of the two rainy seasons (symbolic of the Spirit's outpouring) in Palestine. We are now in the time of "the latter rain." James 5:7 states: "Therefore be patient, brethren, until the coming of the Lord. See how the farmer waits for the precious fruit of the earth, waiting patiently for it until it receives the early and latter rain."

Two-Stage Patterns

Various groups developed the idea that after, or subsequent to, conversion a person could have an additional experience or "second blessing"—an experience that was frequently called baptism in the Holy Spirit. It is not our purpose to discuss this in depth but merely to point out that this general attitude was developing in the Wesleyan churches and others before the Pentecostal movement was launched. Vinson Synan says that "by the time of the Pentecostal outbreak in America in 1901, there have been at least a century of movements emphasizing a second blessing called the baptism in the Holy Spirit."[11] Some of those groups are listed below:

- The Reformed Sealers, made up of many seventeenth-century Puritans, believed that sealing or Spirit-baptism is an inner occurrence subsequent to regeneration that brings assurance of salvation and spiritual power for ministry.[12]
- The Wesleyan Revival, in the eighteenth century, taught a distinct second work of grace subsequent to conversion. John Fletcher, theologian of the early Methodists, used "baptism with the Holy Spirit" in reference to a specific spiritual experience of sanctification and empowerment.
- Edward Irving (1792–1834), popular Presbyterian pastor in London, led in a restoration of tongues and prophecy in 1831. Irving has been called "the morning star of the Pentecostal movement," but interestingly this influential minister himself never spoke in tongues.
- The Revivalists (Finney, Moody and Torrey) strongly emphasized a "baptism with the Holy Spirit," an experience subsequent to conversion, for empowerment in Christian service. The three greatly influenced the Keswick Movement.

- The Keswick "Higher Life" conferences and teaching began after 1867. "This new Keswick emphasis displaced the concept of the second blessing as an 'eradication' of the sinful nature in favor of a 'baptism in the Holy Spirit' as an 'enduement of power for service.'"[13]

Biblical Reasons Confirm Subsequence

Four brief illustrations highlight the fact that regenerated or born again believers need, in addition to conversion, a baptism with the Holy Spirit: (1) Old Testament typology, (2) Jesus' example, (3) the disciples' conversions before Pentecost and (4) examples from Acts and other references.

Old Testament Typology

Perhaps one of the greatest biblical typologies (natural things that illustrate spiritual truths) would be the feasts of Israel. Each symbolizes a major fact of Christ's ministry, and they are separate and sequential in Israel's calendar year. First, Passover finds fulfillment in the cross (see 1 Corinthians 5:7). Christ died for us on the cross, and we come to God in our conversions by the experience of the cross. Secondly, the Feast of Pentecost finds fulfillment in Acts 2 and in our personal experiences of Spirit-baptism. Notice, Pentecost is subsequent (fifty days later) to the cross.

Under the Levitical system, oil was sometimes placed over blood. Blood referred, of course, to salvation through atonement and sacrifice. Oil referred to the anointing of the Holy Spirit. This dual anointing was placed, for instance, on the cleansed leper for his atonement (see Leviticus 14:14–17). Oil over blood, applied after blood, refers to the baptism with the Spirit over the blood of Jesus—Spirit-baptism in addition to salvation.

Jesus' Example

Jesus is our model, our example, our prototype. We are to follow in His footsteps (see 1 Peter 2:21). Jesus was born of the Spirit, then thirty years later He was baptized or anointed with the Holy Spirit.

The Disciples' Conversions before Pentecost

The disciples were New Testament followers of and believers in the Lord Jesus Christ before Pentecost. They had left all to follow Jesus (see Matthew 19:27). They confessed that Jesus was the Christ (see Matthew 16:16). Their names were written in heaven (see Luke 10:20). They were clean through the Word (see John 13:10–11; 15:3). They were chosen and planted (see John 15:16), and they were friends of Jesus (see John 15:14). Jesus had commissioned them to preach (see Acts 1:8). Robert Gromacki says of the disciples' experience at Pentecost: "They were definitely saved men before the events of Pentecost occurred. . . ."[14]

Dick Iverson adds these five thoughts to validate their spirituality: "(1) they were in unity and one accord (Acts 1:14, 21), (2) they were in prayer and supplication (Acts 1:14), (3) they received revelation from the Scriptures (Acts 1:15–22), (4) they were continually in the temple praising and blessing God (Luke 24:53), (5) they were absolutely obedient to the command of Christ to wait for the promise of the Father, even though it meant waiting in prayer and praise for ten days after His final words and ascension. We cannot conclude, then, that they were not saved, nor that they were just waiting to be born again."[15]

I personally believe that when Jesus—after shedding His blood on the cross and returning to heaven—appeared to His disciples in that locked upper room, He imparted the Holy Spirit to indwell them when He breathed on them and said: "Receive the Holy Spirit" (John 20:22). J. Rodman Williams compares the experience of Jesus and His disciples: ". . . in both cases the Holy Spirit came upon those who were 'born' of the Spirit. Jesus Himself was born of the Spirit in the womb of the Virgin Mary; the disciples were born of the Spirit in the room where Jesus breathed upon them and said, 'Receive the Holy Spirit' . . . . In Jesus' case, of course, it was generation; in the disciples' it was regeneration. But for both, being born of the Spirit preceded the coming of the Spirit."[16]

Next to Jesus Himself, the disciples offer the best example for those who follow. They were converted, spiritually alive, having the indwelling Spirit, yet Jesus came several days later and said that they must also wait in Jerusalem to receive the mighty baptism with the Holy Spirit. This is substantial proof that Spirit-baptism follows conversion.

Examples from Acts and Other References

In the next three chapters we will be analyzing in detail the episodes in the Acts of the Apostles and will particularly verify that conversion and the baptism with the Holy Spirit were separate events. It will be obvious that people first put their faith in Christ (conversion) and after that experience received the baptism with the Holy Spirit. Note Ephesians 1:13: "In whom also, having believed, you were sealed with the Holy Spirit of promise."

Galatians 4:6 states: "And because you are [already] sons, God has sent forth the Spirit of His Son into your hearts, crying out, 'Abba, Father!'" (Note also Romans 8:15.) Horton makes this accurate assessment: "The fact they are sons [is] the ground for sending the Spirit."[17]

INITIAL EVIDENCE

Sometimes the term *initial* is used with *evidence* ("initial evidence") to describe the primary manifestation of tongues when Spirit-baptism occurs. This does not mean that tongues are the only evidence; it means they are the initial, outward, observable evidence. My dictionary has three separate listings for *initial,* and it is used here in the sense of being the first thing that happens; it happens at the beginning.

Consider this additional definition. *Initial* also means "authorization," like a manager authorizing a document with his initials or a notary affixing his seal and name (the original thought behind *initial*). The document is declared to be what it claims to be; similarly, the miracle of tongues is an immediate confirmation or validation that the Holy Spirit has truly baptized the person.

Background of the Terminology

Since its beginning in 1901, the Pentecostal movement has considered speaking in tongues as "the initial evidence." This is how it began. "Rev. Charles Parham, head of the Bethel Bible college in Topeka, Kansas, had given his students . . . an assignment of 'studying out diligently what was the Bible evidence of the baptism of the Holy Ghost' . . . . To his surprise they all later reported that the evidence was speaking in other tongues." When Parham prayed for Agnes Ozman, one of the students, she became "the first known person to have received such an experience as a result of specifically seeking a baptism in the Holy Spirit with the expectation of speaking in tongues."[18]

Does this mean that there is biblical proof that tongues are the primary sign? This is the frustrating thing about this study of tongues: The answer can only be found in Acts, and even there we find no absolute, watertight statement. Scholars become irritated at this seemingly obsessive use of Acts by Pentecostals. Donald Gee, one of the prominent, early teachers of the Pentecostal movement, admits that we are "shut up" to the episodes in Acts to prove our point. I like this forthright statement by William MacDonald:

> On this score we constantly infuriate our evangelical brothers by our *ex post facto* approach. They contend that we dogmatize as follows: "Everyone must speak in tongues in order to receive the fullness of the Spirit." And we merrily agree with them that such a precept is not to be found in the New Testament! However—and there was hardly ever a "however" with greater amplitude—we assert forthrightly on the basis of biblical precedents and our own experiences, that all believers in fact do speak in tongues subsequent to their being submerged completely in the Spirit. This they do, and their glossolalia is evidence of what has taken place in them, not the epitome or embodiment of the experience itself.[19]

Our Only Evidence: Biblical Precedent

Since Acts is the only part of the Bible that describes Spirit-baptism accompanied by tongues, that is where we must study. There is a rule of hermeneutics used by Bible scholars that I think fits our situation perfectly. It is called "The Full Mention Principle," and I think Conner words it clearly: "That principle by which the interpretation of any verse is determined upon a consideration of the complete mention of its subject in Scripture."[20] The fact is, God put the sum of His information on Spirit-baptism in the gospels and the Acts and the sum of information on speaking in tongues in Mark, Acts and 1 Corinthians.

This is the complete mention of this very important subject in the Bible. We must, therefore, accept the narratives presented in Acts as trustworthy material to understand God's thinking on the subject. This is how God has chosen to discuss this subject, and Acts does, after all, contain 22 percent of the New Testament verses that mention the Holy Spirit. My chapter 13 will be devoted to the best manner of interpreting the book of Acts.

The Historical Presentation of Acts

There are five major outpourings of the Spirit mentioned in Acts, and in three of the cases speaking in tongues is mentioned. The five cases are: (1) the Jews at Jerusalem, (2) the Samaritans, (3) the conversion of

Saul, (4) the household of Cornelius and (5) the disciples at Ephesus. As I mentioned a moment ago we will be studying these outpourings in the next few chapters, but suffice it to say here that in three of the above cases, the people spoke in tongues—and in the remaining two cases, speaking in tongues is clearly implied. We will see that this material leads to more than assumption; this is the way it was then and what is expected now.

FOURTEEN DESCRIPTIVE TERMS

The following terms, arranged alphabetically, are mainly from the epistles and are descriptive of what is accomplished by the baptism of the Holy Spirit. This is the heritage of the Spirit-filled believer.

Anointing: Clothed with His Authority

It is like the precious, symbolic oil flowing from Samuel's horn down over the head of David, placing God's authority on his life. Jesus was anointed by the Holy Spirit (see Luke 4:18; Acts 34:27; 10:38). God has anointed us as well (see 2 Corinthians 1:21; Hebrews 1:9). John uses two tenses: "the anointing which you have received," and "you have an anointing" (1 John 2:20, 27). It is "the sacred touch and blessing of God upon a person or thing. It is the confirmation I sense in the Spirit whenever I act in the call of God in my life" (Niswander).[21]

Baptism: Submerged into the Spirit

Just as John immersed people in the Jordan River, Jesus the baptizer would immerse people in the Holy Spirit. John declared: "I indeed baptized you with water, but He will baptize you with the Holy Spirit" (Mark 1:8; see also Matthew 3:11; Luke 3:16). Jesus also used the word *baptize* (see Acts 1:5), so did Peter (see Acts 11:16) and so did God (John 1:33)!

Earnest: Sample of the Life to Come

Receiving the Spirit is like receiving a substantial down payment of a huge inheritance to come. The Greek papyri used the word *earnest* and furnished us examples of "earnest money" (a part given in advance of what will be bestowed in full afterward): a woman selling a cow, a mouse catcher receiving partial payment and even an engagement ring.[22] Bauer's lexicon says of the Greek word *arrabon:* "first installment, deposit, down payment, pledge, that pays a part of the purchase price in advance, and so secures a legal claim to the article in question, or makes a contract valid . . . a payment which obligates the contracting party to make further payments."[23] Paul tells us we have been "given the Spirit in our hearts as a deposit" (2 Corinthians 1:22) and "as a guarantee" (2 Corinthians 5:5) and that "the Holy Spirit of promise . . . is the guarantee of our inheritance" (Ephesians 1:13–14). It was "the Spirit who served as the evidence that the future had come and the guarantee of its consummation" (Fee).[24]

Empowerment: Dynamic Strengthening

Most of us have read about a scenario like this one: An accident occurs and a man must lift a car off of his friend. Amazingly, the excitement sends a shot of adrenaline into his bloodstream, and he heroically does what he ordinarily would be incapable of doing. This natural story helps illustrate how the Holy Spirit comes with spiritual empowerment and special strengthening. (See Matthew 10:20; Acts 6:10; 1 Corinthians 2:4; Colossians 1:29; 1 Thessalonians 1:5.)

Enduement: His Presence on Me

When the Spirit came upon the Old Testament judges, they did amazing things. Samson, for instance, not noted for his spirituality, still slew the enemy because "the Spirit of the LORD came mightily upon him" (Judges 14:6). This is the same enduement Jesus meant when He said, "Behold, I send the Promise of My Father upon you; but tarry in the city of Jerusalem until you are endued with power from on high" (Luke 24:49).

Falling Upon: God's Gift Descends on Us from Above

Another term would be *outpouring:* a flow from above. The presence of the Holy Spirit descends over and upon the individual invisibly, as real as a glistening waterfall. (See Matthew 3:16; 12:18; Mark 1:10; Luke 2:25; 3:22; John 1:32–33; Acts 1:8; 8:16; 10:44; 11:15; 19:6; 2 Corinthians 12:9; 1 Peter 4:14.)

Filling: Overflowing Us from Within

As David said, "My cup runs over" (Psalm 23:5). The Spirit is like an artesian well whose waters spring up from within. Jesus said: "He who believes in Me, as the Scripture has said, out of his heart will flow rivers of living water" (John 7:38). (See Luke 1:15, 41, 67; 4:1; Acts 2:4; 4:8, 31; 6:3, 5; 7:55; 9:17; 11:24; 13:9, 52; 15:8; Ephesians 5:18.)

Firstfruits: First Product of the Spirit

"The born again believer receives the firstfruits of the Spirit's operation in the baptism of the Holy Spirit. . . . The firstfruits always speak of the beginning and point to the full harvest yet to come" (Conner).[25] Romans 8:23 states: "We . . . have the firstfruits of the Spirit."

Gift: Given without Merit (Prejudice), Hesitation or Obligation

Think in terms of a benevolent king bestowing a valuable present on an undeserving beggar. The Holy Spirit is a most precious gift, freely and graciously bestowed by the heavenly Father on the born again believer. (See Luke 11:13; John 3:34; 14:16; Acts 2:38; 5:32; 8:18, 20; 10:47; 11:17; Romans 5:5; 1 Thessalonians 4:8.)

Indwelling: A Guest Abides Within

The individual becomes the temple that the Holy Spirit indwells. (See John 14:16–23; Romans 8:11; Ephesians 2:22; Revelation 3:20.)

Outpouring: Flowing from Above

Paul states that God "poured out on us abundantly" the Holy Spirit (Titus 3:6). (See Acts 2:17–18, 33; 10:45.)

Promise: Given by One Who Never Forgets or Fails

As Numbers 23:19 makes clear, "God is not a man, that He should lie, nor a son of man, that He should repent. Has He said, and will He not do? Or has He spoken, and will He not make it good?" (See Luke 24:49; John 14:26; 15:26; Acts 1:4; 2:39.)

Receiving: The Child Accepts the Gift

This term reminds me of a grandchild eagerly reaching out for a new toy. In Acts 8:15 the apostles "prayed for them that they might receive the Holy Spirit." (See John 7:39; Acts 8:17, 19; Galatians 3:2.)

Sealing: The Mark of Ownership

An ancient king would press his signet ring into the fresh glob of wax on the letter. The impression ensured privacy and denoted "ownership and responsibility, and it authenticated and protected" (Holdcroft).[26] We are God's letter, bearing His seal. We belong to Him "who also has sealed us and given us the Spirit in our hearts as a deposit" (2 Corinthians 1:22). "You were sealed with the Holy Spirit of promise" (Ephesians 1:13). Some feel this sealing refers to water baptism. Gordon Fee comments: "There seem to be no grounds in the text . . . for viewing this passage as also referring to water baptism . . . in this text and others Paul designates the Spirit, not baptism, as God's 'seal' of ownership."[27]

SPIRIT ACTIVITY IN ACTS

The fourteen terms that we have just described are glimpses of the various ways in which the Holy Spirit operates. Nine of these terms are used as action words in Acts to illustrate Holy Spirit baptism and infilling. I have placed them in the following chart with their appearances in Acts.

SPIRIT EMPOWERMENT ACTIVITY IN THE BOOK OF ACTS

Received	Baptized	Fell upon	Came upon	Filled	Poured out	Empowered	Anointed	Given
2:38	1:5	8:16	1:8	2:4	2:17–18	6:10	4:27	5:32
8:15	11:16	10:44	19:6	4:8	2:33	8:39	10:38	8:18–20
8:17		11:15		4:31	10:45	20:28		11:17
8:19				6:3, 5				15:8
10:47				7:55				
19:2				9:17				
				11:24				
				13:9, 52				

Although there are nine different terms, it becomes apparent that all describe the wonderful action of the Spirit coming upon and working within people. Actually the terms are synonymous in the sense that they describe the Holy Spirit at work. Each term brings out some special divine perspective or emphasis, yet they all blend marvelously to present the active Holy Spirit. Luke, who used these terms in making his record of events, seems to have had little concern for refined usage or definition. He simply described the Spirit's activity in ways that seemed appropriate at the moment.

There should be no confusion about the ongoing work of the Spirit in the Christian's life. Although the cross is our glory and where we obtain our salvation, the ministry of Jesus continues to the believer through the tomb (water baptism and resurrection) and finds great fulfillment at the throne, from where the ascended Jesus gives (pours out) the promised Holy Spirit. That is not the end, however. The Peter Pattern is the initiation. From that point on the believer will find (as Peter did) that a person will need to have frequent infillings of the Spirit on an ongoing basis.

This is why we can say that we "receive" the Spirit when born again. That is, receive Him in the sense that He is our life-giver in spiritual regeneration. But we continue to "receive" that same Spirit for special empowerment in Spirit-baptism, and "receive" that Spirit in subsequent times of refreshing when God meets our need. Sometimes we are so concerned about the refined definition of such words that we fail to enjoy what God has described in very human, illustrative terms.

How to Receive Spirit-Baptism

Many lists have been made by authors who wish to help people receive the baptism with the Holy Spirit. My list is put in simple terms, but additional suggestions are available in the endnotes.[28]

1. Be sure that you are a Christian.[29]
2. Understand clearly what you wish to receive from God.[30]
3. Prayerfully ask God to bring you the answer.[31]
4. Prepare yourself to be a temple of the Holy Spirit.[32]
5. Set specific times to seek God.[33]

6. Be worshipful and expectant in your seeking.[34]
7. Go with the flow of the Holy Spirit.

As you open yourself to God—which is similar to taking the lid off a vessel—God causes His Spirit to descend (fall, come upon, fill). Your own spiritual nature perceives (becomes vividly conscious of) the presence of God. This awareness occurs in various ways, and a person having such an experience will probably use terms like the nine in the chart to describe it later on. None of us is exactly alike, and we all tend to react differently—whether in touching a live wire, or experiencing the power of God!

The coming of the Spirit is perceived in various ways: deep peace, intense joy and even tumultuous energy. As was mentioned in chapter 7, the baptism with the Holy Spirit does not always necessitate that a person have strong physical reaction. My observation is that most people do have a strong emotional response, but some do so in a fairly placid physical manner. The great thing that happens, regardless of human reaction, is the wonderful, new awareness (or consciousness) of Jesus Christ. You will be thrilled at the spiritual awakening and empowerment that has occurred!

When you are aware of God's astonishing presence in answer to your prayers, open your mouth in audible praise. Your tongue will be given utterance by the Holy Spirit. This is glossolalia or speaking in tongues. Do not be afraid; it is biblical and of the Holy Spirit. It may at first seem strange and even unbelievable, but you will find that it is a truly marvelous way that God has chosen to manifest Himself in us. You will not have to think up words or manufacture jargon. The Holy Spirit gives the utterance! You will be overwhelmed with appreciation; it will rise within your spirit and burst forth in languages never learned. Jesus will be more real than ever to you!

KEEP THE PETER PATTERN ALIVE

As the feasts of Israel (Passover, Pentecost and Tabernacles) were given to maintain Israel's continuity with the past, we Christians are given the Peter Pattern to bond us with our past. Notice in the following chart how the three phases of the Peter Pattern are being "re-presented" constantly for Christians, thereby recalling our awareness of and continuity with the faith of the early Church.

MAINTAINING THE PETER PATTERN

The experience	What we remember	The ordinance of recall
1. Conversion	Calvary: Jesus' death on the cross, His broken body and shed blood	Communion: partaking of the body and blood of the Lord Jesus on regular basis
2. Water baptism	The tomb: The burial and resurrection of Jesus' body	Water baptism: reaffirming our testimony vicariously through the ongoing baptisms of new converts
3. Baptism with the Holy Spirit	Pentecost: Jesus' ascension and the outpouring of the Holy Spirit	Praying in tongues: reminding ourselves daily of the significance of Pentecost

Our special interest in the next three chapters will be to analyze the recordings of the baptism with the Holy Spirit attended by speaking in tongues—a normal experience for Christians of Bible days. What lessons can be learned for the Church today from these exciting episodes?

REVIEW QUESTIONS FOR CHAPTER 9

1. Who were the four who spoke of a "baptism with the Holy Spirit"?
2. How would you describe the literal meaning of being "baptized with/in the Holy Spirit"?
3. What has been your experience with the Holy Spirit?
4. What were the two things that launched the Pentecostal movement?
5. Would you like to receive the Holy Spirit?

PART 4

HOLY SPIRIT ACTIVITY
RECORDED IN ACTS

THE POWER OF PENTECOST SWEEPS ON

10

AMAZING EPISODES IN ACTS
LUKE TELLS IT AS IT WAS

IN THIS CHAPTER

- Examine an unusual chart that illustrates the Peter Pattern in Acts
- Consider why it is logical to believe the Samaritans spoke in tongues
- Learn which evangelist initiated phases 3 and 4 of the Acts 1:8 commission
- Discover who was the first missionary to Africa

The next three chapters focus on Holy Spirit activity in the book of Acts, followed by a closing chapter explaining how the Pentecostal views the book of Acts. Sixty-three verses mention the Spirit (more than any other book in the New Testament), so we must not bypass or neglect this very important fund of information. Keep in mind this comment by William Barclay:

In one sense it is true to say that the Book of Acts is the most important book in the New Testament. It is the simple truth that if we did not possess the Book of Acts, we would have, apart from what we could glean or deduce from the letters of Paul, no information whatever about the early church.[1]

The Holy Spirit's activity is best understood by beginning in the gospels, moving to Acts, and then going to the epistles—and this is the format we will follow. Some feel that starting with the Pauline epistles is the most logical approach, but this is like reading a book for its content—and starting in the last chapter. Those who try to understand the Spirit by concentrating on Pauline academics will find it difficult to understand the experience of the Spirit so carefully laid out in the gospels and then in Acts.

Doctrinal teaching grows from experience, not vice versa; theology generally emerges from ministry. The early Church first experienced the Holy Spirit and then wrote about Him. The epistles were written to people who already were converted, baptized in water and baptized with the Holy Spirit. They do not describe and analyze the baptism with the Spirit any more than they do conversion. They were instructions by the apostles to encourage members of the Body of Christ, those already dedicated and filled with the Spirit.[2] Without first reading the charismatic record of Luke (in Luke and Acts), we cannot understand the later charismatic writings of Paul. The two approaches complement and amplify each other.

Luke's narratives (Luke and Acts) have a clearly stated objective: "Having carefully investigated all of these accounts from the beginning, I have decided to write a careful summary for you, to reassure you of the truth of all you were taught" (Luke 1:3–4, NLT). Luke's narratives in Acts offer three interesting views of the early Church: historical, missiological and theological. Historically "Acts should be read and understood as essentially a missiological document if we are to receive its maximum value" (Wagner).[3]

The theology of Acts is charismatic and is meant to be the foundational understanding for the epistles that will be written later. The theology of the Holy Spirit is woven throughout the historical account as well as the missionary activity of the Church. For our study of Acts, I suggest that Luke's account has this purpose (weaving history, missions and theology together): to show that the life and success of the early Church was the direct result of the Holy Spirit's presence and activity.

THE THREEFOLD PURPOSE OF ACTS

Purpose	Description
1. Historical	A history of the early Church's activity and growth during the time of Holy Spirit empowerment.
2. Missiological	An account of how cultural barriers were broken and the Gospel moved from Jews to non-Jews through the ministry of Spirit-filled believers.
3. Theological	The story of Holy Spirit activity that enabled the early Church to function and gives today's Church a standard of excellence to emulate as well as insight into the nature and activity of the Holy Spirit.

In this chapter and the next, we will view this threefold objective in action by reviewing of some of the key episodes of conversion, water baptism and Spirit-baptism in the Acts. You will recall from the last chapter that these three experiences are actually an apostolic paradigm. I call this the Peter Pattern because it was first articulated by the apostle Peter in Acts 2:38:

> Repent, and let every one of you be baptized in the name of Jesus Christ for the remission of sins; and you shall receive the gift of the Holy Spirit. For the promise [of the Holy Spirit] is to you and to your children, and to all who are afar off [the Gentiles], as many as the Lord our God will call.

Special attention will be given to the baptism with the Holy Spirit accompanied and evidenced by speaking in tongues—a normal and expected experience for Christians in Bible days. Since this interpretation has sometimes been questioned, effort will be made to answer all objections satisfactorily. Those who desire more technical scrutiny are invited to check out the endnote references and suggestions.

Later in chapter 13, principles of biblical interpretation will be applied to the teaching of Acts, showing how these widely accepted concepts substantiate our approach.

ILLUSTRATIONS OF THE PETER PATTERN

Luke gives us in the book of Acts fourteen illustrations in which conversions and at least one of the two other phases of the Peter Pattern are mentioned. I have outlined these in the chart below. In several of these episodes, tongues are implied as it seems that the apostles' expectations of Spirit-baptism are fulfilled. We might also assume that the new believers were baptized in water, whether the text mentions it or not—and could not the assumption for Spirit-baptism be made also? Consider, too, that in the Acts there are another nine accounts of conversions given (not included in the chart) that do not mention either of the other two phases of the Peter Pattern.

We will discuss several of these illustrations in this and the next chapter.

ILLUSTRATIONS OF THE PETER PATTERN IN ACTS

Illustration	Born of the Holy Spirit	Water baptism	Spirit-baptism	Manifestation
1. Jerusalem: the Jews at Pentecost, 2:4	Jesus breathed on them, John 20:2		They were filled with the Holy Spirit	Spoke in tongues
2. Peter preaches at Pentecost: Peter Pattern, 2:38	Repent	Be baptized	Received the Holy Spirit	
3. Three thousand converts at Pentecost, 2:41	Gladly received Peter's word	Were baptized	Told they would receive the Holy Spirit	Continued in apostles' doctrine
4. Samaria: the converted Samaritans, 8:12, 14–18	Believed	Were baptized	Received the Holy Spirit	Showed immediate evidence
5. Road to Gaza: the Ethiopian eunuch, 8:26–39	Believed	Was baptized	Received the Holy Spirit (Western Text)[4]	Rejoiced in the Spirit
6. Damascus: conversion of Saul of Tarsus, 9:1–19, 22, 26	Acknowledged Lordship of Jesus	Was baptized	Filled with the Holy Spirit	Immediately preached Christ (note 1 Cor. 14:18)
7. Caesarea: the household of Cornelius, 10:1–48	Heard the Word	Were baptized	The Holy Spirit fell on them	Spoke with tongues and magnified God
8. Jerusalem: Peter's report, 11:1–18	Heard words by which they were saved		The Holy Spirit fell upon them, they were baptized with the Holy Spirit	As upon the disciples in the beginning (i.e., with tongues)
9. Antioch: Gentiles, 13:48–52	Believed		Filled with the Holy Spirit	Great joy
10. Jerusalem: Peter at council, 15:7–9	Heard the Gospel and believed		Gave them the Holy Spirit	Just as with the disciples
11. Philippi: household of Lydia, 16:14–15	Opened her heart	She and her house were baptized		

Illustration	Born of the Holy Spirit	Water baptism	Spirit-baptism	Manifestation
12. Philippi: household of jailer, 16:30–33	They believed	He and household were baptized		
13. Corinth: household of Crispus, many Corinthians, 18:8	Many believed	Were baptized		
14. Ephesus: twelve disciples, 19:1–7	Believed on Him	Were baptized	The Holy Spirit came upon them	Spoke with tongues and prophesied

The remainder of this chapter will discuss two illustrations found on the chart: numbers 4 and 5—the Samaritans and the Ethiopian eunuch. These fascinating examples are both from the eighth chapter of Acts and both involve the evangelist Philip. Discussions of other illustrations on the chart will follow in the next chapter.

THE SAMARITANS BELIEVE AND RECEIVE

Now when the apostles who were at Jerusalem heard that Samaria had received the word of God, they sent Peter and John to them, who, when they had come down, prayed for them that they might receive the Holy Spirit. For as yet He had fallen upon none of them. They had only been baptized in the name of the Lord Jesus. Then they laid hands on them, and they received the Holy Spirit.

Acts 8:14–17

Good news arrived in Jerusalem! Under the preaching and miracle working of deacon-missionary-evangelist Philip, revival had broken out in a strange place. Samaria had received the word of God! This meant that phase three of Jesus' missionary program, as outlined in Acts 1:8, had been spontaneously launched: "But you shall receive power when the Holy Spirit has come upon you; and you shall be witnesses to Me in [1] Jerusalem, and in all [2] Judea and [3] Samaria, and [4] to the end of the earth." The apostles carefully reviewed the report, rejoicing that the Samaritans had received the message of Christ and been baptized in water, that miracles of healing had occurred, that demons had been cast out, and that there was great joy in the city!

Naturally they were extremely interested in how things were progressing, for it was their apostolic responsibility to oversee this burgeoning movement. They had concern, of course, because of the smoldering hostility between Jews and Samaritans. They remembered their own ministry with Jesus and how a Samaritan village would not receive Him (see Luke 9:51–56). The Samaritans were considered a hybrid people, the result of Jews intermarrying with foreign peoples, and they held a warped theology—a near-Jewish religion corrupted by syncretistic elements.[5] Previously, the Samaritans had not recognized Jerusalem as their religious center, and the possibility existed that the new Samaritan believers might become estranged from the church at Jerusalem and the apostolic leaders.

As Bruner has said: "Samaria was the church's first decisive step out of and beyond Judaism." It was a major event that required special apostolic oversight, so Peter and John (as key leaders and original apostles) were commissioned to welcome and bless the Samaritans, the first people group outside of Judea to be reached, "the crossing of the first threshold into the non-Jewish world."[6]

Key Issue: Reception of the Spirit

Something else about the report was of major importance: It gave no indication that the Holy Spirit had fallen on any of the water-baptized converts.[7] The manifestation (glossolalia) that had accompanied God's gift of the Spirit at Pentecost had not yet occurred in Samaria (compare Acts 2:4; 10:44–46; 11:15; 19:6). Usually, conversion, water baptism and the reception of the Holy Spirit happened about the same time, so the Samaritan situation was unique and challenging.

So far, in the spread of the Gospel, only Jews had been converted and baptized in water and with the Spirit. It was logical and important that apostolic authority be represented in this first Spirit-venture beyond Judea—both for the apostles' peace of mind and the Samaritans'. The laying on of the apostles' hands would link the Samaritans with the Church of Jesus Christ.

It was also important that there be charismatic outpouring, as there was at Pentecost. This would cinch forever in everyone's mind that there were now no barriers or differences between Jews and Samaritans; racial background or prior religion could not hinder or frustrate the grace of the heavenly Father, the bestowal of the Holy Spirit and inclusion in the one Church of the living God.

The Samaritan episode in Acts 8—how faith, baptism and the gift of the Spirit were presented—has been a huge source of debate among Bible commentators who seek to explain the activity of the Holy Spirit. One scholar calls it "an anomaly"—a deviation from the common rule; something peculiar or not easily classified.[8]

The key issue has to do with how and when the Spirit was received. This account clearly presents a "time gap" between the Samaritans' belief in Christ and receiving the Spirit. Verse 16 states: "For as yet He [the Holy Spirit] had fallen upon none of them. They had only been baptized in the name of the Lord Jesus." Those who believe that Spirit-baptism happens at conversion naturally oppose the thought that the Samaritans had a subsequent experience. It would imply that the Samaritans' conversions and baptisms were not genuine. To deal with this difficulty of being filled with the Spirit in a "later" experience, some Bible scholars teach that true conversions did not occur in Samaria until after the apostles arrived.[9]

The question is also raised of whether or not there was miraculous evidence when the Spirit was given (such as speaking in tongues). Acts 8 is a unique passage because it shows that the Samaritans were converted and baptized in water, and then later (when the apostles arrived) were filled with the Spirit—but it does not say they spoke in tongues! The text leaves these important issues open to question.

Were the Samaritans Believers?

Were they, indeed, believers? From our text we see that the apostles did not come to *convert* the Samaritans. This had already been accomplished by evangelist Philip. Note the following verses: Philip went out "preaching the word" (verse 4); he "preached Christ to them" (verse 5); "when they believed Philip as he preached the things concerning the kingdom of God and the name of Jesus Christ, both men and women were baptized" (verse 12); "Samaria had received the word of God" (verse 14). Philip gave a solid salvation message to the Samaritans and the apostles rejoiced to hear it.

And, without a doubt, in light of the way Philip later quizzed the Ethiopian eunuch, he would not have baptized anyone who had not confessed belief in Jesus Christ (see verse 37). Also, although Samaritans were excluded from the first preaching mission of the Twelve (see Matthew 10:5–6), no question is raised about Philip's wisdom or authority in baptizing them—or the authenticity of their experience. We can accept the Samaritans' baptism as authentic because Peter and John did! Notice that they did not rebaptize them as Paul later did with certain Ephesians (see Acts 19).

It was common practice for new converts to confess publicly their new faith in Christ. In fact, "apostolic baptism involved a public confession of commitment to Jesus Christ."[10] Ananias brought this same challenge to Saul (Paul): "Arise and be baptized, and wash away your sins, calling on the name of the Lord" (Acts 22:16). Note this same similarity in the conversion of Lydia and also the Philippian jailer (see Acts 16:14–15, 33–34). There is no reason to doubt the authenticity of Philip's message, approach or results.

The Apostolic Team

Thus, Luke's record shows that the leading apostles came not to bring the message of Christ to Samaria but rather an apostolic presence, contact and seal of approval to cap what had already occurred. Peter and John were the official representatives of the apostolic council to welcome the Samaritan believers into the Church of Jesus Christ. This made the Samaritans' initiation into the Body of Christ complete. The blessing of the two leading apostles, the conferring of the Holy Spirit by their prayer with the laying on of hands and the immediate charismatic reaction of (what I believe was) speaking in tongues would confirm to the Samaritans the validity of their new experience. It would settle their minds that they were truly joined by the same Holy Spirit to the same Church and to the same Messiah. The tangible manifestation of the Spirit—the same that they themselves had experienced—would also cause the Jewish apostles to think the same thing! The Samaritans were no longer despised outsiders. Carl Brumback comments insightfully: "This revival in Samaria was acknowledged by the church at Jerusalem by the sending of the apostles, and acknowledged by God by the sending of the Holy Ghost."[11]

Note that although the apostles laid hands on the Samaritans to receive the Spirit, this was not the only method the Church would employ. At Jerusalem (see Acts 2) and at Caesarea (see Acts 10), hands were not laid on the candidates, but in Ephesus (see Acts 19) they were. In fact, the apostles themselves did not always have to be present for individuals to receive the Holy Spirit (as with Ananias and Saul and with Philip and the Ethiopian).

In this case, however, it was appropriate. The prayer of the apostles over the Samaritans was important, but the communication of their love through actual touching confirmed to the Samaritans their acceptance. They were now truly assured of full participation in the Church.

Was Simon's Faith Genuine?

An unfortunate casualty in this episode was Simon, a magician well versed in the dark secrets of sorcery who had captivated the attention of the entire countryside with his nefarious actions. The Bible states that he too had believed and been baptized, but an ugly attitude suddenly reared within him as he beheld an amazing demonstration. This was something that had not occurred in Philip's ministry or his own past sorcery. It happened when the apostles began laying their hands on the converts and praying for them to receive the Holy Spirit.

Reverting to his past (a magician would pay money to acquire secrets from masters of the magical arts), Simon anxiously asked to purchase (for personal influence) the unusual power he saw displayed. Peter's rebuke was direct and severe, "a vehement expression of horror on the part of St. Peter, an expression that would warn Simon that he was on the way to destruction."[12] The power of the Holy Spirit could not be purchased with money. We hope that Simon repented, but no one can be sure.[13] His name has inspired the everyday term *simony,* an eternal reminder of God's displeasure with those who would buy or sell divine favor and the gifts of the Holy Spirit.

Because Simon's faith was questionable, and his background and that of the Samaritans tainted with false teaching, sorcery, magic and superstition, the faith of the believing Samaritans has been brought into question and even deemed defective. Dunn, for instance, makes the surprising comment: "They all went through the form but did not experience the reality."[14]

We must be careful not to underplay the power of the Gospel at work through Philip. This episode in Samaria was a "power encounter" in which the Lord subjugated the evil sorcery abounding there, finally reducing the sorcerer himself to a whimpering man asking for prayer. Simon's diabolical hold on the people was broken by Philip's power and proclamation. It was not mass hysteria, as some suggest, that brought the people to baptism but the power of God. The fact that "great joy" came to a demon-oppressed city indicates an authentic work of God.[15]

What Did Simon See?

What so fascinated Simon as the apostles laid their hands on the believers? He saw an external, visible sign that was unique, fresh and immediately believable. There is no question in my mind but that the converts spoke in tongues, the unique sign of the continuing presence of the same Holy Spirit that birthed the Church. "This miracle utterance was entirely new to him [Simon] and would arrest his attention as nothing else."[16]

Lutheran scholar R. C. H. Lenski says: "When Peter and John came . . . a gathering of all the believers was probably held, and the apostles laid their hands on some of them, and these began to speak with tongues."[17] Non-charismatic teacher F. F. Bruce writes: "It is clearly implied that their reception of the Spirit was marked by external manifestations such as had marked his descent on the earliest disciples at Pentecost."[18]

Stanley M. Horton, well-known Pentecostal scholar, says of the Samaritan experience:

> Simon had already seen Philip's miracles. Prophecy would have been in his own language and not noticeably supernatural. There remains the same thing that attracted the attention of the crowd at Pentecost. They spoke with other tongues as the Spirit gave utterance. . . . Tongues, here, was not the point at issue. Nor did it have the same effect exactly, since there were not people of various languages present. Thus Luke says nothing about them in order to focus attention on Simon's wrong attitude.[19]

Some feel that other evidence could have occurred. Falling under the power of God and inner spiritual experiences are sometimes proposed, but these would not have been new or dramatically different. Others suggest things that had already occurred in Philip's revival such as healing the sick, casting out devils, great joy, soul winning. These miracles, however, did not impress Simon as much as when the Samaritans received the Holy Spirit. So the obvious number one choice remains speaking in tongues. More than miracles, Simon wanted the power to impart Holy Spirit baptism, which was accompanied by speaking in tongues. Ralph M. Riggs makes this comment:

[Simon] had not offered to buy Philip's evangelistic zeal, nor Philip's gifts of healing, miracles, and faith. But the mighty Baptism of the Holy Spirit which came upon the Samaritan disciples was to his mind more spectacular and wonderful. This explains his offer to buy the power and his neglect to offer to buy the previous working of the Holy Spirit.[20]

Some question this explanation since tongues are not specifically mentioned. Luke's reason, however, seems obvious to a Pentecostal, something we have known for a hundred years. If I tell someone that five people received the baptism of the Spirit in a meeting last night, I do not need to say they spoke in tongues; that is something we take for granted. This is why I believe Luke told his story as he did—that and the fact that he wanted to emphasize the experience and not the immediate evidence.

Another possible confirmation that tongues accompanied the reception of the Spirit is Peter's use of *logos,* which means "word" or "utterance." Rebuking Simon, Peter said: "You have neither part nor portion in this matter [logos]" (8:21). The "matter" he spoke of involved words or utterances—a strong indication of tongues![21]

Great Truths Taught by This Episode

G. Campbell Morgan states the question that readers of this episode invariably ask: "Why did they not receive the Spirit of God immediately?" His conclusion: "There is no answer. There is no reason to be discovered in the Acts of the Apostles for that delay."[22]

Perhaps, but is it not conceivable that the order of events was divinely orchestrated so that succeeding generations might have a clear-cut example? If so, we learn from the early Church that the baptism with the Spirit can indeed be a separate (and often subsequent) experience to conversion and water baptism and it is accompanied by charismatic evidence.[23]

THE ETHIOPIAN EUNUCH

And both Philip and the eunuch went down into the water, and he baptized him. Now when they came up out of the water, the Spirit of the Lord caught Philip away, so that the eunuch saw him no more; and he went on his way rejoicing.

Acts 8:38–39

God took Philip from a revival of multitudes to a solitary, discontented African man riding in his chariot on an infrequently traveled desert road. This was no ordinary man; he was the finance minister of the kingdom of Ethiopia (Nubia)—a rich and important dignitary and powerful official who was traveling home in his royal carriage from a pilgrimage to Jerusalem. His capacity in Jerusalem had been that of an observer and worshiper. His recent visit had apparently left him disquieted, for his spiritual questions were still unanswered and truth eluded him.

This was another divinely orchestrated episode as told in Acts 8:26–40. Philip was summoned by an angel and directed by the Spirit to the eunuch. The eunuch was prepared in heart, the experience was gloriously climaxed by the Spirit and finally both evangelist and convert went their respective ways rejoicing.

The man was probably a God-fearing Gentile like Cornelius. He worshiped the LORD God of the Jews, but he had not (and could not) become a Jewish proselyte, so in spite of his importance he could only go so far as the Court of the Gentiles and worship from afar. Dunn comments: "As a eunuch he could not be circumcised, and therefore not become a proselyte. However ardent his desire to worship in the Temple, it could not be realized, since he was both a Gentile and a eunuch (Deuteronomy 23:1). . . . His degree of commitment had been shown by his journey [a difficult and hazardous two hundred miles]. His degree of enthusiasm was shown by his purchase of a no-doubt expensive scroll, evidently written in Greek."[24]

Philip, a true cross-cultural evangelist-missionary, who had initiated phase three of Jesus' missions program—"and Samaria"—is now used in opening phase four—"and to the end of the earth." Philip found the eunuch reading aloud (a common way of reading in those days) the Greek text of Isaiah 53:7–8, the finest of the messianic predictions. After an opening greeting, Philip (whose native tongue was Greek) was invited to interpret the passage, which he joyfully proceeded to do: "And beginning at this Scripture, [he] preached Jesus to him" (Acts 8:35). The eunuch saw how his amazing text was fulfilled in Christ. He believed and was baptized in a convenient pool of water!

Philip now beheld not an Ethiopian eunuch, forever separated from the people of God, but rather a new brother in the faith—possibly the first true Gentile converted to Christianity! Kistemaker makes this interesting observation: "Philip first brings the Samaritans, who were in between the Jew and the Gentile, into the church. Now he leads the Ethiopian, who was a half-convert to Judaism, into the assembly of the Lord."[25]

Philip, newly come from the mighty outpouring of the Spirit in Samaria, would no doubt be equally concerned about the Ethiopian man receiving the baptism with the Holy Spirit. Previously (I believe), Philip had called for apostles to come and bring the Spirit's baptism to Samaria; circumstances on this desert road precluded such activity. Yet if he felt it was important to bring the experience to the Samaritans, how much more to a new convert going to a far-flung heathen nation like Ethiopia? It is extremely likely that Philip himself prayed for this man to receive the Holy Spirit. Philip, after all, was filled with the Spirit. Could we possibly think he would let the eunuch return to his people without the full experience of the Peter Pattern?

My opinion is that Philip discussed missions expansion with Peter and John while in Samaria. In the light of the Samaritan revival and outpouring of the Spirit—and the obvious zeal of Philip—the apostles must have come to the realization that it would not be necessary for them or other apostles always to be present to lay hands on new converts to receive the Holy Spirit. Peter later did go to the household of Cornelius (by divine direction), but that was a special occasion in the Gentile community—and very close to Jerusalem. In this episode with the eunuch, we see a case where Philip the evangelist was converting and baptizing—and then, without apostolic presence, God stepped in and baptized the eunuch with the Spirit Himself!

Notice the powerful Spirit activity at that pool of water! Although no apostle was present (no time or need to call one), the Holy Spirit came down miraculously as Philip baptized the eunuch and caught Philip away transporting him to Azotus! The Ethiopian went on his way rejoicing—with every indication that he was filled with the Spirit and probably speaking joyfully in tongues.

Linking the Spirit with joy is a natural connection. G. W. H. Lampe, for instance, assumes that when the Ethiopian eunuch went on his way "rejoicing" or when the Philippian jailer "rejoiced" with all his household, Luke was using the word as a synonym for receiving the Spirit.[26]

The Western Text makes a special emphasis: "The Holy Spirit fell on the eunuch, and an angel of the Lord caught up Philip."[27] Although most translations do not make this distinction, as F. F. Bruce says, "Even with the shorter reading it is a reasonable inference that he did receive the Spirit, although it would be an impermissible inference in the thinking of those who believe that the Spirit is bestowed only through the imposition of apostolic hands."[28]

Incidentally, if the eunuch continued his reading through Isaiah 56, he found to his delight that he doubly fulfilled the prophecy that both foreigners (aliens) and eunuchs are to be accepted in God's great house of prayer for all nations (see Isaiah 56:3–7; note also 1 Kings 8:41–43). After arriving in Ethiopia, the eunuch—saved, baptized and filled with the Spirit—became (we assume) the first Gentile missionary to a Gentile nation. Some say this episode is the fulfillment of Psalm 68:31: "Envoys will come out of Egypt; Ethiopia will quickly stretch out her hands to God."

REVIEW QUESTIONS FOR CHAPTER 10

1. What are your impressions after reviewing the chart illustrating the Peter Pattern?
2. How do you feel about the genuineness of the Samaritans' conversions and baptisms?
3. Was it really necessary for Peter and John to go to Samaria?
4. Explain Acts 1:8 in the light of the two episodes involving Philip.

11

MORE EPISODES
THE RAIN KEEPS FALLING

IN THIS CHAPTER

- See who baptized the great apostle Paul
- Learn who spoke in tongues more than any other Christian
- Find out why the Jewish leaders were perturbed with Peter
- Discover how Peter knew the Romans had received the Holy Spirit

This chapter continues our review of several episodes in Acts that describe the activity of the Holy Spirit, particularly Spirit-baptism. So far, we have discussed three illustrations from a chart of fourteen that show the Peter Pattern in operation: the disciples at Pentecost, the Samaritan believers and the Ethiopian eunuch.

Now we will review the conversions of Saul and the household of Cornelius along with Peter's report to the Jerusalem elders. By the end of Acts, we see that Holy Spirit baptism had touched the following ethnic groups: Jews (see chapter 2), Samaritans (see chapter 8), Ethiopians (see chapter 8), Romans (see chapter 10), Syrians (see chapter 13), Greeks and Asians (see chapter 19). Peter's prophetic explanation of the Pentecostal outpouring in Jerusalem is now actually happening among Gentile people groups. They experience the same Spirit, magnifying God in both their native tongues and the miracle tongues of Pentecost.

SAUL OF TARSUS MEETS HIS GOD

> And Ananias went his way and entered the house; and laying his hands on him he said, "Brother Saul, the Lord Jesus, who appeared to you on the road as you came has sent me that you may receive your sight and be filled with the Holy Spirit." Immediately there fell from his eyes something like scales, and he received his sight at once; and he arose and was baptized.
>
> Acts 9:17–18

The remarkable story of the apostle Paul's conversion is a favorite of every Christian and one that should be a part of any study of the Holy Spirit. The narrative combines his conversion with an amazing call to be an apostle to the nations. I like the way Philip Schaff opens his discussion of the event:

> The conversion of Paul marks not only a turning-point in his personal history, but also an important epoch in the history of the apostolic church, and consequently in the history of mankind. It was the most fruitful event since the miracle of Pentecost, and secured the universal victory of Christianity. The transformation of the most dangerous persecutor into the most successful promoter of Christianity is nothing less than a miracle of divine grace.[1]

The story is told in three places. Acts 9 is Luke's account, Acts 22 is Paul's statement to the mob in Jerusalem and Acts 26 is Paul's defense before King Agrippa. The variations in the narrative are easily explained by analyzing the different audiences. Any seeming discrepancies refer mainly to the effects of the event on Paul's companions. Our interest is Paul's conversion, water baptism and baptism with the Holy Spirit.

The Journey to Damascus

It was a trying time for the Church of Jesus. Stephen's bold indictment of the Jewish leaders inflamed the anger of the Sanhedrin—the Jewish ruling body—and birthed a full-scale persecution of the Church (including Stephen's martyrdom). The Christians scattered in various directions with some of the fugitives fleeing to Damascus.

Paul, known as Saul at this time, and his conspirators journeyed from Jerusalem to Damascus under the direct commission of the Sanhedrin. Saul, as a sort of inquisitor-general, had "full authority . . . to stamp out the Christian rebellion, and to bring all the apostates he could find, whether they were men or women, in chains to the holy city to be condemned by the chief priests."[2]

The distant, ancient city of Damascus sat as a bountiful oasis in a barren, sandy wilderness. Their journey was approximately 140 miles and took a full week on foot or horseback. Various authors have made much of Saul's mental state during this trip, wondering if the stoning of Stephen haunted his active mind.

Just outside the city of Damascus, this merciless, fanatical persecutor of the Church was apprehended by One greater than himself. The resurrected Jesus, resplendent in the brilliant light of God's glory, burst upon Saul with such intensity that the poor man fell to the ground stone blind. Jesus asked, "Saul, Saul, why are you persecuting Me?" Saul replied, "Who are You, Lord?" And the Lord said, "I am Jesus, whom you are persecuting. It is hard for you to kick against the goads" (see Acts 9:3–5).

When Was Saul Converted?

Much debate has focused on exactly when Saul was converted. Some say convincingly that Saul's next words indicate his submission to and acceptance of Jesus Christ as Lord: "Lord, what do You want me to do?" Later Paul told the Romans, from personal experience, "if you confess with your mouth the Lord Jesus and believe in your heart that God has raised Him from the dead, you will be saved" (Romans 10:9). Also, Paul told the Corinthians that "no one can say that Jesus is Lord except by the Holy Spirit" (1 Corinthians 12:3).

Did Saul call on the Lord at this encounter or at his baptism? In my mind, there is no contextual evidence for changing the vocative *kurie* from

Lord to *sir* as some translations do in Acts 9:5; 22:8, 10; and 26:15. The word is used by Luke eleven more times in Acts, ten of which mean "Lord Jesus" and once to mean the angel of God. As Howard Ervin argues, "[T]he evidence strongly suggests that whenever Jesus is addressed as kurie, the meaning is 'Lord Jesus,' and not the ambiguous 'Sir.'"[3]

The dramatic appearance of Jesus was like a bomb exploding in Saul's mind. This was not a casual introduction; it was the appearance of the great and only God who would accept nothing short of total, immediate surrender. I vote that he was converted at the encounter.

Then, "like a helpless child, blinded by the dazzling light, he was led to Damascus, and after three days of blindness and fasting he was cured and baptized—not by Peter or James or John, but—by one of the humble disciples whom he had come to destroy."[4]

Luke must have felt that it was immaterial to the story to pinpoint exactly when Saul was truly converted; it is of great importance to biblical scholars because of how it relates to the baptism with the Holy Spirit. Suffice it to say that he was "born again" by the great action of the Holy Spirit.[5] Paul later described the change as being "a new creation; old things have passed away; behold, all things have become new" (2 Corinthians 5:17).

Some suggest that Saul needed time to think his way through this dilemma. No, he needed the power of the transforming Spirit that is released through total surrender! The new birth is based on volitional choice, but conversion is dependent on more than an intellectual exercise; it is the power of God, responding to faith that produces salvation. Many people, chained by addiction, drunkenness, hatred, etc., have found that God's power can save and change them instantly, bypassing even withdrawal symptoms. Saul must have had just such a special visitation, for that alone devastated his religious obsession to destroy Christ's Church.

The Mission of Ananias

Ananias, a devout Jew and disciple of Jesus, was sent by Jesus to the stricken man, and said: "Brother Saul, the Lord Jesus, who appeared to you on the road as you came, has sent me that you may receive your sight and be filled with the Holy Spirit." Immediately Saul could see; quickly he arose and was baptized. Notice that Ananias made no effort to convert Saul; he apparently was already saved. The fact that God had told Ananias in the vision that Saul was "a chosen vessel of Mine" indicates that Saul was converted. Also, when Jesus commissioned Ananias, He said, "He is praying to me right now" (Acts 9:11, NLT). Ananias assumed that Saul was converted.

Also, Ananias addressed Saul as "brother," which many see as signifying that Saul was a Christian. Others say that this word could easily refer to a brother Jew.[6] The simple sense of the story is that Ananias realized that this persecutor was now apprehended by the Lord, so he gratefully welcomed him as a spiritual brother. The purging effect of Saul's repentance was now completed, and he submitted humbly to Ananias's baptism (the representative of the Church he had persecuted).

Saul's Reception of the Holy Spirit

Little is recorded about Saul being baptized in the Holy Spirit—only that Ananias was to pray for Saul and he would receive the Spirit. I believe that Saul spoke in tongues at this time. The whole package—conversion, water baptism, receiving the Spirit—was foundational for his subsequent ministry. Saul was baptized in water, but the text itself is not clear whether it was before or after being filled with the Spirit. *Hayford's Bible Handbook* says: "Ananias . . . is instructed to lay hands on Saul for the restoration of his sight and so that Saul may be filled with the Holy Spirit. In this case, Spirit fullness precedes baptism in water."[7] Here are several considerations of this issue.

Did Saul Speak in Tongues?

First of all, consider that the man who was to be the apostle to the Gentiles—like the converts at Samaria—needed to experience the same Pentecost that the other apostles had experienced and thereby be uniquely joined to them. It is true that the historical happening of Pentecost can never be repeated, but in another sense the coming of the Spirit on Pentecost—the experience and significance of Pentecost—can and should be repeated in the lives of all who would be active members of the Body of Christ.

The same Holy Spirit came down upon rabbi Saul who had come upon fisherman Peter. In this case as in other historical cases, there was no audible wind or visible fire, but the important ingredients of what makes Pentecost *Pentecost* for every generation (the enhanced awareness of Jesus and the ability to speak God's greatness in an unlearned tongue) surely came powerfully upon this penitent soul![18] The Lord would not shortchange His potentially greatest missionary-apostle! Carl Brumback comments:

> It is unthinkable that the chiefest of apostles could have received an experience which did not measure up to the standard. And if Peter and his brethren found assurance in the glossolalic utterances of friendly Gentiles, how great was the assurance which Ananias received upon hearing the arch-persecutor of the church speak with tongues just like the very saints against whom he had been breathing out threatenings and slaughter![19]

What Does Circumstantial Evidence Show?

Second, consider that since the text is silent on the matter of tongues, any interpretation will need to look at circumstantial evidence. Once again, the silence is possible because Luke felt that his readers already knew exactly what he meant. Luke did not feel obligated to explain where Saul was baptized in water and what words were said over him, and Luke apparently felt the same about explaining how Saul received the Spirit. Roger Stronstad notes: "Luke's silence makes it clear that he can be quite indifferent to both the timing and the phenomena associated with the gift of the Spirit."[10]

In fact, the text does not actually say Saul received the Spirit, it merely quotes Ananias as saying he would be filled. We are justified in assuming that he was—so why not also assume that he spoke in tongues as well? This is a great frustration to the academic researcher, but to those of us who have experienced the power of water baptism and instantaneous spiritual tongues, there is no mystery at all! Such an interpretation follows with the other accounts given in Acts.

Was Saul Really Filled?

Third, how would Ananias know Saul was filled unless he spoke in tongues? This, by the way, was how Peter and friends knew that the household of Cornelius had received the Spirit, and it is a simple, wonderful way to determine if people today are filled as well. (See my fourth argument about a universal, uniform experience in chapter 6.)

Ananias must have been overjoyed, strongly assured and greatly relieved to see the great persecutor speaking in tongues just like the saints he had been persecuting. Imagine also how joyfully the news would be received at Damascus and Jerusalem as it spread far and wide along the Christian grapevine. Today, we find such news equally exciting!

Further, in light of the fact that Saul (Paul) would later say: "I thank my God I speak with tongues more than you all" (1 Corinthians 14:18), I conclude that his first experience was when Ananias prayed for him. In other words, Saul likely spoke in tongues at this earliest possible point and this set the course for him to become the Christian who spoke in tongues more than all others. I do not think that he meant necessarily that he had "a gift" of tongues (we do not know for sure about this) but rather that he exercised every opportunity as a Spirit-filled believer to pray in heavenly prayer languages. The fact that Saul began right away to preach powerfully in Damascus indicates a full baptismal experience had occurred.

Thus, Paul, apostle to the Gentiles, fulfilled perfectly the prescribed pattern articulated by Peter, apostle to the Jews: (1) conversion, (2) water baptism and (3) the baptism with the Holy Spirit. And, this is the very principle that characterized Paul's own ministry to others and, I might add, made Paul a Pentecostal!

THE SPIRIT FALLS ON THE HOUSEHOLD OF CORNELIUS

> While Peter was still speaking these words, the Holy Spirit fell upon all those who heard the word. And those of the circumcision who believed were astonished, as many as came with Peter, because the gift of the Holy Spirit had been poured out on the Gentiles also. For they heard them speak with tongues and magnify God. Then Peter answered, "Can anyone forbid water, that these should not be baptized who have received the Holy Spirit just [exactly] as we have?" And he commanded them to be baptized in the name of the Lord. Then they asked him to stay a few days.
>
> Acts 10:44–48

Luke's stories of Holy Spirit outpouring roll powerfully on! It seems the Spirit knew no boundaries as He targeted the great cities and ethnic groups of that day for invasion. The Jews received the Spirit and revival moved through their communities; the Samaritans received the Spirit and basked in His presence; the Ethiopian eunuch was baptized and joyfully went his way. Now it was time for the Gentile community close at hand to meet the Christ and experience God's mighty power.

Note that there are two sovereign-initiated outpourings of the Holy Spirit: the first upon the Jews and the second upon the Gentiles. "All other 'outpourings' were through the Ministries in the Church, and by the Laying on of Hands."[11]

God's Choices

For this breakthrough ministry to the Gentiles, God made careful selection of location and people involved. The strategic city was Caesarea ("by the Sea"), the Roman administrative capital of Palestine, a predominately Gentile city with an influential and powerful minority of Jews. Named in honor of the Roman Caesar, the city had been recently built by Herod the Great. Under construction for ten years, it boasted a theater, an amphitheater, public buildings, a racecourse, a palace, an aqueduct and a magnificent harbor with thriving maritime activity. Here the Roman procurator resided, as did a considerable Roman garrison with some three thousand troops.[12] Visitors to the site today see foundation pillars in the Mediterranean Sea still standing; computer graphics have been used to reconstruct this ancient city from the archaeological findings available, and the picture presented is indeed that of an impressive city with strong military fortification.

A key person in this episode is Cornelius, a noncommissioned officer in command of one hundred men, hence (in Latin), a centurion.[13] In the Roman army, a cohort numbered four to six hundred men, and Cornelius had the segment known as "the Italian cohort" under his command. This specialized unit, composed of Italian volunteers, was considered the most loyal of Roman troops.

A Significant Story for the Church

This story is extremely significant to the whole book of Acts, and in fact to the history of the Church. Unless a Christian is involved in cross-cultural ministry, he or she cannot understand the magnitude of what this story, coupled with the apostolic conference in Jerusalem (see Acts 15), actually means. Ministry to the Samaritans was somewhat natural, as they had common ancestry with the Jews. But this experience meant that even Gentiles were welcome in the—until now—Jewish Christian Church without meeting traditional Hebrew requirements. Jesus the Messiah of the Jews was now the Christ of all nations! It was an epochal step of momentous significance.

In the story of the Ethiopian eunuch I mentioned that he was possibly the first missionary to the Gentiles. I think this is true, but it need not depreciate the significance of the event at Cornelius's household. This was a recognized, publicized, uncontested people-event with apostolic sanction that established the open-door policy in the heart of Judea. It did not at all upset God's program to slip a hungry African man into His program beforehand! Incidentally, the peripatetic evangelist Philip ended up in the very city where Cornelius lived (see Acts 8:40; 21:8)—and was possibly (dare we speculate?) the reason for Cornelius's receptive heart!

Wagner points out that three stories take up the most space in Acts, all incidents crucial to breaking cultural barriers that hinder the Gospel moving to non-Jews.[14] This particular one is the longest narrative with 77 verses, a fact that underlines its importance. Lenski says: "Luke devotes so much space to the story of Cornelius because it marks a new departure in the work of the Apostles."[15] Johannes Munck comments in the Anchor Bible: "Luke has treated the narrative as one dealing with an event of fundamental importance."[16]

I see three important results of Luke's according such importance to the story:

- "[It] tells how Peter used the keys of the kingdom to open a door of faith to the Gentiles" (Bruce)[17]
- It settles the question of requirements for Gentile believers who seek admission into the Church (circumcision and dietary laws, for instance, will not be imposed)
- It affirms that whether Jews or Gentiles, the full circle Peter Pattern of conversion, water baptism and baptism with the Holy Spirit is essential to every ethnic group in every generation

Two Men Gain New Understanding

The account is basically about two men, two visions and two major conversions. One involves the Roman centurion Cornelius (and his household) accepting Christ, receiving the Holy Spirit and being baptized in water. The other involves Peter undergoing a major conversion in his understanding of how God viewed the non-Jewish world, a change in outlook destined to alter the future of the Church. Each man was changed dramatically by interlocking visions inspired by the Holy Spirit.

Cornelius, a soldier, was a dedicated Roman and commander of an elite group of Rome's finest troops. He was a well-to-do man of influence, but he was also a devout believer in the God of the Jews. He was considered a "God-fearer," a person who had not fully embraced the Jewish religion (that is, had not submitted to the Mosaic regulations of circumcision, baptism and sacrifices), so was classified as neither pagan nor proselyte.[18]

Although he did not know Jesus Christ, his godly manner of living and praying strongly influenced his military associates, friends and household. He gave alms generously, prayed faithfully and shared his religious convictions diplomatically—but he was not admitted fully into the worship and fellowship of the Jewish community. F. F. Bruce feels that "he had every qualification, short of circumcision, which could satisfy Jewish requirements."[19] He was similar to the Ethiopian eunuch, a "proselyte of the gate"—one who believed in the God of Israel but was allowed only into the Court of the Gentiles where ominous signs at the gates warned Gentiles to proceed no farther on penalty of death. Like the eunuch, Cornelius was ready to hear the Good News of Jesus Christ and believe.

In stark contrast, the apostle Peter was a devout, dedicated Jew, "thoroughly loyal to ancestral traditions" (Dunn).[20] He had some social contact with Gentiles, that is, non-Jews, but such contact instantly rendered him ceremonially unclean (such as, entering a Gentile house or handling their articles). A strict Jew could not eat the most ordinary Gentile food, such as bread, oil or milk, and the most intolerable thing was sitting at a meal with Gentiles.[21]

The laws of cleanliness were not just hygienic but also spiritual. Following the laws given by Moses, the devout Jew ate only certain kosher food that met strict standards. Peter had followed these absolute laws all his life. He had never had bacon and eggs, meat from the local butcher shop, a birthday cake—or any foods that most non-Jews would take for granted. Traveling for a Jew was a trying experience, for his attitude and actions always seemed hostile and antisocial.

It was not like my experience in Zimbabwe where I was graciously offered worms that had been deep-fried. Trying to be courteous, I ate one (it was crunchy)—but did not care for more. It was a matter of choice and being socially agreeable. Peter, in contrast, was commanded by divine law not to eat anything in a Gentile home. There was a deep, personal revulsion against it but also an even deeper sense of spiritual uncleanness and separation from God. I could eat the worm and thank God for it. Peter, in contrast, would feel as though he was losing his soul!

Both men in our story followed the Jewish custom of praying daily at scheduled times, a routine that deeply affected their spirituality and provided God an excellent channel of communication.[22] Prayer provided both men their divine encounter. Because of it, attitudes changed and the Spirit was able to bring about the conversions of a Roman household and seven dyed-in-the-wool Jews. Prayer precipitated the meeting of two worlds.

Two Places of Abode

The two men lived in different locations. Peter resided temporarily by the sea, just outside the city limits of the ancient city of Joppa, the guest in the humble home of a tanner. It seems strange that Peter would stay in such a place for tanneries were notorious for foul odors, dyes, general disarray and public disapproval. He had been evangelizing effectively throughout the area; only recently he had healed a paralyzed man and raised a woman from the dead (see Acts 9). Yet he stayed in the most humble of circumstances, possibly seeking privacy to wait on God. Simon the fisherman must have felt somewhat akin to Simon the tanner, and for all his seeming brashness, Peter graciously accepted the hospitality of a man many Jews considered to be unclean.

Joseph Parker shares an interesting insight about Peter's temporary abode in Joppa:

> [T]he Jews would not have tanneries in the towns. . . . [It was] A hated and detested necessity. . . . The tanner was not allowed to have his place of business within fifty cubits of a town. . . . If a man married without telling his bride that he was a tanner, she could instantly demand release from the nuptial vow. The law which provided that the childless widow was to marry the brother of a deceased husband was actually set aside in the event of that brother following the occupation of a tanner. You see then how stubborn were the prejudices which the higher Jews entertained against the occupation of tanning, and yet we read as if it involved no extraordinary principle or secret, that Peter lodged or "tarried many days with one Simon a tanner."[23]

Peter was pleased to stay with his ostracized Christian friend and was unconsciously already traveling the road toward fellowship with the unclean Gentiles.

Meanwhile, Cornelius lived some thirty miles north in a well-to-do villa by the seacoast in newly built Caesarea, surrounded by family, household servants and military guards. Everything was immaculate (as was expected of a military leader), the envy of even the Roman community. The ensuing story is a remarkable case of simultaneous preparation, the Spirit working at both ends to bring together two unlikely people to fulfill divine purposes. Two interlocking visions produce one of Luke's most amazing illustrations.

The Two Visions

At midafternoon prayer time, an angel in a dazzling robe appeared in a vision to Cornelius. He was told that his abundant alms and diligent prayers were a delight to God. He was to send for Peter who was residing in Joppa. The frightened man ("numinous awe," Dunn[24]) quickly dispersed two household servants and a devout soldier (each devoted to Cornelius) to find this mysterious man who would explain the ways of God.

Meanwhile, the next day about noon the apostle Peter ascended to the flat roof of the house to pray, meditate and wait for his lunch. There, moved upon by the Holy Spirit, he saw a vision. The strange sight was repeated two more times. In the vision a great four-cornered canvas or sheet was lowered down to the earth filled with all manner of clean and unclean animals, reptiles and birds. The "four corners" was a way of scripturally describing the whole earth (four is the number of earth, the worldwide, universal number). Three times was God's way of confirming that the vision was divinely given and confirmed (see Genesis 41:32; 2 Corinthians 13:1); it also allowed the truth to sink in and convince Peter. The various animals not only referred to dietary habits but, in a deeper sense, symbolized all nations before God (see Daniel 7:17; 8:20–21; Revelation 13).

A voice said, "Rise, Peter; kill and eat." Peter protested vigorously—just as Ezekiel had done! (Compare Acts 10:13 and Ezekiel 4:14.) "Not so, Lord! For I have never eaten anything common or unclean."[25] That recognizable voice spoke again: "What God has cleansed you must not call common." After this sequence was done three times, suddenly, the sheet was taken up! As Peter reflected on the vision, the Spirit said to him, "Behold, three men are seeking you. Arise therefore, go down and go with them, doubting nothing; for I have sent them."

The Trip to Caesarea

After greeting the three Gentile visitors and hearing their story, Peter did the unthinkable: He invited them to stay at the tanner's house that night! It was a stretching experience for both the humble Jews and the fastidious Romans! The next day a party of ten left for Caesarea (the three Romans, Peter and six of his Jewish friends). "This is significant: as the apostles Peter and John went to Samaria and welcomed the Samaritans as full members of the Christian church, so Peter travels to Caesarea and welcomes the Gentiles as full members in the church" (Kistemaker).[26]

The group from Joppa apparently arrived about noon on the fourth day. Cornelius welcomed the party with profuse thanks and bowed before Peter. The apostle immediately lifted him to his feet, assuring him that he himself was just an ordinary man (on the same level before God). To Peter's surprise a good-sized group of Cornelius's relatives and friends awaited his arrival. Peter greeted everyone, explaining the unlikelihood of an orthodox Jew like himself being there, and then Cornelius explained why Peter had been summoned. Truly a unique situation!

Peter began his first message to the Gentile audience with a startling statement, no doubt said for the benefit of both Romans and Jews present: "God has shown me that I should not call any man common or unclean." This was a profound confession for Peter to make, and although people today may not fully appreciate the depth of emotion, it was truly significant and heartwarming to the household of Cornelius. Peter had finally fully grasped this marvelous insight that reflected the heart of Jesus: There is no race superiority and no religious superiority. There are no inferior races.[27] The barriers that God had once erected to separate His people from surrounding nations were removed!

The message that followed was brief (it probably took about a minute and a half) but sparkled with key thoughts about Jesus, of whom these Romans were well aware (see Acts 10:37–38). Then, as Peter declared, "'Whoever believes in Him will receive remission of sins' . . . the Holy Spirit fell upon all those who heard the word" (Acts 10:43–44).

For the first time the Holy Spirit poured forth on a group of Gentiles! *Fell* indicates suddenness and descent from above. There is "visible impact of the Spirit" (Dunn).[28] The awestruck Jewish friends of Peter gasped as they saw a replica of the Jewish Pentecost occur before their very eyes—in a Gentile house! "For they heard them speak with tongues and magnify God." To complete the full circle of initiation, Peter had them water baptized in the name of the Lord Jesus Christ, an action that would have raised a challenging question by the Jewish Christians present if done before they received the Spirit. They now have an irrefutable sign of God's acceptance and Holy Spirit blessing of the Gentiles.

Walls Are Broken Down

The apostle Peter had now been present at three Pentecostal group outpourings: first, the Jewish disciples at Pentecost; second, the Samaritan believers; and, now, the Roman community. In each of these cases the Spirit of God performed an identical outpouring accompanied by charismatic signs.[29] Peter as the leading apostle and member of the original Twelve was used by God to open the door of invitation to the Jews, the half-Jews and the Romans, three groups that symbolized all nations everywhere. Peter was given the keys of the Kingdom (see Matthew 16:19), and he used them! In each instance, the people were converted, baptized in water and received the Holy Spirit. Here was the full-circle Peter Pattern in operation!

All commentators see this significance and recognize that the Spirit had broken down the wall of separation; now all nations are welcome to accept the salvation Jesus Christ offers. Some, however, feel that since these occasions were symbolic, there is no further need (in our time) for dramatic charismatic manifestation. The door is now open, why do we need any more Holy Spirit verification?

But wait! Could this episode be more than a token symbol of a historic event? Could these events also be the ongoing chain reaction of an active Holy Spirit bonding new converts (whether individually or in groups) to the same salvation, the same baptism in His name and the same baptism with the Holy Spirit?

The Cornelius episode, with its two conjoining visions, was a statement that the Romans were accepted—they were given the experience of speaking in tongues to confirm it. But, let us not overlook that this was the life of the Spirit at work: SOP, standard operating procedure. Consider the possibility that this Peter Pattern is actually made available for all people in every nation and throughout this present age. How wonderful if every other Roman in Caesarea, or anywhere in the Gentile world for that matter, would have the opportunity to experience the bonding power of the Pentecostal Spirit! This promise for every Christian seems implicit in Peter's statement: "For the promise is to you and to your children, and to all who are afar off, as many as the Lord our God will call" (Acts 2:39).

The Importance of Tongues

Several years ago when the charismatic renewal was just getting started in the Philippines, the World Missionary Assistance Program team arrived to conduct ministers' conferences. I was part of the ministering team. We soon discovered that the Spirit was working, especially in the Catholic Church, but very few spoke in tongues because it was not taught as part of the Spirit-filled life. As we all ministered we announced that this gift of the Holy Spirit was available.

On two different occasions I saw five hundred people (who had not spoken in tongues) instantly begin speaking in tongues at almost the same moment! Priests and nuns began dancing with joy in the aisles, side by side with Pentecostals and other denominational representatives. To see a group of Gentiles have the Spirit poured upon them is indeed a glorious experience! Like the Jews with Peter, we had no doubt that they were filled with the Spirit because they spoke with tongues!

There is an intrinsic need for every believer to have a personal full-circle experience with the Holy Spirit that makes Calvary, the tomb and Pentecost real in their lives. Simply taking it by faith is not sufficient. Faith is certainly essential and fundamental; however, without the scriptural authentication of that faith, something wonderful is missing. To continue the experience of water baptism but discount this marvelous baptism with the Holy Spirit is really inconsistent.

Did Cornelius speak in tongues again? Did future converts in Caesarea receive the Spirit in the same way and speak in tongues also? The Bible does not say, but the corroborating evidence of Acts and 1 Corinthians indicates that it was so. Why should today's Christian be deprived of an experience that was so vital and essential to the early Church?

Peter Explains His Actions

When the news got out that Peter was hobnobbing with the Gentiles down in Caesarea, the fat hit the fire! You see, up until now the whole Christian Church had been Jewish. All the leaders were Jews and they were as fanatical as Peter had been about not eating with Gentiles. In fact, that was their biggest problem with Peter at the moment! As Bruce points out, it is most "remarkable that nothing was said about water baptism."[30]

When Peter was challenged by the Jerusalem apostles and leading brethren about what had happened, he simply gave his testimony. Carefully reviewing all that had happened, he told of his time of prayer in Joppa and the awesome vision that had occurred. He told of the voice that spoke and then how the Holy Spirit told him to go with the messengers. He relayed Cornelius's vision and how the angel had said to send for Peter "who will tell you words by which you and all your household will be saved." Then he told how, "as I began to speak, the Holy Spirit fell upon them, as upon us at the beginning" (Acts 11:15).

Peter had no heavy-duty theology to argue; this was not his forte. Nor would such debate have been beneficial. He simply told his story, but he did insert two quick but significant arguments.

The first one was: "Then I remembered the word of the Lord, how He said, 'John indeed baptized with water, but you shall be baptized with the Holy Spirit.'"[31] Peter and the other leaders were well aware that Jesus had said the Holy Spirit would bring His words to remembrance and give understanding of their meaning (see John 14:26). This was definitely one of those times!

These words of Jesus had flashed into Peter's memory with brilliant meaning, and he had understood instantly; the others apparently had the same experience as Peter repeated the story. The Holy Spirit was doing a deep work in each leader: They began to comprehend that the Gentiles had experienced what they themselves had experienced at Pentecost. The light broke upon their minds as they realized that God made no distinction between believing Jews and believing Gentiles. They also realized that Jesus' saying ("you shall be baptized with the Holy Spirit") actually included this Gentile household and—can we dare believe?—every other Gentile in every successive generation right up to our own! The elders were just as interested in the fact that the Spirit was given to all as they were the fact that all were now welcome. Usually the latter thought receives the most emphasis.

The second quick argument Peter presented was this: "If therefore God gave them the same gift as He gave us when we believed on the Lord Jesus Christ, who was I that I could withstand God?" They now realized by the Spirit that the intrusive Jewish legal system was now obsolete. God had initiated a new approach to Himself. The Jerusalem leaders immediately realized, along with Peter, that they could not "thwart God" (WILLIAMS). The common experience declared common acceptance; one Spirit, many nations, one Body of Christ!

Such a great step merited a special introductory Gentile Pentecost, just as the Jews had experienced. Should this also be the case for the Church of succeeding generations? Should not our experience today be more than a casual memory of history? Surely more is needed to maintain the Pentecostal presence in our day! It seems obvious, there being nothing scriptural to disprove it and the testimony of millions to confirm it, that the Peter Pattern was not just for the Jews and Samaritans but also the Gentiles—in every generation that will claim it!

Some years will pass, and once again Peter will find himself before the Church leaders in Jerusalem, defending the "open-door" policy of admitting Gentiles into the Church. Paul will also be there, and an important decision will be made. We will discuss this in the next chapter, along with Paul's experience in Ephesus.

REVIEW QUESTIONS FOR CHAPTER 11

1. When do you think Saul was converted?
2. Why do you think God chose Ananias to baptize Saul?
3. Have you ever had a vision?
4. After Cornelius's household received the Spirit, do you suppose this experience was repeated again with other Romans?

12

THE SPIRIT FOR ALL PEOPLE
THE NEWS SPREADS EVERYWHERE

IN THIS CHAPTER

- Discover the source of the word *Christian*
- Learn which three men saved the day at Jerusalem
- Find out why twelve men who had been baptized were rebaptized
- Discover whether or not the manifestation of tongues ended shortly after Pentecost

The great tide of the Spirit rolled irresistibly forward. Already many communities and ethnic groups were experiencing the power of the blessed Holy Spirit. The Good News of Jesus now spread wondrously toward the end of the earth. The activity of the Spirit was profoundly affecting Jews, Samaritans, Ethiopians, Romans and Greeks. This chapter focuses on the Council at Jerusalem, the unusual development at the church of Ephesus and the manifestation of tongues among some hungry candidates.

Our last chapter closed with a discussion of Peter's first report to the Jerusalem elders and apostles. God had gloriously poured out His Spirit upon the Romans, making it apparent that Gentiles were welcome in the Body of Christ.

About this same time, the Gospel spread northward to the city of Antioch in Syria. This major city, about fifteen miles from the Mediterranean and some three hundred miles north of Jerusalem, is tucked in the northeast corner of the Mediterranean basin and made an appealing target for energetic Christian evangelists. The refugee preachers opened the Gospel to Greeks as well as Jews (see Acts 11:20) and the response was astounding and unexpected. E. A. Judge comments that "the mass movement of Gentiles at Antioch clearly took the church in Jerusalem by surprise."[1]

THE CHRISTIANS AT ANTIOCH

The Church leaders, concerned by this sudden, great influx of Gentiles into the faith, sent Barnabas, a beloved, Spirit-filled man to check out the situation. He was delighted with what he saw but soon realized that a strong leader was needed in this unusual situation. Barnabas fetched Saul, the converted archenemy of the Church, to come and help: "So it was that for a whole year they assembled with the church and taught a great many people" (Acts 11:26). This activity soon drew the attention of the general public and caused a distinctive name to be attached to the followers of Jesus: "And the disciples were first called Christians at Antioch" (verse 26). Although the text does not discuss spiritual manifestations among the new converts, this new title reflected the fact that these people were touched or anointed with the Spirit of Jesus the Christ.

Later, in Acts 13, during a meeting in which prophets and teachers were present, an inspired word of prophecy announced that the time had come for Barnabas and Saul, now called Paul, to launch out on their first missionary journey. The Gospel was to be taken westward to the synagogues and the Gentiles of Cyprus and central Asia Minor. So off they went attended by great blessings of the Lord. When they returned, their testimony of God's grace to the Gentiles was received with tremendous enthusiasm.

Dissension Arises

Meanwhile, certain Jewish Christians in Jerusalem began to fear for the purity of the Jewish messianic community. The Cornelius episode, significant as it was, apparently was not a numerically strong threat to the established Church at Jerusalem. After Paul and Barnabas had returned from their Western mission, however, some legalistically minded Jewish Christians took it upon themselves to journey to Antioch and other Galatian congregations to set these many Gentile converts straight on the matter of circumcision and commandment keeping (see Acts 15:1). Paul and Barnabas were present to defend the Gospel they preached, and a huge dispute erupted. It was finally settled that Paul and Barnabas would be commissioned by the church of Antioch to consult with the leadership in Jerusalem on this question.

After being received by the church, apostles and elders, Paul and Barnabas reported all that God had done through their ministry. Some of the listeners, however, were Pharisees, and they voiced a strong stand for circumcision of the Gentiles.

Three presentations won the argument for a continued "open-door" policy. First, Peter recounted the famous story of Cornelius's household receiving the Holy Spirit, and then Paul and Barnabas told of the miracles and wonders done among the Gentiles. Finally, when everyone became silent and reflective, James, the arbitrating apostle, sealed the matter with the remarkable quotation from Amos 9:11–12 and proposed that minimal restrictions should be put on the new converts. James suggested that the converted Gentiles should abstain from idolatry, immorality, eating blood and eating things strangled. The leaders gave immediate approval to his suggestion and announced the confirmation of the Holy Spirit upon it (see Acts 15:28).

Peter's Story Revisited

It is notable, and pertinent to our discussion, to emphasize that Peter retold his experience of being sent to the household of Cornelius. He described again how God "acknowledged them by giving them the Holy Spirit, just as He did to us, and made no distinction between us and them" (Acts 15:8–9). In other words, Peter was stating that there could be no doubt of the Gentiles' inclusion into the community of faith. Just as the Spirit fell upon the Jewish disciples at Pentecost and they were filled with the Holy Spirit and spoke in tongues, so the Spirit fell on the Gentiles producing the same hallmark evidence.

This Jerusalem conference occurred some fifteen years after Pentecost. Our concern is whether or not the baptism with the Holy Spirit was still happening. Were the previous, recorded manifestations among Jews, Samaritans and Gentiles only token affirmations—with later converts assuming the experience of Spirit-baptism by faith alone? Are we to believe that the multitudes of people who were converted later received the Spirit without charismatic evidence? Did God mean for there to be only one Pentecost or, as some believe, one Pentecost in three stages (the Jews in chapter 2, the Samaritans in chapter 8 and the Gentiles in chapter 10)?

In this next and last episode, 21 years after Pentecost, we find that another group of Jews experienced Spirit-baptism and spoke in tongues.[2] What does this indicate for us today?

Paul at Ephesus

The decision of the Church leadership was a great relief to Paul. He redoubled his efforts to reach both Jews and Gentiles with the Good News of Jesus Christ. His second missionary journey took him to many places; he spent about a year and a half in Corinth and then a hasty two-week stopover in Ephesus where he reasoned with the Jews in the synagogue.

After returning to Antioch, Paul began his third missionary journey. He passed through the regions of Galatia and Phrygia, finally arriving in Ephesus again. He then spent two years of ministry in that key city. We must remember that Paul, although a first-class theologian, was also an on-fire charismatic apostle-evangelist-pastor. His example challenges Christian leaders to guard against academic euphoria that robs ministers of spiritual zeal and charismatic activity. Paul's sterling example gives no indication that charismatic activity was beginning to wane and cease. His life and writings indicated just the opposite!

One of my professors in seminary was a world-class theologian. I made a major effort to get into his class and greatly enjoyed every moment of his teaching—except when he answered a certain question by one of the students. One young man who was part of a Vineyard Church asked the professor about whether or not "casting out devils" was for today—a logical question following a teaching on the powerful advance by the Kingdom of God against Satan. I had, at this point, spent many years in the field and was aware of many cases of deliverance. Thus I was surprised at his answer. The great man replied that he did not know about such things. He said that he lived in his ivory tower at the seminary and spent his time ensuring that doctrine was correct.

In contrast, Paul lived in no ivory tower. Read Acts 18 and 19 and look at the setting for the churches of Galatia, Corinth and Ephesus—and the epistles that Paul later wrote to those churches. A quick summary of Paul's spiritual activities shows that although he, too, was concerned about doctrine, he knew it was equally important to keep the spiritual fires burning. Paul's activities in just these two chapters can be summarized by the words, "So the word of the Lord grew mightily and prevailed" (Acts 19:20). He worked tirelessly:

- Making tents (undoubtedly witnessing in the marketplace)
- Arguing in the synagogue on the Sabbath
- Splitting synagogues and then teaching his new followers
- Baptizing converts
- Being dragged before the Roman judgment seat
- Traveling over the whole region of Galatia and Phrygia strengthening believers
- Preaching
- Laying hands on believers to receive the Holy Spirit
- Declaring boldly the Kingdom of God in the synagogue for three months
- Drawing disciples from the synagogue to hear his teaching (for two years)
- Propagandizing all of Asia, both Jews and Greeks
- Performing unusual miracles to heal the sick and cast out spirits
- Being recognized by evil spirits
- Sponsoring confession and book-burning meetings
- Inciting a major riot because of his teaching

An absence of speaking in tongues in the epistle to the Ephesians does not indicate charismatic manifestations had ceased or were deliberately ignored. The activity in these two chapters alone shows that the context of those New Testament churches was full-blown Holy Spirit revival and power. Paul knew what Charles Finney found out later, that "the indispensable ingredient for revival was the outpouring of the Holy Spirit."

Paul Questions Some Followers of "the Baptist"

In Paul's yearlong absence from Ephesus, his coworkers Priscilla and Aquila infiltrated the synagogue congregation and raised the messianic expectancy. Apparently no church was yet established in Ephesus. Messianic Jews met regularly at the synagogue and privately in homes. And everyone in the synagogue anticipated a visit from Paul.

Meanwhile, an educated, eloquent Jew from Alexandria[3] named Apollos arrived in Ephesus and spoke forcefully and persuasively in the synagogue of his understanding of John the Baptist's message.[4] Since he knew only the baptism of John (see Acts 18:25), Aquila and Priscilla wisely took him aside and explained the way of God more fully. Apparently he learned quickly. With the believers' blessings and recommendation, Apollos the Fervent traveled on to Greece and—with expanded insights—was a great help to the new believers there.

At this point Paul arrived back at Ephesus. In the biblical text, after noting that he had come to Ephesus, Luke states in the next sentence that he found "some disciples." Personally I think that upon arrival Paul first visited his friends in the Jewish quarter,[5] particularly Aquila and Priscilla who had been quietly working with the Jews of the local synagogue. It seems likely that the husband-wife team knew of this group of disciples and hastily directed Paul to them (after giving him a report on Apollos and the state of the congregation). Paul did not just stumble across these men when he arrived in Ephesus, but he wasted no time in getting to them!

These twelve men were disciples of John the Baptist and probably represented the most responsive, ready people in Ephesus to believe in Christ and be the foundation for a new church. They had been baptized, either by John (25 years before) or more likely by Apollos (before he received more insight from Aquila and Priscilla) or another recent preacher into John's baptism of repentance.

There is some debate as to the meaning of the word *disciple* here. Some argue that only believers in Christ were called disciples, and if we review the ten times that the word *disciple* occurs in Acts 18–21,[6] we see that this is the general use of the word. The context here, however, gives a different picture.

The context indicates that they are not yet born again Christians but rather sincere Jews who believed in and were concerned about the advent of the Messiah.[7] They possibly knew that Jesus had been declared that Messiah. The question is relevant because of the issue of whether or not they received the Holy Spirit after they were born again.[8]

What Did They Believe?

These "disciples" believed John's doctrine, which included two significant thoughts:

- They should repent of their sins and prepare their hearts for the coming Messiah and His Kingdom
- Just as they had been immersed by John into water baptism, they could expect to be immersed by the coming Messiah into His baptism with Holy Spirit and fire

Paul knew immediately that what was lacking. He perceived that these men were living under Old Testament expectancy (John was the last of the Old Testament prophets), and three things were needed. Once again the Peter Pattern is practiced! Actually, since Paul practiced it, too, we could call it the Pauline Pattern. In fact, it was the paradigm of the whole Church. Remember, this episode is happening 21 or more years after Pentecost, but the truth of Acts 2:38 was as vital at that moment as it was when Peter first annunciated it during his Pentecostal sermon.

These baptists need to do three things:

1. Truly believe in and accept Jesus Christ as Savior, Lord and Messiah. This they probably had not done (according to verses 4–5, regardless of how one interprets verse 1). They needed to change their belief (or mental wonderment) about a coming Messiah to a Spirit-quickened, present belief in Jesus as the Messiah who had come and brought salvation.

2. Be rebaptized in the name of Jesus who is both Lord and Messiah (see verse 5).[9]
3. Receive the Holy Spirit baptism, which was foretold by John the Baptist (see Matthew 3:11; Mark 1:8; Luke 3:16).

Regarding number 2 above, this means, of course, that anyone who had been baptized with John's baptism (including any of Jesus' own disciples who had been so baptized) needed to be rebaptized. John's baptism was a call to repentance. The Jews who responded were accustomed to ritual baptism by submersion for cleansing from sin, and some of them could have been proselytes who had been baptized upon acceptance into Judaism. To accept John's invitation (or that of his disciples) was a logical way to express public repentance. This was not Christian baptism but rather an act of public repentance in preparation for the coming Messiah. That was the point of John's baptism. He was calling the nation to a state of repentance and readiness, and used a method common to the Jewish people to accomplish his purpose.

All who became Christians needed to repent, but they also submitted to the Lordship of Jesus Christ. Such baptism was for those who were born again. We do not know for sure, of course, about the baptism of the hundred and twenty disciples on the day of Pentecost. It seems logical that they used the large water basins in the Temple precincts into which people were commonly immersed. My opinion is that the key apostles baptized each other, then baptized the rest of the hundred and twenty, and then the hundred and twenty baptized the three thousand. And, while we are speculating, imagine the excitement as that many people were being baptized and many—if not all—were also baptized in the Spirit and speaking in tongues!

Did the twelve disciples of John receive the Holy Spirit after they were born again? The mysterious question is easily understood in the light of John the Baptist's doctrine that the people of God would be baptized with the Holy Spirit and fire. They were expecting this baptism to occur at some future time, just as they were expecting the Messiah to come soon. Paul announced that both were now available! They simply believed and accepted. Their question to Paul was not whether or not the Holy Spirit existed; rather they were asking about the fulfillment of John's preaching on the Holy Spirit.

Notice that the three-step, full-circle experience proceeded in orderly fashion: believing, being baptized, receiving the Holy Spirit baptism. They did not receive the Spirit-baptism until after they had believed. This, by the way, did not startle the veteran apostle. He fully expected it to happen when he laid his hands on them (probably as they were standing in the river dripping wet from baptism).

Paul's belief on this matter is highlighted in a message written later to this very church in Ephesus (and possibly reminiscent of this episode): "In Him you also trusted, after you heard the word of truth, the gospel of your salvation; in whom also, having believed, you were sealed with the Holy Spirit of promise, who is the guarantee of our inheritance" (Ephesians 1:13–14).

Although speaking in tongues in this illustration seems to appear a long time after the previously recorded occurrence, it indicates, as Dennis Bennett has pointed out, that this spiritual activity did not die out.[10] The promise is, after all, "to you and to your children, and to all who are afar off, as many as the Lord our God will call" (Acts 2:39).

This account of the baptism with the Holy Spirit offers no ethnic or "special occasion" significance. It merely shows that the Peter Pattern was standard operating procedure in the early Church wherever and whenever new converts were made. It also illustrates that the baptism of John was merely a harbinger of another, superior baptism—one performed by Jesus in which the believer would be immersed into the Holy Spirit!

This episode also shows that John's baptism was important in its time, but it would not suffice for the Christian life. Even though John's disciples believed to the best of their ability in a coming Messiah, the baptism did not suffice once Christ did actually come. It is sad to think that we have baptized churchgoers today (similar to John's disciples) who have experienced a form of baptism but have lacked the reality that comes with sincere faith in Christ. Paul realized all of this, and apparently the twelve men did also, because Paul baptized these "disciples" of John upon their confession of faith in Jesus as Lord—and they experienced the baptism with the Holy Spirit. In a sense this was not rebaptism, because they had never been baptized according to the Christian faith.

If Paul could be among us today, he would be surprised that more churches are not promoting the amazing apostolic prescription given by Peter in Acts 2:38. He knew firsthand the benefits to both individuals and the local churches when the baptism with the Holy Spirit was advocated. I believe that it is detrimental to people's faith for commentators who have not spoken in tongues to give the impression that this experience is unnecessary or was a temporary occurrence for that day only or was a strange, unexpected phenomenon that occurred only rarely. The gift and promise of the Holy Spirit are now available for all people everywhere. Only believe!

In our next chapter, the last of the book, we will discuss some basic hermeneutical principles that will add credence to our use of the Acts of the Apostles as a proof text in our discussion of the baptism with the Holy Spirit. Also, you will find in the Appendix a brief summary of seven viewpoints about when the baptism of the Holy Spirit takes place.

REVIEW QUESTIONS FOR CHAPTER 12

1. Explain how speaking in tongues was such an important factor in accepting the Gentiles into the Christian Church.
2. Why would it be wrong to think of Paul as merely a theologian?
3. Do you think that the twelve men in Acts 19 were Jews or Gentiles?
4. Is it significant that the Peter Pattern is being mentioned and illustrated twenty years after Pentecost?

13

WHY THE FUSS OVER ACTS?
LET'S READ IT RIGHT

IN THIS CHAPTER

- Check out your "hermeneutics"
- Face the deeper significance of a "literal" reading of the Bible
- Learn how history is important in charismatic theology
- Discover the principle of universal application

Hermeneutics, the art and science of interpreting the Bible, provides us with a number of helpful principles that scholars have developed over the years. The words of the whole Bible are the words of God, and proper interpretative guidelines give us a better understanding of these divine thoughts.

Thus we ask: Is it scripturally sound to believe in an experience of Spirit-empowerment that occurs after conversion and that is made evident by glossolalia?

221

INTERPRETING ACTS

We face a unique challenge with our subject because Acts is generally considered a historical book, and yet it is here that we have the greatest concentration of material on Holy Spirit activity. Some commentators question that the accounts given of the early Church are suitable for drawing conclusions about how the Church today should operate, particularly in regard to the baptism with the Holy Spirit. Does Luke indicate how he wanted his material to be received?

The answer depends, in large part, on the mind-set of the scholar or student. If one is sufficiently prejudiced, it is nearly impossible to be open to new insights. We see this in the way that supernatural accounts in the Bible are handled. If a person believes in the miraculous accounts of Old and New Testaments but is convinced that miracles do not happen today, then he or she will naturally relegate the possibility of miracles of healing or deliverance to the past only. For those who do not believe the Bible accounts, much less their happening today, any discussion of the relevance of Acts will appear ludicrous. Sometimes a well-meaning student can be so colored by his or her church tradition that significant New Testament teachings are overlooked simply because they do not fit into the expected ecclesiastical pattern.

Instead, let us emulate the Jews of Berea: "These were more fair-minded than those in Thessalonica, in that they received the word with all readiness, and searched the Scriptures daily to find out whether these things were so. Therefore many of them believed" (Acts 17:11–12).

Do Hermeneutics Support a Pentecostal Theology?

This much discussed question has already received a resounding no! from some,[1] a qualified yes from others and some are still searching. Pentecostals hold to a theological center that is common with all orthodox believers, as listed below. I might add that we also hold in common the belief that the Holy Spirit is active in our time, particularly in causing people to be born again. We believe in:

1. The inspiration and infallibility of Scripture
2. The deity of Jesus Christ
3. The virgin birth and miracles of Jesus Christ

4. Jesus' physical death for our sins and His physical resurrection
5. His personal return to earth again

Pentecostals add two more points:

6. Spiritual gifts exist today—they did not cease to exist with the close of the first-century Church.
7. Every born again believer can also experience "the baptism with the Holy Spirit," a dynamic empowerment subsequent to the salvation experience. It is accompanied by speaking in tongues.

The heart of a Pentecostal hermeneutic is a literal belief in the book of Acts and an acceptance of its accounts as a valid pattern for Christian living. It follows that the teaching of the epistles instructs those already initiated into the Body of Christ.

Luke's Objective

It is wise to ask ourselves, What did the writer have in mind when he penned this document? Luke told his story the way the people of that day viewed it—simple and direct without apology for the Holy Spirit's unpredictable, miraculous behavior or the apostles' ministry. He wanted succeeding generations to remember that the Church started at Pentecost.

As we have noted, Luke wrote his account in two parts, the first being the gospel of Luke and the second the Acts of the Apostles. In his opening remarks, Luke explained why he was writing these books:

> Inasmuch as many have taken in hand to set in order a narrative of those things which have been fulfilled among us . . . it seemed good to me also, having had perfect understanding of all things from the very first, to write to you an orderly account . . . that you may know the certainty of those things in which you were instructed.
>
> Luke 1:1–4

Immediately we are told that we have here both authentic history and instructive material. Acts conveys important information that the author wants his readers to understand.

Luke has not presented his story in such a way that every question is specifically and thoroughly answered, so we must assume that he expected his readers to be understanding and go with the flow of his narrative. It is as we take his entire record into account and seek the conclusions that best fit with the tenor of the whole presentation that we arrive at what is "the most natural, clear, evident meaning"[2] (McQuilkin).

Luke's account of the Spirit among the various ethnic groups leads the reader to believe that there was a basic consistency of ministry and expectation by the apostles. The reader perceives a procedure of initiation into the Body of Christ that was to be perpetuated wherever the Gospel was preached—the consistent application of what I call the Peter Pattern. There is no indication in the Bible that the apostles and early Church felt that those things were meant to stop; rather, there is a contention and effort that they should continue.

The book of Acts seems to lack closure, as though Luke expected the story to flow on in history. Acts starts in Jerusalem and ends in Rome, a triumphant story that leaves the Church a marvelous pattern to maintain in subsequent history; may we preserve it and persevere in its proclamation.

FIVE HELPFUL PRINCIPLES OF HERMENEUTICS

Acts is different from the epistles because of its historical review, but it is of particular value for instructing us on how the Holy Spirit is meant to operate in and through the Church on an ongoing basis. Think of the epistles as an overlay of the Acts. It shows how the dynamic experience of the early Church was to be maintained.

The Literal Interpretation Principle: The Bible Is Literature

The Bible is to be read like any other book.[3]

R. C. Sproul

Whenever we read a book, an essay, or a poem we presume the literal sense in the document until the nature of the literature may force us to another level.[4]

Bernard Ramm

The Bible is uniquely inspired and infallible, but it is still literature and is meant to be read and interpreted like literature. This does not mean we must compromise the integrity or inspiration of the Bible, but it does mean that we must know the type of material in the Bible we are studying and react accordingly; for instance, is the text poetry, a parable, prophecy, a letter, a historical account? Leland Ryken gives this sound advice:

> Each literary genre has its distinctive features. Each has its own "rules" or procedures. This, in turn, affects how we read and interpret a work of literature. As readers we need to come to a given text with the right expectations. . . . An awareness of genre will program our reading of a work, giving it a familiar shape and arranging the details into an identifiable pattern.[5]

Acts and the Old Testament historical books form a special genre of literature. These books are historical, but they have the further objective of perpetuating faith in the miraculous, and this is something very difficult for the secular historian to accept.

The Historical Narrative Principle: God Teaches through Examples

> Christianity is built not only upon precepts but also upon examples. God has revealed His will not only by giving orders but by having certain things done in His church, so that in the ages to come others might simply look at the pattern and know His will. God has directed His people not only by means of abstract principles and objective regulations but by concrete examples and subjective experience. God does use precepts to teach His people, but one of His chief methods of instruction is through history. God tells us how others knew and did His will, so that we, by looking at their lives, may not only know His will but see how to do it, too.[6]

> Watchman Nee

Larry Christenson comments that the book of Acts simply records the occurrence of speaking in tongues, and it makes no theological statement or precept about the phenomenon. Those occurrences, he adds, are not random or arbitrary; there is a definite pattern with significant implications for how we are to understand speaking in tongues.[7]

The Context Principle: Study Every Verse in the Light of Its Context

[T]he interpretation of any verse is determined upon a consideration of its context.[8]

Kevin J. Conner

The context of any verse is the entire Scripture.[9]

Bernard Ramm

[God] will not set forth any passage in His Word which contradicts any other passage.[10]

J. Edwin Hartill

The divine, organic unity of the whole Bible dispels the possibility of any unexplainable contradiction in Scripture, and no verse of the Bible is meant to be an island unto itself. The book of Acts is not an "upcropping" of mystifying activity protruding from the stolid academic sea of Pauline theology. Bible scholars insist on the correlation of other subjects, so why stalemate our inquiry by insisting that Peter, Paul, Luke and John all held differing approaches to Spirit-baptism? As McQuilkin has said, "[B]ecause all parts of Scripture are true, the harmony is already there, and our task is to search it out."[11] Also, "It is through the context of any passage, in the final analysis, that we determine meaning."[12]

Nothing in Acts or in the rest of the New Testament indicates that the Peter Pattern enjoyed by Jews, Samaritans, Romans, Ethiopians, Greeks and Ephesians was meant to be for just the first-century Church. If churches today preach and attempt to apply the total New Testament, does it not seem strange to disregard the Acts of the Apostles?

This principle urges us to value the contribution of Acts and to understand that it is not in conflict with the epistles; rather, it is a complementary book that throws much light on why the epistles developed as they did. Remember that these epistles were written in the context of Pentecostal-charismatic revival; for instance, consider Acts 19 and 20 as the context for interpreting the books of Ephesians and Corinthians. Paul's intellect did not establish the New Testament churches but rather the dynamic ministry of the Holy Spirit working miraculously through him! Do you think he would forget all of that as he wrote to the churches? No, he invited scriptural interpretation in the light of the disciples' experience in the Holy Spirit.

The Full Mention Principle: Determine the Complete Mention of a Subject

God declares His full mind upon any subject vital to our spiritual life. Somewhere in the Word, God gathers together the scattered fragments that have to do with a particular truth, and puts them into one exhaustive statement. That is His full mind concerning that truth.[13]

J. Edwin Hartill

Some say we should go by the didactic, more academic approach of the epistles rather than attempt to establish doctrine from the historical record of Acts. Here is a wrong corollary: Look to Luke for history; turn to Paul for theology. Stronstad calls such thinking an "illegitimate identity transfer."[14]

When Paul wrote to the Corinthians about decorum in a charismatic worship service, he was not writing about a far-out experience that was strange to all the other churches of that time. The fact is, God put the sum of His information on Holy Spirit baptism in the gospels and the Acts, and the sum of His information on speaking in tongues in Mark, Acts and 1 Corinthians.

This is the complete mention of this subject in the Bible. We must, therefore, consider it as authoritative on the matter, giving the benefit of any doubt to the clear implication in Acts. Remember, Acts contains 22 percent of the New Testament verses that mention the Holy Spirit.

The Universal Truth Principle: Identify the Audience

Every teaching of Scripture is to be received universally, unless the Bible itself limits the audience, either in the context of the passage itself or in other biblical teaching.[15]

J. Robertson McQuilkin

For history to be used as a model it must have universal application, and for any historic event to be so named there must be an authorized spokesman for God (McQuilkin).[16] If there was ever a universal statement given by an authorized spokesman, it is Acts 2:38, the famous Peter Pattern Scripture. Peter opened the door for the Gospel age. God's message is to go forth without ethnic, color, social or sexual division. And it is to continue as long as God desires. How could we think of limiting this great plan once God released it to the nations? The message of Pentecost (salvation, water baptism and Spirit-baptism) is now available to all—from generation to generation and to people from every nation and tongue!

REVIEW QUESTIONS FOR CHAPTER 13

1. Discuss the hermeneutical principles that you feel best apply to Acts.
2. Why do you think that an antimiraculous attitude is sometimes adopted?
3. How would you define Luke's objective?
4. Explain why or why not you think that the early Church considered the epistles as teaching for a Spirit-led lifestyle.

Appendix

The Church Body's Diverse Views on the Baptism with the Holy Spirit

Seven leading positions held in the Body of Christ on the baptism with the Holy Spirit are presented below.

SACRAMENTARIAN

The baptism is receiving the strengthening gifts of the Holy Spirit.

Sacramentalists believe that the Holy Spirit is received at the time of infant baptism with renewal of dedication at confirmation. J. Rodman Williams, a leading renewal theologian, gives this summary:

> In the sacramental tradition there is little or no emphasis on such crisis categories as "conversion" or "baptism with the Holy Spirit." Rather it is assumed that through the proper sacramental action there is conversion-regeneration and the gift (or baptism) of the Holy Spirit. . . . [T]he sacramentalist may see Spirit-baptism either as occurring in and with water-baptism, or as taking place at the moment of the second rite (confirmation/chrismation). . . . The sacramentalist . . . cannot understand how any action of the Holy Spirit outside the sacraments may be properly viewed as baptism in the Holy Spirit. . . . From the sacramentalist perspective all on whom the proper

sacramental action has been bestowed are thereby Christians. Rebirth occurs in baptism: one does not need later to be regenerated. Spirit-baptism occurs with water baptism or in the sacrament of confirmation/chrismation. There is no nominal Christianity: through the power of the sacraments the full Christian reality is conveyed.[1]

Veli-Matti Kärkkäinen summarizes the sacramental view:

Spirit-baptism is a breakthrough to a conscious awareness of the Spirit already received and present through water baptism. Rather than being a new imparting, it is an actualization of the graces already received.[2]

Sacramental churches include: Roman Catholic, Orthodox, Anglican/ Episcopal, Lutheran.

Roman Catholic Church

- Pope Paul VI (1971): "Through the sacrament of confirmation, those who have been born anew in baptism receive the inexpressible Gift, the Holy Spirit himself, by which they are endowed . . . with special strength."[3]
- "In Catholic doctrine [confirmation is] the second of the seven sacraments, in which the Holy Spirit is received by the anointing of the bishop for strength to profess, to defend, and to practice the faith."[4]
- "[T]he ritual of baptism itself communicates the Spirit, though this does not imply that the Spirit is fully appropriated at the time of baptism."[5]
- "In Roman Catholic and Anglican circles the sacrament of confirmation is usually seen as an impartation of the Holy Spirit by the laying on of hands by a bishop."[6]
- "[Confirmation] confers an indelible character upon the recipient, it is administered but once."[7]

Eastern Orthodox Church

This summary is by Fr. Athanasios F. S. Emmert:

The baptism in the Holy Spirit is primarily understood as taking place in the sacraments of water-baptism and "chrismation." Chrismation is a "sealing" of the gift of the Spirit in baptism, the imparting of the Spirit—who comes to dwell in the one baptized through the act of the anointing with the oil of chrism. One must be careful, however, not to confuse the rite of chrismation with the rite of confirmation in Western usage. Chrismation is understood and practiced in a much broader sense and is not exclusively a sacrament of initiation.[8]

Episcopal Church

In the Episcopal Church confirmation "is a sacramental rite completing baptism."[9] Dennis Bennett says: "[T]he term 'confirmation' is used of the traditional rite intended to confer the experience of the baptism in the Holy Ghost. 'Confirm' literally means 'to strengthen.' The Episcopal Prayer Book says: 'The Church provides the Laying on of Hands, or Confirmation, wherein . . . I receive the strengthening gifts of the Holy Spirit.'"[10] This concept is strengthened by the reading of Acts 8:14–17 at the confirmation service.

Lutheran Church

"In the Lutheran Church confirmation is a rite rather than a sacrament, and the recipient offers it as a confirmation in his own heart of those baptismal vows which his parents assumed on his behalf."[11]

WESLEYAN/HOLINESS

The baptism is sanctification.

According to the Wesleyan doctrine, the baptism with the Holy Spirit is a distinct second work of grace subsequent to conversion, "a second blessing," usually called sanctification. This is "the instantaneous replacement of all evil motives of the heart by perfect love and pure intention."[12]

John Wesley (1703–1791), ordained to the Anglican priesthood at the age of 25, found his greatest acceptance with the masses and not the church hierarchy. John found peace with God while listening to a reading of Luther's Preface to Romans at Aldergate Street in London. He began enthusiastically to preach justification through faith in Christ alone; the ensuing Methodist revival swept many souls into the Kingdom of God. John began to preach a work of grace subsequent to regeneration, which was called sanctification. Such an approach had not been emphasized since the fourth century. John Fletcher, who became the systematic theologian of early Methodism, preferred "baptism in the Holy Spirit" to Wesley's "sanctification," so gradually this Pentecostal language was incorporated into their teaching and writing. Eddie L. Hyatt comments:

> Wesleyan terminology was thus replaced by his [Fletcher's] Pentecostal terminology. This helped set the stage for the twentieth century Pentecostal movement which emerged out of the nineteenth century Holiness movement. Early Methodism, a charismatic movement in its own right, thus became the womb that gave birth to the Pentecostal/Charismatic movement of the twentieth century.[13]

Donald G. Bloesch says: "In the mainstream Holiness movement the baptism of the Holy Spirit is understood as a crisis experience of sanctifying grace after conversion. This experience has been variously called 'the second blessing,' 'heart purity,' 'full salvation,' 'scriptural holiness,' 'Christian perfection,' 'perfect love,' 'entire sanctification' and 'the fullness of the blessing.' The Holiness groups, emerging from Methodism, believed in entire sanctification."[14]

The Holiness revival gave birth to new and sometimes separatist churches, such as: The Salvation Army, the Christian and Missionary Alliance, the Church of the Nazarene, the Free Methodist Church, the Wesleyan Methodist Church, the Church of God (Anderson, Indiana) and others.

THE REVIVALISTS (FINNEY, MOODY, TORREY)

The baptism is the filling.
For Finney, Moody and Torrey, the baptism with the Holy Spirit was an empowerment of the Spirit, distinct from and subsequent to regeneration, particularly given for service and testimony. Evidence was the manifestation of God's power and a greater revelation of Christ to the person involved.

Charles G. Finney (1792–1875)

Perhaps the greatest revivalist of all time was Charles Grandison Finney, a converted lawyer who became a Presbyterian minister and later a college president. Through his ministry a revival of great proportions came to New York State from 1820 until 1831.

As a teenager I had the good fortune to acquire his astounding autobiography, one of the most influential books I have ever read. The stories of conversions, revival meetings and prayer times left a tremendous impact on my life that has stayed with me for sixty years. I would like to quote the account of Finney's own baptism of the Holy Spirit:

> I returned to the front office, and found that the fire that I had made of large wood was nearly burned out. But as I turned and was about to take a seat by the fire, I received a mighty baptism of the Holy Ghost. Without any expectation of it, without ever having the thought in my mind that there was any such thing for me, without any recollection that I had ever heard the thing mentioned by any person in the world, the Holy Spirit descended upon me in a manner that seemed to go through me, body and soul. I could feel the impression, like a wave of electricity, going through and through me. Indeed it seemed to come in waves and waves of liquid love, for I could not express it in any other way; it seemed like the very breath of God. I can recollect distinctly that it seemed to fan me, like immense wings.
>
> No words can express the wonderful love that was shed abroad in my heart. I wept aloud with joy and love; and I do not know but I should say, I literally bellowed out the unutterable gushings of my heart. These waves came over me, and over me, and over me, one after the other, until I recollect I cried out, "I shall die if these waves continue to pass over me." I said, "Lord, I cannot bear any more;" yet I had no fear of death.[15]

John Gresham, a researcher of Finney theology, makes this comment:

Charles G. Finney understood the Baptism in the Holy Spirit as an experience of the Holy Spirit's presence and power subsequent to conversion. It brought a greater revelation of Christ that produces a deeper union with him. As a result of this experience, believers are established in their consecration and obedience, and are anointed with power in their prayer life and ministry.[16]

Finney himself said:

> The fact that the baptism of the Holy Ghost is a thing universally promised or proffered to Christians under this dispensation, and that this blessing is to be sought and received after conversion, was not so distinctly before my mind formerly as it has been of late. I am satisfied that this truth is abundantly taught in the Bible.[17]

Dwight L. Moody (1837–1899)

Dwight L. Moody, founder of Chicago's Moody Bible Institute, was another world-class evangelist. He was a strong believer in a baptism of the Holy Ghost subsequent to conversion, although he did not advocate tongues. He himself had a powerful Holy Spirit experience in 1871, fifteen years after conversion, which transformed his ministry.

Moody made this statement:

> In some sense, and to some extent, the Holy Spirit dwells with every believer; but there is another gift, which may be called the gift of the Holy Spirit for service. This gift, it strikes me, is entirely distinct and separate from conversion and assurance. God has a great many children that have no power, and the reason is, they have not the gift of the Holy Ghost for service.[18]

Donald W. Dayton makes this interesting comment about Moody:

> Moody had a sure instinct for avoiding controversy and kept his public statements, some have suggested, deliberately vague, especially on disputed issues. He certainly shied away from the characteristic vocabulary of the Holiness movement and was reluctant to speak in public of his experience of 1871 [when he had a baptism of the Holy Spirit], though he sometimes relented in private. But his teaching of a special "Pentecostal enduement of power for service" seems to have been a relatively constant theme of his preaching and apparently did not significantly change between the mid-1870s and the late 1890s.[19]

R. A. Torrey (1856–1928)

The Moody Bible Institute opened in 1899, the year of Moody's death. R. A. Torrey, a powerful preacher, popular evangelist and author in his own right, became head of the institute. Torrey was a strong advocate of a baptism of the Holy Spirit that is separate from conversion and is connected with testimony and service. This was a theme that occurred frequently in his sermons and books.

R. A. Torrey said: "The baptism with the Holy Spirit is the Spirit of God coming upon the believer, taking possession of his faculties, imparting to him gifts not naturally his own but which qualify him for the service to which God has called him."[20]

Evangelical

The baptism is being made part of the Body.

For evangelicals, the expression *baptism with the Holy Spirit* is another way of expressing the new birth or the new life in Christ. It occurs when a person repents of sin and believes in the Lord Jesus as Savior; thus, it is identical with conversion, and all Christians are considered to be Spirit-baptized. Following conversion, there can be subsequent fillings with the Spirit.

Churches: Evangelical, Reformed (including Presbyterian), Baptist, Methodist.

- Robert Gromacki: "Both the baptism in the Holy Spirit and the indwelling presence of the Spirit occur at the moment of salvation."[21]

- John R. Stott: "[T]he gift of the Holy Spirit is a Universal Christian experience because it is an initial Christian experience. All Christians receive the Spirit at the very beginning of their Christian life."[22]

- Ray C. Stedman: "[T]he baptism of the Holy Spirit takes place at conversion, unquestionably so. It is that which adds us to the body of Christ. . . . The baptism of the Holy Spirit is not accompanied by any signs at all. It is an unexperienced reality by which the believer's life is made one with the life and being of Jesus Christ. There is no feeling attached to it, or sense of it happening at all."[23]

- Billy Graham: Although Billy Graham believes that baptism with the Holy Spirit was synonymous with conversion, he nevertheless had a very meaningful and definite empowering experience with the Spirit (subsequent to conversion) that transformed his ministry. Billy was in Wales, and the 28-year-old evangelist was not having the success that he wished to have. Fortunately, Steven Olford, a Welsh evangelist, was in the area and they got together for fellowship and prayer. Olford himself had been led into a rich experience of the Holy Spirit under the influence of the Keswick movement. Olford led Billy into a Bible study that expounded the power that comes to the submitted believer.

As he spoke, Billy Graham replied with tears streaming down his face, "Steve, I see it. That's exactly what I want. It's what I need in my life." He then began pouring out his heart in prayer of total dedication to the Lord. Finally, he turned to Steven Olford. "My heart is so aflood with the Holy Spirit, I want to laugh and praise God all at the same time," he said. Graham then got up and began pacing back and forth across the narrow room declaring, "I have it. I'm filled." Finally he turned and grasped Steven Olford's hand. "This is a turning point in my life," he said, his eyes shining brightly. That night the meeting was packed and at the end the aisles were jammed with people wanting to accept Christ. Olford attended the meeting, then afterward at home he said to his father, "Dad, something has happened to Billy Graham. The world is going to hear from this man. He is going to make his mark in history."[24]

PENTECOSTAL

The baptism is the experience of Pentecost.
Spirit-baptism occurs after (sometimes at) conversion and is accompanied by speaking in tongues, as it was in the Acts of the Apostles. It is an experience given for empowerment in service and spiritual enhancement.

Churches: Assemblies of God, Church of God (Cleveland), Church of God in Christ, Foursquare Gospel, Open Bible Standard, Pentecostal Holiness, the Apostolic Church, United Pentecostal Church, and many independent churches and movements.[25]

Every Christian has the Holy Spirit—one cannot be born again without the working of the Holy Spirit. The baptism with the Spirit is an experience that enhances the reality of Jesus Christ and is a special enduement of Holy Spirit power for service.

Speaking in tongues is considered a normal part of the baptism with the Holy Spirit and is an immediate, observable evidence that a miraculous work of God has just occurred. The person begins to speak in a language never before learned. This uniquely affirms that the candidate has received the same Holy Spirit that started the Church and is a part of that same worldwide Church that continues today. Tongues are a miraculous point of contact that unites the new believer with the Holy Spirit that fell on Pentecost. The same evidence (tongues) bonds the believer to the same Church—and Spirit—that was begun by Christ and His apostles.

Lederle calls the Pentecostal position "a theology of subsequence," because the experience is after conversion.[26] Bloesch describes it as "the need for a second work of the Spirit after conversion in which we are empowered for ministry."[27]

He also says, "the gift of the Spirit after baptism imparts not perfection in character but power for witnessing. The visible sign of this spiritual endowment is speaking in other tongues (glossalalia)."[28]

Sometimes the expression "an immediate evidence" is used to describe speaking in tongues. This means that although tongues are one of several visible signs or evidence that a person is baptized with the Holy Spirit, by divine design it does happen immediately as a confirmation that this supernatural happening has occurred. It is "an objective, externalized, and physical manifestation of the Spirit" (R. Stronstad).[29]

Baptist pastor John Osteen had a remarkable baptism in the Spirit that transformed his ministry.

> [I]n an air-conditioned room, with my hands lifted . . . and my heart reaching up for my God, there came the hot, molten lava of His love. It poured in like a stream from Heaven and I was lifted up out of myself. I spoke in a language I could not understand for about two hours. My body perspired as though I was in a steambath: the Baptism of Fire![30]

As an example of classic Pentecostal belief, here are two of sixteen fundamental truths of the Assemblies of God denomination, taken from their web site:

> 7. WE BELIEVE . . . the Baptism in the Holy Spirit is a Special Experience Following Salvation that empowers believers for witnessing and effective

service, just as it did in New Testament times [one of the four cardinal doctrines of the A/G].

8. WE BELIEVE . . . The Initial Physical Evidence of the Baptism in the Holy Spirit is "Speaking in Tongues," as experienced on the Day of Pentecost and referenced throughout Acts and the Epistles.[31]

CHARISMATIC

The baptism is life in the Spirit.

For many denominational charismatics, the baptism with the Holy Spirit experience is an actualization of the Holy Spirit who was given in conversion/confirmation. Generally, speaking in tongues is considered "a" sign of the baptism, not necessarily "the" sign. My observation is that most charismatics think that speaking in tongues indicates being baptized with the Spirit. Bloesch comments about Catholic Pentecostals: "Tongues are accepted as one of the gifts of the Spirit but not as a proof of having the Spirit."[32]

The Pentecostal experience began penetrating the historic denominations in the 1960s (including Baptist, Methodist, Lutheran, Presbyterian, Roman Catholic and others). Larry Christenson (Lutheran pastor) states: "Many people have received the baptism with the Holy Spirit as a definite experience and reality. In their life and ministry there has been the unmistakable evidence of increased power and effectiveness."[33]

Dennis Bennett (1917–1992)

In 1960, while he was rector of St. Mark's Church in Van Nuys, California, Dennis Bennett experienced a baptism in the Spirit and speaking in tongues. That experience is generally credited with launching the charismatic renewal. This is how he describes his initial experience of speaking in tongues:

The language was being given me from the central place in me where God was, far beyond the realm of my emotions. Speaking on and on, I became more and more aware of God in me. . . . God living in me was creating the language. I was speaking it—giving it voice, by my volition, and I was speaking it to God Who was above and beyond me. God the Holy Spirit was giving me the words to talk to God the Father, and it was all happening because of God the Son, Jesus Christ.[34]

Catholic Pentecostal (Began at Duquesne University in 1967)

Donald L. Gelpi, S. J. (Catholic theologian) stated: "In the Catholic [charismatic] prayer groups with which I am familiar, Spirit-baptism is presented as a renewal of one's confirmation."[35] When hands are laid on candidates for Spirit-baptism, it is not considered a new sacrament but rather an activation (a catalyst, an experiential moment) that now causes baptism and confirmation to function in a conscious way.[36]

A very impressive three-volume review of the beliefs and reactions to the charismatic renewal (1960–1980) by various Christian churches and religious bodies was published in 1980. Edited by Catholic scholar Kilian McDonnell, these volumes give a quite complete review of the documents on the charismatic renewal during a twenty-year period.[37]

THIRD WAVE AND OTHER NEO-PENTECOSTALS

The baptism is being in Christ.

Generally, neo-Pentecostals believe that the baptism with the Holy Spirit happens at conversion and is not a second work of grace subsequent to the new birth. Tongues are not rejected but are considered one of many spiritual gifts and not the only evidence of the Spirit.

Begun with the Vineyard movement led by John Wimber in 1980–1990, this approach stresses power evangelism and signs and wonders to attest the Gospel, but speaking in tongues is minimized. Generally, these advocates are conservative evangelicals, theologians and pastors who seek to relate their experience of the Holy Spirit's power to conservative, evangelical beliefs.

A number of charismatic groups and organizations have sprung up, each with its own distinctives. One such group would be the Charismatic Presbyterians. Two of their ministers, Zeb Bradford Long and Douglas McMurray, tell of their unique approach in the recent book *Receiving the Power,* where they particularly adopt four propositions about the baptism with the Holy Spirit that were advocated by R. A. Torrey.[38]

Note: The following chart gives only a general idea. The checkmarks are not accurate for every subgroup within the seven listings.

COMPARISON OF EXPERIENCES IN THE GROUPS

	1. Sacramentarian	2. Wesleyan/Holiness	3. Revivalists	4. Evangelical	5. Pentecostal	6. Charismatic	7. Neo-Pentecostal
Infant baptism	✔						
Confirmation/Chrismation	✔						
Conversion	✔	✔	✔	✔	✔	✔	✔
Water baptism	✔	✔	✔	✔	✔	✔	✔
Second blessing/Sanctification		✔			✔		
Baptism with Holy Spirit subsequent but no tongues		✔	✔				
Baptism with Holy Spirit with tongues					✔	✔	
Tongues optional						✔	✔
Continuing infillings		✔	✔	✔	✔	✔	✔

AUTHOR'S CONCLUDING REMARKS

I have friends in each of the seven groups just discussed. These people are all devoted Christians and have a high regard for the Holy Spirit, but they all do not speak in tongues. I do believe we can all be "filled" with the Spirit in the sense that God will empower us if we will humble ourselves and seek the Lord. To me, this is the prerogative of every Christian, although it does not replace the initial Spirit-baptism.

As you know, I have experienced and advocate the Pentecostal Spirit-baptism accompanied by tongues. My discovery has been that this has been both a wonderful encounter with Jesus as well as a truly dynamic experience. I have also had repeated "infillings" of the Spirit that enhanced the original experience even more.

I think it is counterproductive to compare myself with other sincere Christians who do not speak in tongues. It is much better to compare myself before Spirit-baptism to myself after Spirit-baptism—rather than to compare my experience with that of someone else. I do know that I am a transformed, upgraded Christian, and for this I am grateful.

When I read the testimonies of people like Finney, Moody, Graham and many others who have had powerful experiences of Holy Spirit empowerment after conversion—some of them without speaking in tongues—I realize that God will be pleased to bless whenever people will humble themselves and wait for spiritual empowerment. It does seem a shame, however, that such people do not rest in the Spirit and allow the miracle of tongues to occur. My observation is that such reticence is based on unwarranted prejudice or fear, and this is enough in many cases to keep the miracle from happening.

Sincere people who seek God will receive Holy Spirit empowerment and God will use them. Even Peter and the others who had the mighty baptism in the Holy Spirit and spoke in tongues on the Day of Pentecost found themselves a few days later needing to seek God and be refilled with the Holy Spirit. From time to time, we all must return to our source of replenishment. I hope that every reader will join me in a sincere attempt to "walk in the Spirit" every day of our lives.

NOTES

Introduction

1. Vinson Synan, in his monumental book *The Century of the Holy Spirit,* says the total group is composed of classical Pentecostals and millions of mainline denominational and nondenominational churches, both Roman Catholic and Protestant. "The combined number now stands at more than five hundred million people. This growth has caused some historians to refer to the 20th century as the 'Pentecostal century.'" (Nashville: Thomas Nelson Publishers, 2001), 2.

2. Stanley M. Burgess and Gary B. McGee, *Dictionary of Pentecostal and Charismatic Movements* (Grand Rapids: Zondervan Regency, 1988), 250. Seven and a half columns are devoted to his remarkable life.

3. In 1970 two significant books were published that challenged the spread of Pentecostal theology on many of the world's seminary campuses. Almost any book on the Holy Spirit with scholarly footnotes (in the past thirty years) will invariably quote from one or both of these books: (1) James D. G. Dunn, *Baptism in the Holy Spirit* (Philadelphia: The Westminster Press, 1970); and (2) F. Dale Bruner, *A Theology of the Holy Spirit* (Grand Rapids: Eerdmans, 1970).

In the light of the continued dramatic growth of the Pentecostal/charismatic movement, it seems that we are not the only ones who are unconvinced by their arguments. Various scholarly replies have been given from the Pentecostal perspective, such as: Harold D. Hunter, *Spirit-Baptism: A Pentecostal Alternative* (Lanham, Md.: University Press of America, 1983); and Howard M. Ervin, *Conversion-Initiation and the Baptism in the Holy Spirit* (Peabody, Mass.: Hendrickson Publishers, Inc., 1984). My low-key response is given in the text with more technical comments in the endnotes.

A strong group of Pentecostal-charismatic scholars are rising to the challenge of research, discussion and publication. An impressive journal is *Pneuma: The Journal of the Society for Pentecostal Studies.*

4. Gordon D. Fee, "Baptism in the Holy Spirit: The Issue of Separability and Subsequence," *Pneuma: The Journal of the Society for Pentecostal Studies* 7, no. 2 (fall 1985): 93–94.

Chapter 1: Jesus' Preparation

1. See G. Campbell Morgan, *The Crises of the Christ* (Old Tappan, N.J.: Fleming H. Revell Co., 1903), particularly chapter 4, "The Great Mystery—The God-Man."

2. Ibid., 76. He says the Greek word *morphe* [form] occurs only here and in Mark 16:12 where Jesus (in resurrected body) was "manifested in another form" unto two of the disciples.

3. John Rea, *The Holy Spirit in the Bible: All the Major Passages About the Spirit* (Lake Mary, Fla.: Creation House, 1990), 136.

4. "Son of Man" was a favorite expression of Jesus for describing Himself; it veiled His divine glory by emphasizing His humanity and relationship to the human race. The term occurs 32 times in Matthew, 15 times in Mark, 26 times in Luke and 12 times in John. All (but two) occasions are spoken by Jesus Himself. The first three gospels do not record that Jesus referred to Himself as "the Son of God."

There were also episodes that showed Jesus to be the divine Son of God. Some examples: forgiving sin, transfiguration, three-time affirmation of the Father's voice, descriptions of His Second Coming, the great "I AM" statements (such as when He called Peter to walk on water or when the guards came to take Him in Gethsemane and they fell back as He declared Himself to be "I AM"), declarations of "Truth" and "Amen," upgraded interpretation of Scripture, tasting death for all and recognition by demons.

5. Kaari Ward, ed., *Jesus and His Times* (Pleasantville, N.Y: Reader's Digest Association, Inc., 1990), 31. "By the first century A.D., about a million Jews were living in Egypt. They were concentrated in Alexandria but were also found in smaller communities throughout Egypt," 30.

6. "In secular Gk. *tekton* means a craftsman or builder in wood, stone or metal . . . [the word] appears only in the identification of Jesus by the people of Nazareth as 'the carpenter' (Mk. 6:3), 'the carpenter's son' (Matt. 13:55). Though 'carpenter' is the common rendering here, *tekton* could equally mean 'mason' or 'smith' (as indeed some of the Fathers took it); or it could mean that Joseph and Jesus were builders, so that both carpentry and masonry would have been among their skills." J. I. Packer, *"Tekton,"* in *The New International Dictionary of New Testament Theology,* vol. 1, ed. Colin Brown (Grand Rapids: Zondervan, 1975), 279.

7. Alfred Edersheim, *The Life and Times of Jesus the Messiah,* vol. 1 (Grand Rapids: Eerdmans, 1950), 227.

8. I. Howard Marshall, "The Gospel of Luke: A Commentary on the Greek Text," in *New International Greek Testament Commentary* (Grand Rapids: Eerdmans, 1978), 126.

9. Ward, *Jesus,* 123.

10. W. Phillip Keller, *Rabboni . . . which is to say, Master* (Old Tappan, N.J.: Fleming H. Revell Co., 1977), 72–73.

11. J. W. Shepard, *The Christ of the Gospels* (Grand Rapids: Eerdmans, 1939), 53.

12. Alfred Plummer, "The Gospel According to St. Luke," in *The International Critical Commentary* (1896; reprint, Edinburgh: T & T. Clark, 1951), 76.

13. A. T. Robertson, *Word Pictures in the New Testament: Luke,* vol. 2 (Nashville: Broadman Press, 1930), 33.

14. J. W. Doeve, quoted by Walter L. Liefeld, *The Expositor's Bible Commentary,* vol. 8 (Grand Rapids: Zondervan, 1984), 852.

15. Plummer, "St. Luke," 77.

16. Raymond E. Brown, *The Birth of the Messiah: A Commentary on the Infancy Narratives in the Gospels of Matthew and Luke* (New York: Doubleday, 1993), 490.

17. Shepard, *Christ,* 55.

18. Philippians 2:5–11; Hebrews 2:9–11, 14–17; 10:5–7; 1 Timothy 3:16.

19. NLT: "was shown to be righteous"; CEV: "the Spirit proved that He (Jesus) pleased God"; MESSAGE: "proved right by the invisible Spirit."

20. Brown, *Birth,* 495. He suggests: "The growth in favor may be related to the obedience that Jesus, the Son of God, shows his parents at Nazareth. The son who is obedient and keeps the commandments is assured in Prov 3:1–14: 'You will find favor . . . . in the sight of God and men.'"

21. Fulton J. Sheen, *Life of Christ* (New York: McGraw-Hill, 1958), 49.

22. Isaiah 42:1–4; 49:1–6; 50:4–9; 52:13–53:12. See F. F. Bruce, *The New Testament Development of Old Testament Themes* (Grand Rapids: Eerdmans, 1982).

23. Psalms 2, 8, 16, 22, 45, 69, 72, 89, 110, 118, 132.

24. Isaiah 4:2; 11:1, 10; 53:2; Jeremiah 23:5; 33:15–16; Zechariah 3:8; 6:9–15.

Chapter 2: Jesus' Ministry

1. George M. Lamsa, *Gospel Light: Comments on the Teachings of Jesus from Aramaic and Unchanging Eastern Customs*, rev. ed. (Philadelphia: A. J. Holman Co., 1936), 19–20.

2. John 1:33: "I did not know Him, but He who sent me to baptize with water said to me. . . ." The sign of the descending Spirit would identify Christ to John. It is possible that many years have passed since they had met each other in childhood, but this is uncertain.

3. Thomas L. Holdcroft, *The Holy Spirit: A Pentecostal Interpretation*, rev. ed. (Abbotsford, Canada: CeeTeC Publishing, 1999), 47.

4. A. T. Robertson, *Word Pictures in the New Testament: Matthew & Mark,* vol. 1 (Nashville: Broadman Press, 1930), 255–56.

5. Henry Barclay Swete, *The Holy Spirit in the New Testament* (1910; reprint, Grand Rapids: Baker Book House, 1976), 54.

6. Keller, *Rabboni,* 133.

7. I. H. Marshall, *Luke,* 180.

8. Jesus had just read "To proclaim the acceptable year of the LORD," which referred to His ministry and the Church age, but He stopped just before reading "And the day of vengeance of our God," which refers to His Second Coming (see Isaiah 61:2).

9. Matthew 7:29; 21:23–24, 27; Mark 1:22, 27; 11:28–29; Luke 4:32, 36; 20:2, 8; John 7:45–46.

10. My reference to 35 miracles—"17 Bodily Cures," "9 Miracles over Forces of Nature," "6 Cures of Demoniacs" and "3 Raised from the Dead"—is based on Henry H. Halley, *Halley's Bible Handbook,* 24th ed. (Grand Rapids: Zondervan, 1965), 469–70.

11. Ernest B. Gentile, *Worship God! Exploring the Dynamics of Psalmic Worship* (Portland, Ore.: City Bible Publications, 1994), 16.

Chapter 3: Jesus' Promise

1. F. F. Bruce, *The Gospel of John* (Grand Rapids: Eerdmans, 1983), 303.

2. Rea, *Holy Spirit,* 155.

3. Catherine Marshall, *The Helper* (Waco, Tex.: Word Books, 1979), 22.

4. Bruce says: "The word paracletos is best understood as a verbal adjective with passive force, denoting one who is called alongside as a helper or defender, a friend at court." *Gospel of John,* 301.

When the pioneers took covered wagons across deep rivers, they strapped logs on either side of the wagons enabling the wagons to float! Just as the logs were alongside to lift and support, so we have the Holy Spirit close beside and supporting us.

5. George T. Montague, *The Holy Spirit: Growth of a Biblical Tradition* (New York: Paulist Press, 1976), 350.

6. Wilbur Smith, *Peloubet's Select Notes on the International Bible Lessons* (Natick, Mass.: W. A. Wilde Company, 1960), 97.

7. C. F. D. Moule, *The Holy Spirit* (Grand Rapids: Eerdmans, 1978), 36.

8. Kenneth S. Wuest, *Wuest's Word Studies from the Greek New Testament* (1973; reprint, Grand Rapids: Eerdmans, 2002), 91.

9. Rea, *Holy Spirit,* 154–55.

10. William Barclay, *The Acts of the Apostles* (Philadelphia: The Westminster Press, 1955), 2.

11. A. B. Simpson, *The Holy Spirit: Power from on High* (Camp Hill, Pa.: Christian Publications, 1994), 353.

12. Albert Barnes, *Notes on the New Testament: Explanatory and Practical,* vols. Luke and John (Grand Rapids: Baker Book House, 1976), 330.

13. Kenneth S. Wuest, *The New Testament: An Expanded Translation* (1961; reprint, Grand Rapids: Eerdmans, 2002), 253 ff.

14. Ernest B. Gentile, *Awaken the Dawn!* (1990; reprint, Columbus, Ga.: The Eastwood Company Publications, 2001).

15. C. Marshall, *Helper,* 33.

16. Derek Prince, *The Holy Spirit in You* (New Kensington, Pa.: Whitaker House, 1987), 45.

17. Sheen, *Life,* 321.

18. Michael Green, *I Believe in the Holy Spirit* (Grand Rapids: Eerdmans, 1975), 45.

19. Swete, *Holy Spirit,* 4.

20. Green, *Believe,* 43.

21. As suggested by Swete, *Holy Spirit,* 148.

22. In addition to His teaching on the coming Spirit, Jesus foretold the advent of the Holy Spirit in the following statements. The first ten listings below are verses already discussed in the Farewell Discourse.

John 14:16
John 14:17
John 14:18
John 14:26
John 15:26
John 16:7
John 16:8
John 16:13
John 16:14
John 16:15
Matthew 3:11
Mark 1:8
Luke 3:16
Luke 11:13
Luke 24:49
John 1:33
John 4:13
John 7:38
John 7:39
John 20:22
Acts 1:4
Acts 1:5
Acts 1:8
Acts 11:16

23. The John 17 prayer provides some insight to Jesus' present intercession in heaven. The disciples heard Him pray these things, and undoubtedly remembered them later with great appreciation. Eleven things are mentioned: (1) Glorify the disciples, v. 1; (2) Give eternal life, v. 21; (3) Ask on their behalf, v. 9; (4) Keep them in Thy Name, v. 11; (5) My joy made full in them, v. 13; (6) Keep them from the evil one, v. 15; (7) Sanctify them in the truth, v. 17; (8) Also ask in behalf of their followers, v. 20; (9)

Oneness or unity of believers that world may believe, vv. 21–23; (10) Be with Me, v. 24; (11) God's love may be in them, v. 26. Another reference, Luke 22:31–32, tells of Jesus' intercession for Peter and the other disciples. This surely reflects in some way His present activity in heaven.

24. J. Rodman Williams has an excellent discussion on the Holy Spirit's Personhood. He points out that the Spirit has intelligence (see Acts 8:29), will (see Acts 16:6), feelings (see Ephesians 4:30) and personal relationships. *Renewal Theology: Systematic Theology from a Charismatic Perspective,* vol. 2 (Grand Rapids: Zondervan, 1990), 151–52.

25. See Raymond E. Brown, "The Paraclete in the Fourth Gospel," *NTS* 13 (1966–67): 113–132.

26. Max Turner, *The Holy Spirit and Spiritual Gifts* (Peabody, Mass.: Hendrickson Publishers, 1998), 79–81.

27. Barnes, *Notes,* 331.

28. Green, *Believe,* 14.

29. Barnes, *Notes,* 333.

30. See chapter 2 of Charles Spurgeon, *Holy Spirit Power* (New Kensington, Pa.: Whitaker House, 1996).

31. Turner, *Holy Spirit,* 83.

32. E. Y. Mullins, "Holy Spirit," in *The International Standard Bible Encyclopaedia,* gen. ed. James Orr (Grand Rapids: Eerdmans, 1974), 1414.

Chapter 4: The Miracle of Pentecost

1. Joseph Parker, "Acts I–XII," in *Preaching Through the Bible,* vol. 23 (Grand Rapids: Baker Book House, 1978), 43.

2. John Rea says: "At the great Jewish feasts as many as 180,000 came to worship, and 120,000 to 150,000 of these might be pilgrims from other countries speaking other languages as their native tongue." *Holy Spirit,* 167.

C. Peter Wagner says: "On the Day of Pentecost, when the Holy Spirit came, 100,000 Hellenists would easily have been visiting Jerusalem, possibly 200,000." *Acts of the Holy Spirit: A Modern Commentary on the Book of Acts* (Ventura, Ca.: Regal, 1994), 71.

3. Sholem Asch, *The Apostle* (New York: G. Putnam's Sons, 1943), 4–5. This description introduces activity not usually mentioned in commentaries. The festival of Pentecost was actually both that of wheat harvest and firstfruits. Thanksgiving for the conclusion of wheat harvest was celebrated by the priest offering two loaves of new wheaten flour baked with leaven (which he waved before the Lord). Afterward, the pilgrims would bring their baskets of firstfruits produce, carried on their shoulders, to the court of the temple (note Exodus 23:16; Leviticus 23:16–17). Asch's colorful description is confirmed in *Smith's Comprehensive Dictionary of the Bible,* ed. Samuel W. Barnum (New York: D. Appleton Co., 1884), 308.

4. Shepard, *Christ,* 52.

5. Alec Garrard, *The Splendor of the Temple: A Pictorial Guide to Herod's Temple and Its Ceremonies* (Grand Rapids: Kregel Publications, 2000), 31.

6. My chart is based on the discussion of Alfred Edersheim in *The Temple: Its Ministry and Services,* updated ed. (Peabody, Mass.: Hendrickson Publishers, 1994), 38–39.

7. Ibid., 34.

8. Ibid., 33.

9. As pictured by Torger G. Thompson in his magnificent mural (120' long x 20' tall) called "Miracle at Pentecost" and housed in Dallas, Texas, at the Biblical Arts Center. See his book *Creation of a Masterpiece* (Dallas: Biblical Arts Center, circa 1981).

See also "The Temple Porches," in Edersheim, *Temple,* 20–22. He comments: "These 'porches,' or cloisters, were among the finest architectural features of the Temple. They ran all round the inside of its wall, and bounded the outer enclosure of the Court of the Gentiles. They consisted of double rows of Corinthian pillars, all monoliths, wholly cut out of one block of marble, each pillar being 37 1/2 feet high. A flat roof, richly ornamented, rested against the wall, in which also the outer row of pillars was inserted," 20.

10. G. Campbell Morgan, *The Acts of the Apostles* (Old Tappan, N.J.: Fleming H. Revell Co., 1924), 25–26.

11. F. F. Bruce, "The Book of Acts Revised," in *The New International Commentary on the New Testament* (Grand Rapids: Eerdmans, 1988), 49. Note the following references: Exodus 23:16; 34:22; Leviticus 23:15–21; Numbers 28:26–31; Deuteronomy 16:9–12; Philo, *Spec. Leg.* 2.176–88; Josephus, *Ant.* 3:252 ff.

12. Wagner, *Acts,* 66.

13. Edersheim, *Temple,* 206.

14. James 1:25; Romans 8:2; 2 Corinthians 3:3.

15. Swete, *Holy Spirit,* 69.

16. James D. G. Dunn, *The Acts of the Apostles* (Valley Forge: Trinity Press International, 1996), 23.

17. "Such upper rooms were quite common. Sometimes they were merely booths that were erected on the flat roof of a building. . . . Sometimes they were roomy and even ornate like the one with its tiled floor that is mentioned in Luke 22:12 . . . a place that was free from interruption and disturbance." R. C. H. Lenski, *The Interpretation of the Acts of the Apostles* (Minneapolis: Augsburg Publishing House, 1934), 39.

18. G. Campbell Morgan, *Great Chapters of the Bible* (London: Marshall, Morgan & Scott, 1946), 224–25.

19. Garrard, *Temple,* 33.

20. Bruce notes that any theory requires reading more into the text than what is actually recorded. One possible suggestion that he mentions is that they were in the Upper Room, went out into the streets speaking in tongues and then led people to the Temple; this seems an unwieldy interpretation to me. See his full discussion in "Acts Revised," 51.

I think John Rea gives a good summary of why the "one place" or "house where they were sitting" was the Temple rather than an upper room (*Holy Spirit,* 169). My quick summary of his clues: (1) No typical Jewish rooftop room in (already crowded) Jerusalem could accommodate 120 people; (2) Luke 24:53 says Jesus' followers "were continually in the temple, praising God"; (3) As devoted Jews the disciples were expected to be present in the Temple area for the feast-day ceremonies; (4) Luke referred to the Temple by the term "house" (Luke 11:51; 19:46; Acts 7:47, 49); (5) The great crowd came to the disciples right away upon hearing the sound of praise in many tongues (note: The streets of Jerusalem were narrow, winding alleys, unable to sustain such a multitude); and (6) The traditional house containing the Upper Room is on the opposite side of the city from the Temple site.

One of the most interesting discussions is by Donald Lee Barnett and Jeffrey McGregor in their chapter "Where Were the Disciples Praying on the Day of Pentecost?" in *Speaking in Other Tongues* (Seattle: Community Chapel Publications, 1986), 52–57.

21. The word *house (oikos)* is used of both a private house as well as the Temple. Note: Acts 7:47; Mark 11:17; John 2:16; Isaiah 6:4.

22. Lenski comments: "The Jews stood when praying; sitting implies that the assembly of disciples was listening to some discourse that was being uttered, let us say, by one of the apostles [possibly being led in prayer?] . . . the assembly was sitting on the floor in Oriental, cross-legged fashion." *Interpretation,* 57.

23. I have explained this in detail in my book *Your Sons and Daughters Shall Prophesy* (Grand Rapids: Chosen Books, 1999), in chapter 5, "How Did Prophecy Come to a Prophet?"

24. David Ewert, *The Holy Spirit in the New Testament* (Kitchener, Ontario: Herald Press, 1983), 105.

25. Compare: God breathed into His clay-formed man Adam the breath of life and he came alive (see Genesis 2:7). Also, Jesus breathed on His disciples, saying, "Receive the Holy Spirit" (John 20:22)—and they were born of the Spirit and became part of the new creation. This naturally raises the oft-asked question, Is this experience of Acts 2 supplemental to that of John 20?

Note how Holy Spirit is taken literally to mean "Holy Breath" by some, such as Catholic scholar Donald L. Gelpi. See his chapter "Breath-Baptism in the Synoptics," in *Charismatic Experiences in History*, ed. Cecil M. Robeck (Peabody, Mass.: Hendrickson Publishers, 1985).

26. Herbert Lockyer, *All the Divine Names and Titles in the Bible* (Grand Rapids: Zondervan, 1975), 322.

27. As in a recent book by Robert Gromacki, *The Holy Spirit: Who He Is What He Does* (Nashville: Word Publishing, 1999), 147–48. Also, a popular book by Arthur W. Pink, *The Holy Spirit* (Grand Rapids: Baker Book House, 1970), 39–40. Their arguments about antecedents are not conclusive for me and do not reflect the majority of commentators (see following endnote).

28. James D. G. Dunn says: "The 'all' of 2:1 is almost certainly the 120 and not just the twelve. The *pantes* [all] most naturally refers to the whole body involved in the preceding verses; that more than twelve languages were heard implies that there were more than twelve speakers; 2.15, and perhaps 2.33, probably refers to other than the eleven . . . the 'us' of 11.15 includes 'the brethren who were in Judea' (11.1). There is certainly no room for the Catholic view which singles out the apostles for special or exclusive endowments of the Spirit . . . and which makes it possible to regard the apostles as the sole 'channel' of the Spirit to others. The one gift and the same gift was common to all." *Baptism,* 40.

Personally, I think that the one hundred and twenty disciples speaking in tongues illustrates the universal priesthood of *all* believers. Also, the one hundred twenty priests at the dedication of Solomon's Temple blowing trumpets in one accord (see 2 Chronicles 5:11–14) is undoubtedly a prophetic illustration of the coming Day of Pentecost when the one hundred twenty disciples declared the glory of the Lord.

29. I could be wrong about this being a prophetic, visionary experience. Roger Stronstad, in contrast, stresses that the descent of the Spirit upon Jesus was "an objective, externalized, and physical manifestation of the Spirit." He feels also that the descent and the voice showed that God is restoring the broken communication between Himself and Israel. *The Charismatic Theology of St. Luke* (Peabody, Mass.: Hendrickson Publishers, 1984), 40.

30. Sheen, *Life,* 57.

31. Maynard James makes an interesting comparison between the fire on the disciples and the dove on Jesus: "When the Holy Ghost came at Pentecost to fill the hearts of the hundred-and-twenty, the visible symbol was not a dove. It was a cloven tongue like fire—the emblem of dynamic purification. Jesus had no need of purification from inbred sin: He had no taint of depravity. Hence the symbol of the Holy Spirit who came 'without measure' to the spotless Son of God was a dove." *I Believe in the Holy Ghost* (Minneapolis: Bethany Fellowship, Inc., 1965), 48.

32. Rea says: "The term for 'utterance' in Acts 2:4 also suggests that the newly empowered Christians were speaking forth the praises of God with a prophetic ring in their voices. The Greek word, *apophthengesthai,* means to speak forth boldly as a prophet or other inspired person . . . it occurs several times in the septuagint in a prophetic context (Ezek. 13:9; Mic. 5:12; Zech. 10:2; and 1 Chr. 25:1, the clearest Old Testament example)." *Holy Spirit,* 174.

33. A. T. Robertson, *Word Pictures in the New Testament: Acts,* vol. 3 (Nashville: Broadman Press, 1930), 21.

34. Morgan, *Great Chapters,* 226.

35. Flavius Josephus, "The Wars of the Jews" (2, 16, 4), in *The Works of Josephus,* trans. William Whiston (Lynn, Mass.: Hendrickson Publishers, 1980), 490.

36. Lawrence O. Richards, *The Illustrated Concise Bible Handbook* (Nashville: Thomas Nelson, 2000), 570.

37. Barclay, *Acts,* 16. These converts to Judaism became members of Israel by a threefold rite: (1) male circumcision; (2) a self-baptism of purification witnessed by others; and (3) offering a sacrifice.

Chapter 5: Great Balls of Fire!

1. Some include 1 Corinthians 12:13, but I do not agree. See my explanation in chapter 7. Since only two of the six references use "and fire," and since fire was not repeated in the rest of the episodes of Acts, we must assume that visible fire is not to be an expected manifestation.

2. For a quite complete review of scholarly opinion, see chapter 7, "Spirit-and-Fire Baptism," in James D. G. Dunn, *The Christ and the Spirit* (Grand Rapids: Eerdmans, 1998). Also, see I. H. Marshall, *Luke,* 146–48.

3. George Eldon Ladd, *A Theology of the New Testament* (Grand Rapids: Eerdmans, 1974), 36–37. The sources can be found there.

4. E. W. Bullinger, *Word Studies on the Holy Spirit* (Grand Rapids: Kregel Publishers, 1979), 44.

5. Stanley M. Horton, *What the Bible Says About the Holy Spirit* (Springfield, Mo.: Gospel Publishing House, 1997), 86.

6. Ladd, *Theology,* 37.

7. Parker, "Acts," 49.

8. F. B. Meyer, quoted by Smith, *Peloubet's Select Notes,* 266.

9. Quoted from Lewis Drummond, *Spurgeon: Prince of Preachers* (Grand Rapids: Kregel Publications, 1992), 349. Originally quoted from Charles Ray, *The Life of Charles Haddon Spurgeon.*

10. Quoted by Graham Truscott, *You Shall Receive Power* (Poona, India: New Life Centre, 1967), 258.

Chapter 6: Speaking in Tongues

1. First Corinthians 13:1 intimates that there are tongues "of angels," suggesting the possibility that the early Church considered some prayer languages to be angelic languages.

2. W. E. Vine, *An Expository Dictionary of New Testament Words,* vol. 4, 17th ed. (Westwood, N.J.: Fleming H. Revell Co., 1966), 142.

3. R. Spittler, "Glossolalia," in Burgess and McGee, *Dictionary,* 336.

4. Jack Hayford, *The Beauty of Spiritual Language* (Nashville/Atlanta: Thomas Nelson Publishers, 1996).

5. Larry Christenson, Lutheran charismatic, makes these comments in *Speaking in Tongues* (Minneapolis: Dimension Books, 1968), 23–24: "[P]eople jump rather too quickly to the conclusion that a person is speaking gibberish simply because they themselves do not understand it. This writer had the opportunity to visit with Professor Eugene Rapp, world-famous linguist at the University of Mainz, Germany. He speaks some 45 languages and is a specialist in West African dialects. He gave me a practical demonstration of coming into contact with a completely unfamiliar language. He read some lines out of one of his recent works: The Gospel of John in the language of a small West African tribe. To my unschooled ear it sounded like little more than a series of animal grunts. I have never heard any speaking in tongues which sounded so primitive. If I had heard sounds like that in a prayer meeting, I might have been tempted to dismiss it as gibberish. Yet this was a known language of earth. The fact of the matter is, even a trained linguist cannot determine whether a brief utterance of unfamiliar sounds

is in fact a language. Professor Rapp said: 'I have once in my life heard someone speak in tongues. My impression was that it was no nonsense or gibberish. However, one cannot determine that from hearing just a few sentences. I would need at least sixteen pages of phonetically transcribed script to study and analyze before I could make a certain judgment.' If a trained linguist cannot make that judgment, certainly a layman in the field could not."

6. Christopher Forbes suggests five main options: (1) the miraculous ability to speak unlearned human languages; (2) the miraculous ability to speak heavenly or angelic languages; (3) some combination of 1 and 2; (4) a kind of sub- or prelinguistic form of speech or a kind of coded utterance; or (5) an archaic or idiosyncratic language. *Prophecy and Inspired Speech: In Early Christianity and Its Hellenistic Environment* (Peabody, Mass.: Hendrickson, 1997), 56–65.

7. Hayford, *Beauty,* 74.

8. Marion Meloon, *Ivan Spencer: Willow in the Wind* (Plainfield, N.J.: Logos, 1974), 210.

9. Dennis J. Bennett, "The Gifts of the Holy Spirit," in *The Charismatic Movement,* ed. Michael Hamilton (Grand Rapids: Eerdmans, 1975), 27.

10. For documented accounts of utterances by the Spirit, see Ralph W. Harris, *Spoken by the Spirit* (Springfield, Mo.: Gospel Publishing House, 1973). For stories of people in India speaking in English, which they had never learned, see chapter 14 of Truscott, *Receive.* Also, the interesting article by historian Stanley M. Burgess, "Medieval Examples of Charismatic Piety in the Roman Catholic Church," in *Perspectives on the New Pentecostalism,* ed. Russell Spittler (Grand Rapids: Baker Book House, 1976), 14.

11. Wagner, *Acts,* 76.

12. Christenson, *Speaking,* 20.

13. C. S. Lovett, *Lovett's Lights on Acts* (Baldwin Park, Ca.: Personal Christianity, 1972), 138.

14. Bruner, *Theology,* 163–64.

15. Wagner, *Acts,* 165.

16. Carl Brumback, *What Meaneth This?* (Springfield, Mo.: Gospel Publishing House, 1947), 239.

17. George Canty, *Hallmarks of Pentecost: Discerning the True Spiritual Gifts* (London: Marshall Pickering, 1989), 17.

18. Brumback, *Meaneth,* 240. The Assemblies of God for a number of years conducted summer camps for the deaf in the Minnesota, Wisconsin, Michigan areas. North West Bible College in Minneapolis developed a strong department to teach ministry to the deaf, which was responsible for this kind of results.

19. William G. MacDonald, "Pentecostal Theology: A Classical Viewpoint," in *Perspectives on the New Pentecostalism,* ed. Russell Spittler (Grand Rapids: Baker Book House, 1976), 66.

20. Don Basham, *A Handbook on Holy Spirit Baptism* (New Kensington, Pa.: Whitaker House, 1969), 86.

21. Gordon D. Fee, *God's Empowering Presence: The Holy Spirit in the Letters of Paul* (Peabody, Mass.: Hendrickson Publishers, 1994), 731.

22. Wagner, because of his activity in church growth and missions, has given much thought to clarifying spiritual gifts. His insights on "roles" vs. "gifts" and also the "situational" vs. the "constitutional" view of gifts is extremely helpful. I have used his concept of "role" and applied it to praying in tongues. See his book *Spheres of Authority* (Colorado Springs: Wagner Publications, 2002), 51–54.

23. Fee, *Presence,* 270.

24. Dennis and Rita Bennett, *The Holy Spirit and You,* rev. ed. (Gainesville, Fla.: Bridge-Logos Publishers, 2001), 60.

25. In the excitement of a charismatic meeting, some inadvertently begin speaking in tongues because they are accustomed to releasing privately that particular avenue of Spirit expression. Such

behavior, however, is usually not the gift of tongues (which should be accompanied by interpretation), but more of an inappropriate, personal devotion.

26. Some make a major argument against the use of this verse, because it is suggested that this verse and others may not have been part of the gospel when it was first written. Wagner makes this comment in *Acts*, 201, footnote: "Kurt Aland, a leading textual scholar and organizing editor of both modern editions of the Greek testament, observes that Mark 16:9–20 'is found in 99 percent of the Greek manuscripts,' and therefore over the centuries has by many Christians been regarded as Scripture. [See his comments in *The Text of the New Testament*, 2d ed. (Grand Rapids: Eerdmans, 1989), 292 ff.] . . . If the longer ending were a later addition, it must mean that the Christians responsible felt it important enough to include these charismatic words of Jesus. Acts 20:35 shows that there were true words of Jesus that did not get recorded in the four Gospels (compare John 21:25), so this would not be out of order."

27. Synan, *Century*, ix.

Chapter 7: Answers to Pesky Questions

1. Christenson, *Speaking*, 31.

2. Closing statements taken from Charles F. Stanley, *Charles Stanley's Handbook for Christian Living: Biblical Answers to Life's Tough Questions* (Nashville: Thomas Nelson Publishers, 1996), 54–57.

3. Ibid., 56.

4. See Gordon Fee's comments in the last chapter.

5. Anyone who reads Acts 18 and 19 will see the busy activity of Paul in both Ephesus and Corinth. The prolific manifestation of the Spirit in both these places and the time Paul spent there clearly indicates his involvement in Holy Spirit activity.

6. Stanley, *Handbook*, 56.

7. Ronald A. N. Kydd, *Charismatic Gifts in the Early Church* (Peabody, Mass.: Hendrickson Publishers, 1984), 87.

8. Stanley, *Handbook*, 57.

9. Ibid.

10. Ervin, *Conversion*, 102.

11. Stanley, *Handbook*, 54.

12. Ibid.

13. "[T]he reason prophecy is greater is related to the edification of the community . . . it is not inherently greater, since all gifts come from the Spirit and are beneficial. It is greater precisely because it is intelligible and therefore can edify." Fee, *Presence*, 221.

Chapter 8: The Peter Pattern

1. The expression *baptism with the Holy Spirit* is based on the following six references: Matthew 3:11; Mark 1:8; Luke 3:16; John 1:33; Acts 1:5; 11:16.

The three things of the Peter Pattern are expected to happen, but not necessarily in a three-stage sequence that must always happen in that 1-2-3 order. I will explain why I believe Scripture teaches that conversion comes first—and then the other two events can occur in either order. The Holy Spirit is active at each step.

2. John R. W. Stott suggests four parts in his discussion, *Baptism & Fullness: The Work of the Holy Spirit Today*, 2d ed. (Downers Grove, Ill.: InterVarsity Press, 1964), 40. Although most commentators understand the importance of definition, they do not all agree on the answers!

3. Matthew 20:22; Mark 10:38–39; Luke 12:50. Jesus foretold a time of great suffering that would come upon Him like an overwhelming baptism, ending with His death on the cross. The Passion Week

would be the culmination of persecution and rejection, but He would triumph (see Hebrews 2:9–11, 14, 17)! Jesus' disciples might undergo this baptism as well.

4. John the Baptist preached to the Jews a message of repentance in preparation for the "at-hand" Kingdom of God. He demanded genuine repentance—sealed by public confession and public baptism. He told the crowds to believe in the Coming One who would replace him, and that He would baptize with the Holy Spirit and fire just as John had baptized in water. This was not Christian baptism, but rather a prophetic act of that which was to come. (See Matthew 3:5–6; Mark 1:4; John 1:25; 3:22–23; Acts 1:5; 11:16.)

5. A spiritual whelming of the sinful soul by the precious blood of Christ (see 1 John 1:9). This is the fountain of cleansing (see Zechariah 13:1). John called Jesus "The Lamb of God who takes away the sin of the world" (John 1:29). In the first Passover, Israel baptized their doorways with the blood of the Lamb and were saved. Blood covered the Mercy Seat of the Ark of the Covenant. Great hymns testify of the cleansing baptism of Christ's blood that can wash away all sin and present us faultless before the throne of God. Revelation 1:5 states: "To Him who loved us and washed us from our sins in His own blood." Revelation 19:13 says Jesus was clothed with a robe dipped (baptized, immersed, dyed) in blood. Also note Revelation 7:14: "These are the ones who come out of the great tribulation, and washed their robes and made them white in the blood of the Lamb."

6. See chapter 5 on the fire of God, where several interpretations are discussed. L. Thomas Holdcroft comments: "Holiness preachers of the nineteenth century commonly expounded this promise to teach a special once-for-all experience in which spiritual fire would utterly consume the dross of sin. . . . Some saw fire baptism as an experience separate from Spirit baptism; others saw it as a particular aspect of Spirit baptism. In this interpretation, the fire aspect was for purposes of purifying, cleansing, and refining." *Holy Spirit*, 128–29.

The cleansing, sanctifying work of the Spirit can appropriately be likened to fire. It is best, I feel, to see "the baptism with fire" in a dual role: as a spiritual part of Spirit-baptism for the believer and also as a literal fiery judgment on sin and the ungodly in the last days (as, 1 Thessalonians 1:7–8). I feel it is confusing and counterproductive to seek for a specific baptism of fire.

7. Although Passover and blood is not mentioned in 1 Corinthians 10:1–2, it must be included. Exodus 12 introduces the Passover as foundational to the Exodus. Israel could not become the people of God without the Passover. An event so major, it was memorialized; see Exodus 12:24. Paul's references to the blood of Christ are significant: Romans 3:25; 5:9; 1 Corinthians 10:16; 11:25, 27; Ephesians 1:7; 2:13; Colossians 1:14, 20.

8. F. W. Grosheide, *Commentary on the First Epistle to the Corinthians* (Grand Rapids: Eerdmans, 1953), 220.

9. Simon J. Kistemaker, *New Testament Commentary: Exposition of the First Epistle to the Corinthians* (Grand Rapids: Baker Books, 1993), 429.

10. J. I. Packer, for instance: "[I]n all seven passages the same preposition (en) is used, making the Spirit the 'element' in which Christ baptizes, so that the distinction is linguistically baseless." *Keep in Step with the Spirit* (Grand Rapids: Fleming H. Revell, 1984), 203.

Stanley M. Horton, a well-known Pentecostal theologian, says: "They argue that the Greek word en always means 'in' when it is used with the word baptize. This is true of the six cases that compare John's baptism in water with Jesus' baptism in the Holy Spirit. . . . [however] the word en often does mean 'by.' In some cases it is used with the Holy Spirit to mean 'by the Holy Spirit.' Luke 4:1 uses it of Jesus led by the Spirit into the wilderness. Mark 1:12 confirms emphatically that the Spirit was indeed the agent. Luke 2:27 is a similar case—'came by the Spirit.' So is Ephesians 3:5—'revealed by the Spirit.' . . . An examination of the whole passage gives a firm backing for the usual KJV, 'by one Spirit.'" Horton, *Bible Says*, 215.

11. Ervin, *Conversion*, 99.

12. Kevin J. Conner, *Understanding and Distinguishing the New Birth and the Baptism of the Holy Spirit* (Victoria, Australia: K.J.C. Publications, 1998), 20.

13. David Shibley, "Four Christmas Wonders," *Update* (November–December 2002): 1.

14. Millard J. Erickson, *The Concise Dictionary of Christian Theology,* rev. ed. (Wheaton: Crossway Books, 2001), 10.

15. Vine, *Dictionary,* 32.

16. *First Principles: A Study of the Elementary Principles of Christ* (Grand Prairie, Tex.: Shady Grove Church Publications, 1989), 17.

17. Truscott, *Receive,* 82.

18. Moses was the first man to receive the revelation of God's name (see Exodus 3:14); previously God was known as "the true God" or "God Almighty" (see Exodus 6:3). The name that God gave Moses is the famous four-lettered name called the Tetragrammaton, and it means "I AM." The name was considered so sacred that no one could pronounce it (on penalty of death! See Leviticus 14:16.). The ancient rabbis carefully identified it in the Scriptures by putting the vowel points of the Hebrew word Adonai (Lord) over the four-lettered name JHVH or YHVH (this is where JeHoVaH came from in A.D. 1520, a hybrid word that is unacceptable to Jews as an authentic revelation of God's name). LORD in the Old Testament (capitalized) means that the original Hebrew text uses the Tetragrammaton in that particular place. This is the most frequent name of God in the Scriptures (it appears 6,823 times in the Hebrew Old Testament) and easily qualifies to fulfill "the name of the Father." Apparently Peter felt so, for he said God made Jesus Lord. Lord is not capitalized in the New Testament, but when quoted from the Old Testament (where it is capitalized) or referring to Jesus, it could be! Notice the impact of "LORD Jesus Christ" or "JEHOVAH Jesus Christ."

The title *Messiah* or *Christ* (the Greek form) was such a well-known, talked-about term that it became like a personal, loving name. It meant the Anointed One, the One upon Whom the Spirit Rested. The Holy Spirit provided this beautiful appellation to Jesus to complete the sacred name of Christian baptism. After the Philippian jail had broken apart, the trembling jailer cried out, "Sirs, what must I do to be saved?" The apostle Paul, knowing the full significance of the name (as Peter did), declared the majestic words, "Believe on the Lord Jesus Christ, and you will be saved, you and your household." In what name do you suppose they were baptized (see Acts 16:30–33)?

Now out of print, this little book is the best presentation of the significance of the name of the Lord Jesus Christ that I have read. William Phillips Hall, *A Remarkable Biblical Discovery or "The Name" of God According to the Scriptures* (New York: American Tract Society, 1929). A second book on the same subject deserves mention, although it too is out of print. W. H. Offiler, *God and His Name: A Message for Today* (Seattle: Bethel Temple, 1932).

19. The apostle Paul apparently was not baptized in public, but the news of his conversion, water baptism and baptism with the Holy Spirit undoubtedly became a major source of rejoicing in the Christian community.

Chapter 9: The Baptism with the Holy Spirit

1. Foretold in Joel 2:28; Ezekiel 36:25–27; 39:29.

2. Joyce Meyer, *Filled with the Spirit* (Tulsa: Harrison House, 2001), 13–14.

3. Henry I. Lederle, *Treasures Old and New: Interpretations of "Spirit-Baptism" in the Charismatic Renewal Movement* (Peabody, Mass.: Hendrickson Publishers, 1988), 236.

4. Basham, *Handbook,* 120.

5. Christenson, *Speaking,* 104.

6. MacDonald, "Theology," 66.

7. John H. Osteen, "Pentecost Is Not a Denomination: It Is an Experience," *Full Gospel Business Men's Voice,* 8 (June 1960); 4–9.

8. R. Hollis Gause, "Issues in Pentecostalism," in *Perspectives on the New Pentecostalism,* ed. Russell Spittler (Grand Rapids: Baker Book House, 1976), 108.

9. Fee, "Baptism in the Holy Spirit," 87.

10. Burgess and McGee, *Dictionary,* 2.

11. Synan, *Century,* 3. Also, see Donald W. Dayton, *Theological Roots of Pentecostalism* (Peabody, Mass.: Hendrickson Publishers, 1987).

12. Discussed by Lederle, *Treasures,* 5–9.

13. Ibid., 29. Also see 11–15.

14. Gromacki, *Holy Spirit,* 149. I do not agree with James D. G. Dunn when he says: "Cornelius' experience of salvation and forgiveness was precisely that of the 120 at Pentecost, but also that the spiritual state of the 120 prior to Pentecost was precisely that of Cornelius prior to his reception of the Spirit." *Baptism,* 51. Cornelius and friends were open to hearing the Gospel, and they probably knew of Jesus' ministry in Palestine, but the disciples were already in direct, life-giving relationship with Jesus.

15. Dick Iverson, *The Holy Spirit Today* (Portland, Ore.: City Bible Publications, 1976), 41.

16. Williams, *Renewal,* 174.

17. Horton, *Bible Says,* 173.

18. Williams, *Renewal,* 212.

19. MacDonald, "Theology," 65.

20. Kevin J. Conner and Ken Malmin, *Interpreting the Scriptures* (Portland, Ore.: City Bible Publications, 1976), 119.

21. Dwight L. Niswander, *Handbook on Christian Terminology* (Author's publication, 1974), 1.

22. James Hope Moulton and George Milligan, *The Vocabulary of the Greek Testament Illustrated from the Papyri and Other Non-Literary Sources* (Grand Rapids: Eerdmans, 1976), 79.

23. Walter Bauer, *A Greek-English Lexicon of the New Testament and Other Early Christian Literature,* trans. and ed. W. F. Arndt and F. W. Gingrich (Chicago: University of Chicago Press, 1957), 109.

24. Gordon Fee, *Paul, the Spirit, and the People of God* (Peabody, Mass.: Hendrickson Publishers, 1996), ix.

25. Conner, *Understanding,* 24.

26. Holdcroft, *Holy Spirit,* 28.

27. Fee, *Presence,* 294–95.

28. The idea of listing conditions to receive the Holy Spirit has been criticized by some (as, Bruner, *Theology,* 93–111). If you feel that you received everything you need at conversion, there will, of course, be no incentive to seek the Lord for more. A person can certainly get bogged down by concentrating on things to do rather than seeking more of the Spirit of Jesus. I have seen at least a dozen lists, each reflecting the particular bias of the author. Most would list in some way the importance of: conversion, obedience, prayer and faith. The incidents in Acts that describe people receiving the Spirit do indicate that there was a spiritual hunger in the people's hearts; there was repentance and consecration; prayer was in evidence as well as worship; there was an expectancy of faith; and there was genuine openness to receive gratefully the gift that God would give.

29. Sincerely repent of your sin and make Jesus Lord and Savior of your life. If you have not been baptized in water, do so as soon as possible, keeping in mind the things mentioned in chapter 8.

30. This does not mean you must become a scholar on the subject, but you should realize the basics of the subject and understand you are seeking more than just a blessing—God Himself!

31. Use the Scripture in your prayer, such as: Luke 11:9–13; John 14:13–14, 16–17, 26; 15:7, 16; 16:23–24, 26; 1 John 5:14. Do not hesitate to be specific in asking God to fill you with His Spirit.

32. Make the adjustments to accommodate the Spirit—at least be willing to present to God your desire to be free of harmful addictions, sinful habits and bad attitudes. This is what is involved

in repentance. Dennis and Rita Bennett make a significant point in chapter 4 of *The Holy Spirit and You* about preparing to receive the Holy Spirit by renouncing all types of mind science, pagan religions and metaphysics, occult or psychic. It would be ideal if people would do this before water baptism.

33. All of us should set time to seek the Lord in prayer. This will particularly help you if you are attempting to open your mind to God's will for your life. Many Pentecostals emphasize "tarrying" as the disciples did before Pentecost. We do not see this policy mandated in Scripture, but all of us should realize the great importance of spending undistracted time in God's presence. Sometimes it helps to pray with Sprit-filled friends. Stanley Horton makes the point: "There was no necessary waiting after the Day of Pentecost." (*Bible Says,* 139). As you pray to God you should open your heart in faith and simply receive the gift that God extends to you.

34. "Without faith it is impossible to please Him, for he who comes to God must believe that He is, and that He is a rewarder of those who diligently seek Him" (Hebrews 11:6). Have expectant faith, and be fervent in your worship and seeking. As you sense the presence of the Spirit, do your best to yield yourself in open adoration. If there is weeping or trembling or a desire to cry out to God, do not be alarmed by this. To have physical reactions to God's presence is very common. In this kind of atmosphere you will find your tongue moving from an English mode into speaking in a language not previously learned. You will find yourself speaking in tongues as your heart bursts with a new love for Jesus!

Chapter 10: Amazing Episodes in Acts

1. Barclay, *Acts,* xiii.

2. There is great significance in teaching by illustration and historical record, and God has inspired Luke to write an account with historical clarity, missiological insights and theological significance. The almost total absence of tongues in the epistles (except for 1 Corinthians) does not mean tongues are not important but rather acknowledges that Luke's record is accurate, informative, exemplary and need not be revised.

3. Wagner, *Acts,* 222–23.

4. F. F. Bruce describes the Western Text: "[I]t is represented mainly by the bilingual Codex Bezae (a Graeco-Latin MS. of the Gospels and Ac., written probably in the fifth century in some part of Western Europe, possibly Sicily), the African Latin version (represented in Ac. by the sixth century Codex Floriacensis), and quotations in Tertullian, Cyprian, the Latin translation of Irenaeus, and Augustine." *The Acts of the Apostles: The Greek Text with Introduction and Commentary* (1951; reprint, Grand Rapids: Eerdmans, 1970), 41–42.

5. Simon J. Kistemaker comments: "The Scriptures of the Samaritans consisted of the five books of Moses that, in the light of the entire Old Testament, gave them only a segment of religious truth. The Jews forbade the Samaritans to worship in Jerusalem; therefore, they worshiped in their own temple on top of Mount Gerizim. They also expected the coming of the Messiah, whom they called Ta'eb." *New Testament Commentary: Exposition of the Acts of the Apostles* (Grand Rapids: Baker Book House, 1990), 295.

6. Bruner, *Theology,* 175.

7. We do not know when Peter and John discovered that Samaria lacked the outpouring of the Spirit. It appears that the report contained that information, because the senior apostles were sent, and what they did fulfilled exactly their purpose in coming.

8. Stronstad, *Charismatic Theology,* 63.

9. I disagree with James D. G. Dunn that "Luke suggests that their faith was defective" because of certain "hints" in the text. See his chapter 16 in *The Christ and the Spirit* (Grand Rapids: Eerdmans,

1998). Catholic scholar George T. Montague gives similar comment: "[T]here is some evidence in the text that Luke had reservations about the Samaritans' dispositions." *Holy Spirit,* 294.

Note that Dunn hangs his argument on *pisteuein* ("believe") with a dative object. Linguistic scholar Howard M. Ervin, I believe, has thoroughly and effectively challenged this approach with seemingly irrefutable answers and references. His whole book, in fact, is "an engaging critique of James D. G. Dunn's *Baptism in the Holy Spirit.*" *Conversion,* 28–32. Stronstad challenges Dunn's approach, calling it a "contrived interpretation." *Charismatic Theology,* 64.

10. Ervin, *Conversion,* 29.

11. Brumback, *Meaneth,* 205.

12. R. J. Knowling, "The Acts of the Apostles," in *The Expositor's Greek Testament,* vol. 2 (Grand Rapids: Eerdmans, 1951), 218. Kevin J. Conner says: "Simon's experience was external and not of the heart." He then lists nine things from the text, such as, evil thought of his heart, neither part nor lot in this matter, heart not right, told to repent, told to pray for forgiveness, gall of bitterness, bond of iniquity. Conner's conclusion: "The whole language above reveals the condition of Simon's heart, even though he had professed faith and was baptized in water." Conner and Ken Malmin, *The Book of Acts* (Portland, Ore.: City Bible Publications, 1973), 65–66.

13. F. F. Bruce says: "The nature of his belief must remain uncertain. No doubt it was sincere as far as it went, but it was superficial and inadequate." "Acts Revised," 167.

14. Dunn, *Baptism,* 66.

15. Wagner sees this episode as a "power encounter." *Acts,* 174–77.

16. Brumback, *Meaneth,* 207.

17. Lenski, *Interpretation,* 327.

18. Bruce, "Acts Revised," 169. It is noteworthy that many outstanding scholars who wrote their commentaries before the twentieth-century Pentecostal revival expressed their belief that the Samaritans spoke in tongues.

19. Horton, *Bible Says,* 155.

20. Ralph M. Riggs, *The Spirit Himself* (Springfield, Mo.: Gospel Publishing House, 1949), 52.

21. See 2 Corinthians 8:7; Ephesians 6:19; Colossians 3:19; translated "speech" in ten places. John Rea confirms this thought: "A clue in the Greek text that tongues indeed were in evidence at Samaria may be found in 8:21. . . . The word for 'matter' is Greek logos, 'word,' 'speaking' or 'kind of speaking' as in 1 Corinthians 1:5, where Paul says the Corinthians were enriched 'in all your speaking' (NIV)." *Holy Spirit,* 197–98.

22. Morgan, *Acts,* 204–5.

23. Dunn's approach is that the Samaritans had not been truly converted. Bruner feels that the Samaritan episode shows God's intention for water baptism and reception of the Spirit to be one. On this occasion—and only on this occasion—it was delayed so that the apostles could see with their own eyes and thereby confirm the acceptance of the Samaritans into the Christian community (175–76). Both arguments, it seems to me, are not conclusive.

24. Dunn, *Apostles,* 114.

25. Kistemaker, *Acts,* 312.

26. G. W. H. Lampe, "The Holy Spirit in the Writings of St. Luke," in *Studies in the Gospels,* ed. D. E. Nineham (n.p., n.d.), 198.

27. Bruce M. Metzger, *A Textual Commentary on the Greek New Testament* (New York: United Bible Societies, 1971), 360. Metzger explains the unusual text as "accidental omission" or "deliberate excision" because of its variance with the account in verses 15–18, where it is implied that the Holy Spirit was bestowed only through the laying on of the apostles' hands. Most scholars accept the shorter text, but admit the probability that the words were added "to make explicit that the baptism of the Ethiopian was followed by the Gift of the Spirit."

28. Bruce, "Acts Revised," 178.

Chapter 11: More Episodes

1. Philip Schaff, *History of the Christian Church,* vol. 1 (Grand Rapids: Eerdmans, 1950), 296.

2. Ibid., 297.

3. Ervin, *Conversion,* 42–43.

4. Schaff, *History,* 298.

5. To make a doctrinal point, an author will sometimes ignore the simple beauty and meaning of a biblical account. Some will not concede that Paul could be truly converted several days before he was baptized and received the Spirit, thereby postponing his actual time of conversion until the three days were completed. I believe that Luke realized that the three days of fasting and prayer empowered by the blinding glory of God and the voice of Jesus had somehow accomplished God's purpose. That, after all, was the main point of recording the conversion.

Some cannot make this concession because conversion, water baptism and baptism of the Spirit are considered one unified initiatory experience, and allowing for conversion to be three days before baptism would be an unacceptable time gap. I agree that the ideal occurs when the three experiences happen as one continuous event; however, it was not always that way in Acts and it is not always that way in real life. Each of the three experiences of the Peter Pattern can stand alone if need be, but the closer they are in occurrence, the greater impact on the person's initiation into the Body of Christ.

6. Dunn, *Baptism,* 74.

7. Jack W. Hayford, gen. ed., *Hayford's Bible Handbook* (Nashville/Atlanta: Thomas Nelson Publishers, 1995), 334.

8. On Pentecost the wind was an attention-getter, the fire the confirmation of God's acceptance and the lighting of the Church's candelabra. Tongues, however, was the hallmark of Pentecost and continued through the early history of the Church, reappearing dramatically in great proportion during the last one hundred years. So, of the three original signs only tongues continues as a consistent verification.

9. Brumback, *Meaneth,* 217.

10. Stronstad, *Charismatic Theology,* 66.

11. Conner, *Acts,* 76. Notice that there is no consistency in the so-called three-stage Pentecost since only two of the occasions were without laying on of hands.

12. See descriptions by Bruce, "Acts Revised," 201–3; and Kistemaker, *Acts,* 370.

13. The qualifications of a centurion are given by the historian Polybius: "Centurions are required not to be bold and adventurous so much as good leaders, of steady and prudent mind, not prone to take the offensive or start fighting wantonly, but able when overwhelmed and hard-pressed to stand fast and die at their post." Polybius, *History* 6.24.

14. Wagner, *Acts,* 222. The other two stories are Stephen's speech and death (Acts 6–7), 67 verses, and Paul's conversion (Acts 9, 22, 26), 61 verses.

15. Lenski, *Interpretation,* 393.

16. Johannes Munck, *The Anchor Bible: The Acts of the Apostles* (Garden City, N.Y.: Doubleday & Co., 1967), 96.

17. Bruce, "Acts Revised," 202.

18. Kistemaker, *Acts,* 374.

19. Bruce, "Acts Revised," 203.

20. Dunn, *Apostles,* 137.

21. Bruce, "Acts Revised," 222.

22. Private prayer for Jews was morning, noon and evening (see Psalm 55:17; Daniel 6:10). Public prayer at the Temple in Jerusalem was made at the time of the morning sacrifice and also the offering made mid-afternoon at three o'clock.

23. Parker, "Acts," 255.

24. Dunn, *Apostles,* 136.

25. Lenski comments: "Peter's is not a mild protest, nor is it a downright refusal; it is a shocked declining of the very idea . . . revealing to us the deep hold the old Jewish regulations about ceremonial cleanness had even upon the apostles, and how much was necessary to break this hold to open the door of the church to the ceremonially unclean Gentiles." *Acts,* 403.

26. Kistemaker, *Acts,* 373.

27. This succinct thought from Morgan, *Acts,* 277–79.

28. Dunn, *Apostles,* 146.

29. The spiritual experience and the speaking in tongues, but without the wind and fire of the day of Pentecost.

30. Bruce, "Acts Revised," 233.

31. This statement by Jesus is recorded in Acts 1:5. Acts 10:16 in the NASB uses this wording: "how He used to say," indicating that Jesus had repeated the saying more than once.

Chapter 12: The Spirit for All People

1. E. A. Judge, "Antioch in Syria," in *The Zondervan Pictorial Encyclopedia of the Bible,* ed. Merrill C. Tenney, vol. 1 (Grand Rapids: Zondervan, 1975), 186.

2. This breaks the pattern of a three-stage Pentecost that was poured out on Jews, Samaritans and Romans. Admittedly, the three occasions were special in their missiological import, but we must not minimize the ongoing recurrence of the Pentecostal experience in both individuals and groups—even up to this present time! Salvation, water baptism and the baptism with the Spirit are as important to us as Passover, the Red Sea and Abiding Cloud were to Israel.

3. Alexandria was one of the largest cities in the Roman Empire, second only to Rome itself. There was a very large colony of Jews there, probably larger than the population of Jews at Jerusalem.

4. Apollos's message was "The way of the Lord," an expression quoted from Isaiah 40:3 in Matthew 3:3 and Mark 1:3. God's people are to prepare a way for the Lord; Apollos, in obedience to John the Baptist's burning message, was baptized unto repentance and the expectation of the coming Messiah. Although his motives and beliefs were pure, he knew neither the meaning of the cross, nor the fact of the resurrection or the outpoured Holy Spirit.

5. G. Campbell Morgan disregards the chapter heading, making the section Acts 18:24–19:7. *Acts,* 435. This approach gives the episode full coverage.

6. Acts 18:23, 27; 19:1, 9, 30; 20:1, 7, 30; 21:4, 16.

7. These twelve undoubtedly became part of Paul's great two-year evangelistic crusade, which brought the word of the Lord Jesus to all the Jews and Greeks who dwelt in Asia (see Acts 19:10).

8. Much of the focus on interpreting this episode is upon verse 2 and how the aorist (past) participle should be translated since it is in conjunction with a main verb that is also aorist (past). The Greek is literally, "Having believed, did you receive?" Some modern versions generally take this to mean "when you believed." The King James translators took the believing to mean that it preceded the receiving: "Have you received the Holy Ghost since you believed?" Modern Greek scholars, such as Dunn, *Baptism,* 86, challenge this. Dunn gives examples from the Greek to prove his point; however, they are quite successfully countered by other Greek text examples offered by Horton, *Bible Says,* 159–62, and Ervin, *Conversion,* 61–66. The proper conclusion is probably found in a tighter analysis of the context.

9. John's baptism was certainly ordained by God and was in fact identical in element and mechanical form with Paul's baptism. Jesus knew that John's baptism was from heaven and so did Paul—but it was of a different era. W. H. Offiler comments: "The difference was not in the method or mode. There was no lack there. But there was a very vital lack and it was this lack that the Apostle supplied. The moment it was supplied the Holy Ghost witnessed the divine approbation and they were filled with the Holy Ghost and spake with other tongues. They were Baptized in the Holy Spirit." *Name,* 100.

10. Bennett, *Holy Spirit,* 27.

Chapter 13: Why the Fuss over Acts?

1. William Menzies, "Synoptic Theology: An Essay on Pentecostal Hermeneutics," *Paraclete* 13, no. 1 (winter 1979): 14. He insists that a Pentecostal theology is simply a theology that restores the experience of Pentecost to its rightful place in Christian theology.

2. J. Robertson McQuilkin, *Understanding and Applying the Bible* (Chicago: Moody Press, 1983), 63.

3. R. C. Sproul, *Knowing Scripture* (Downers Grove, Ill.: InterVarsity Press, 1977), 63.

4. Bernard Ramm, *Protestant Biblical Interpretation* (Grand Rapids: Baker Book House, 1970), 123.

5. Leland Ryken, *How to Read the Bible as Literature . . . and Get More Out of It* (Grand Rapids: Zondervan Academic Books, 1984), 25.

6. Watchman Nee, *The Normal Christian Church Life,* (n.p., n.d.), introduction.

7. Christenson, *Speaking,* 31.

8. Conner and Malmin, *Interpreting,* 85.

9. Ramm, *Protestant,* 138.

10. J. Edwin Hartill, *Principles of Biblical Hermeneutics* (Grand Rapids: Zondervan, 1947), 84.

11. McQuilkin, *Understanding,* 48.

12. Ibid., 123. Also see Louis Berkhof's discussion on "Unity and Diversity in the Bible," in *Principles of Biblical Interpretation* (Grand Rapids: Baker Book House, 1950), 53–57.

13. Hartill, *Principles,* 76.

14. Stronstad, *Charismatic Theology,* 9.

15. McQuilkin, *Understanding,* 239.

16. Ibid., 240.

Appendix: The Church Body's Diverse Views on the Baptism with the Holy Spirit

1. J. Rodman Williams, "Pentecostal Theology: A Neo-Pentecostal Viewpoint," in *Perspectives on the New Pentecostalism,* ed. Russell Spittler (Grand Rapids: Baker Book House, 1976), 79–80.

2. Veli-Matti Kärkkäinen, *Pneumatology* (Grand Rapids: Baker Academic, 2002), 97.

3. From the Apostolic Constitution on the Sacrament of Confirmation (1971).

4. John L. McKenzie, S.J., *Dictionary of the Bible* (New York: Simon & Schuster, Touchstone Books, 1965), 146.

5. Donald G. Bloesch, *The Holy Spirit* (Downers Grove, Ill.: InterVarsity Press, 2000), 53.

6. Lederle, *Treasures,* 4.

7. Walter A. Elwell, *Evangelical Dictionary of Theology,* 2d ed. (Grand Rapids: Baker Academic, 2001), 289.

8. Athanasios F. S. Emmert, "Charismatic Developments in the Eastern Orthodox Church," in *Perspectives on the New Pentecostalism,* ed. by Russell Spittler (Grand Rapids: Baker Book House, 1976), 37–38.

9. Elwell, *Dictionary,* 289.

10. Bennett, *Holy Spirit,* 15.

11. Elwell, *Dictionary,* 289.

12. Lederle, *Treasures,* 11. See pages 9–11 for an interesting discussion.

13. Eddie L. Hyatt, *2000 Years of Charismatic Christianity* (Dallas, Tex.: Hyatt International Ministries, Inc., 1996), 113–14.

14. Bloesch, *Holy Spirit,* 132–33.

15. Charles G. Finney, *Memoirs of Rev. Charles G. Finney* (New York: Fleming H. Revell Co., 1903 copyright renewed), 20–21.

16. John Gresham, *Charles G. Finney's Doctrine of the Baptism of the Holy Spirit* (Peabody, Mass.: Hendrickson Publishers, 1987), 12.

17. Ibid.

18. Dayton, *Roots,* 102.

19. Ibid.

20. R. A. Torrey, *The Baptism with the Holy Spirit* (Minneapolis: Bethany House Publishers, 1972), 25–26.

21. Gromacki, *Holy Spirit,* 171.

22. Stott, *Baptism,* 36.

23. Ray C. Stedman, "The Gift of Tongues: True or False?" *Theology, News and Notes* (March 1974): 18.

24. Lewis A. Drummond, *The Evangelist: The Worldwide Impact of Billy Graham* (Nashville: Word Publishing, 2001), 19–20. See Graham's own book *The Holy Spirit: Here Is the Power to Change Your Life* (New York: Warner Books, 1978).

25. For the most complete history on Pentecostalism see Walter J. Hollenweger, *The Pentecostals* (Peabody, Mass.: Hendrickson Publishers, 1988).

26. Lederle, *Treasures,* 66.

27. Bloesch, *Holy Spirit,* 50.

28. Ibid., 55.

29. Stronstad, *Charismatic Theology,* 40.

30. Osteen, "Pentecost," 4–9.

31. <http://www.ag.org/top/beliefs/truths_condensed.cfm>

32. Bloesch, *Holy Spirit,* 187.

33. Christenson, *Speaking,* 55.

34. Dennis Bennett, *Nine O'clock in the Morning* (Plainfield, N.J.: Logos, 1970), 23.

35. Donald L. Gelpi, "Pentecostal Theology: A Roman Catholic Viewpoint," in *Perspectives on the New Pentecostalism,* ed. Russell Spittler (Grand Rapids: Baker Book House, 1976), 87.

36. Bloesch, *Holy Spirit,* 187.

37. Kilian McDonnell, ed., *Presence, Power, Praise: Documents on the Charismatic Revival* (Collegeville, Minn.: The Liturgical Press, 1980).

38. Zeb Bradford Long and Douglas McMurray, *Receiving the Power: Preparing the Way for the Holy Spirit* (Grand Rapids: Chosen Books, 1996).

BIBLIOGRAPHY

Archer, Gleason L. *Encyclopedia of Bible Difficulties.* Grand Rapids: Zondervan, 1982.

Asch, Sholem. *The Apostle.* New York: G. Putnam's Sons, 1943.

Barclay, William. *The Acts of the Apostles.* 2d ed. Philadelphia: The Westminster Press, 1955.

Barker, Kenneth, gen. ed. *The NIV Study Bible: New International Version.* Grand Rapids: Zondervan, 1946.

Barnes, Albert. *Notes on the New Testament: Explanatory and Practical.* Vols. Luke and John. Grand Rapids: Baker Book House, 1976.

Barnett, Donald Lee, and Jeffrey McGregor. *Speaking in Other Tongues.* Seattle: Community Chapel Publications, 1986.

Basham, Don. *A Handbook on Holy Spirit Baptism.* New Kensington, Pa.: Whitaker House, 1969.

Bauer, Walter. *A Greek-English Lexicon of the New Testament and Other Early Christian Literature.* Translated and edited by W. F. Arndt and F. W. Gingrich. Chicago: University of Chicago Press, 1957.

Bennett, Dennis, and Rita Bennett. "The Gifts of the Spirit." In *The Charismatic Movement,* edited by Michael Hamilton. Grand Rapids: Eerdmans, 1975.

———. *The Holy Spirit and You.* Gainesville, Fla.: Bridge-Logos Publishers, 1971.

———. *Nine O'clock in the Morning.* Plainfield, N.J.: Logos International, 1970.

Berkhof, Louis. *Principles of Biblical Interpretation.* Grand Rapids: Baker Book House, 1950.

Bloesch, Donald G. *The Holy Spirit: Works & Gifts.* Downers Grove, Ill.: InterVarsity Press, 2000.

Brown, Raymond E. *The Birth of the Messiah.* New York: Doubleday, 1977.

———. "The Paraclete in the Fourth Gospel." *NTS* 13 (1966–67): 113–32.

Bruce, F. F. *The Acts of the Apostles: The Greek Text with Introduction and Commentary.* 1951. Reprint, Grand Rapids: Eerdmans, 1970.

———. "The Acts of the Apostles." In *The New Bible Commentary,* edited by D. Guthrie and J. A. Motyer. Grand Rapids: Eerdmans, 1970.

———. *Answers to Questions.* Grand Rapids: Zondervan, 1973.

———. "The Book of Acts Revised." In *The New International Commentary on the New Testament.* Grand Rapids: Eerdmans, 1988.

———. "The Epistles to the Colossians, to Philemon, and to the Ephesians." In *The New International Commentary on the New Testament.* Grand Rapids: Eerdmans, 1984.

———. *The Gospel of John.* Grand Rapids: Eerdmans, 1983.

———. *The New Testament Development of Old Testament Themes.* Grand Rapids: Eerdmans, 1983.

Brumback, Carl. *What Meaneth This?* Springfield, Mo.: Gospel Publishing House, 1947.

Bruner, Frederick Dale. *A Theology of the Holy Spirit.* Grand Rapids: Eerdmans, 1970.

Bullinger, E. W. *Number in Scripture.* 1894. Reprint, Grand Rapids: Kregel Publications, 1973.

———. *Word Studies on the Holy Spirit: A complete concordance and concise commentary on every occurrence of pneuma (Spirit) in the New Testament.* Grand Rapids: Kregel Publications, 1979.

Burgess, Stanley M. *The Spirit & the Church: Antiquity.* Peabody, Mass.: Hendrickson Publishers, 1984.

Burgess, Stanley M., and Gary B. McGee, ed. *Dictionary of Pentecostal and Charismatic Movements.* Grand Rapids: Zondervan, 1988.

———. "Medieval Examples of Charismatic Piety in the Roman Catholic Church." In *Perspectives on the New Pentecostalism,* edited by Russell Spittler. Grand Rapids: Baker Book House, 1976.

Canty, George. *Hallmarks of Pentecost: Discerning the True Spiritual Gifts.* London: Marshall Pickering, 1989.

Christenson, Larry. *Speaking in Tongues.* Minneapolis: Dimension Books, 1975.

Conner, Kevin J. *Understanding and Distinguishing the New Birth and the Baptism of the Holy Spirit.* Victoria, Australia: K.J.C. Publications, 1998.

Conner, Kevin J. *The Book of Acts.* Portland, Ore.: City Bible Publications, 1973.

———— and Ken Malmin. *Interpreting the Scriptures.* Portland, Ore.: City Bible Publications, 1976.

Dayton, Donald W. *Theological Roots of Pentecostalism.* Peabody, Mass.: Hendrickson, 1987.

Drummond, Lewis. *The Evangelist: The Worldwide Impact of Billy Graham.* Nashville: Word Publishing, 2001.

————. *Spurgeon: Prince of Preachers.* Grand Rapids: Kregel Publications, 1992.

Dunn, James D. G. *The Acts of the Apostles.* Valley Forge, Pa.: Trinity Press International, 1996.

————. *Baptism in the Holy Spirit.* Philadelphia: The Westminster Press, 1970.

————. *The Christ & the Spirit.* Grand Rapids: Eerdmans, 1998.

————. *Jesus and the Spirit.* Philadelphia: The Westminster Press, 1975.

Edersheim, Alfred. *The Life and Times of Jesus the Messiah.* Vol. I. Grand Rapids: Eerdmans, 1950.

————. *The Temple: Its Ministry and Services.* Updated ed. Peabody, Mass.: Hendrickson Publishers, 1994.

Elbert, Paul, ed. *Essays on Apostolic Themes: Studies in Honor of Howard M. Ervin.* Peabody, Mass.: Hendrickson Publishers, 1985.

Elwell, Walter A. *Evangelical Dictionary of Theology.* 2d ed. Grand Rapids: Baker Academic, 2001.

Emmert, Athanasiaos. "Charismatic Developments in the Eastern Orthodox Church." In *Perspectives on the New Pentecostalism,* edited by Russell Spittler. Grand Rapids: Baker Book House, 1976.

Erickson, Millard J. *The Concise Dictionary of Christian Theology.* Rev. ed. Wheaton: Crossway Books, 2001.

Ervin, Howard M. *Conversion-Initiation and the Baptism in the Holy Spirit: An Engaging Critique of James D. G. Dunn's Baptism in the Holy Spirit.* Peabody, Mass.: Hendrickson Publishers, 1984.

Ewert, David. *The Holy Spirit in the New Testament.* Kitchener, Ontario: Herald Press, 1983.

Fee, Gordon. "Baptism in the Holy Spirit: The Issue of Separability and Subsequence." *Pneuma: The Journal of the Society for Pentecostal Studies* 7, no. 2 (fall 1985): 87–99.

———. *God's Empowering Presence: The Holy Spirit in the Letters of Paul.* Peabody, Mass.: Hendrickson Publishers, 1994.

———. "Hermeneutics and Historical Precedent—A Major Problem in Pentecostal Hermeneutics." In *Perspectives on the New Pentecostalism,* edited by Russell Spittler. Grand Rapids: Baker Book House, 1976.

———. *Paul, the Spirit, and the People of God.* Peabody, Mass.: Hendrickson Publishers, 1996.

First Principles: A Study of the Elementary Principles of Christ. Grand Prairie, Tex.: Shady Grove Church Publications, 1989.

Forbes, Christopher. *Prophecy and Inspired Speech: In Early Christianity and Its Hellenistic Environment.* Peabody, Mass.: Hendrickson Publishers, 1997.

Garrard, Alec. *The Splendor of the Temple: A Pictorial Guide to Herod's Temple and Its Ceremonies.* Grand Rapids: Kregel Publications, 2000.

Gause, R. Hollis. "Issues in Pentecostalism." In *Perspectives on the New Pentecostalism,* edited by Russell Spittler. Grand Rapids: Baker Book House, 1976.

Gelpi, Donald L. "Breath-Baptism in the Synoptics." In *Charismatic Experiences in History.* Edited by Cecil M. Robeck Jr. Peabody, Mass.: Hendrickson, 1985.

———. "Pentecostal Theology: A Roman Catholic Viewpoint." In *Perspectives on the New Pentecostalism,* edited by Russell Spittler. Grand Rapids: Baker Book House, 1976.

Gentile, Ernest. *Awaken the Dawn!* 1990. Reprint, Columbus, Ga.: The Eastwood Company Publications, 2001.

———. *Worship God! Exploring the Dynamics of Psalmic Worship.* Portland, Ore.: City Bible Publications, 1994.

———. *Your Sons and Daughters Shall Prophesy.* Grand Rapids: Chosen Books, 1999.

Graham, Billy. *The Holy Spirit: Here Is the Power to Change Your Life.* New York: Warner Books, 1978.

Green, Michael. *I Believe in the Holy Spirit.* Grand Rapids: Eerdmans, 1975.

Gresham, John L. Jr. *Charles G. Finney's Doctrine of the Baptism of the Holy Spirit.* Peabody, Mass.: Hendrickson Publishers, 1987.

Gromacki, Robert. *The Holy Spirit: Who He Is What He Does.* Nashville: Word Publishing, 1999.

Grosheide, F. W. *Commentary on the First Epistle to the Corinthians.* Grand Rapids: Eerdmans, 1953.

Hall, William Phillips. *A Remarkable Biblical Discovery or "The Name" of God According to the Scriptures.* New York: American Tract Society, 1929.

Halley, Henry H. *Halley's Bible Handbook.* 24th ed. Grand Rapids: Zondervan, 1965.

Harris, Ralph W. *Spoken by the Spirit.* Springfield, Mo.: Gospel Publishing House, 1973.

Hartill, J. Edwin. *Principles of Biblical Hermeneutics.* Grand Rapids: Zondervan, 1947.

Hayford, Jack. *The Beauty of Spiritual Language.* Nashville: Thomas Nelson Publishers, 1996.

———. gen. ed. *Hayford's Bible Handbook.* Nashville: Thomas Nelson Publishers, 1995.

Henry, Matthew. *Matthew Henry's Commentary on the Whole Bible.* Vol. 6. Reprint, Fleming H. Revell Co. N.p., n.d.

Hickey, Marilyn. *He Will Give You Another Helper.* Tulsa: Harrison House, 2001.

Hodge, Charles. *Commentary on the First Epistle to the Corinthians.* Grand Rapids: Eerdmans, 1969.

Holdcroft, L. Thomas. *The Holy Spirit: A Pentecostal Interpretation.* Rev. ed. Abbottsford, Canada: CeeTeC Publishing, 1999.

Hollenweger, Walter J. *The Pentecostals.* Peabody, Mass.: Hendrickson, 1988.

Horton, Stanley M. *What the Bible Says About the Holy Spirit.* Springfield, Mo.: Gospel Publishing House, 1997.

Hunter, Harold D. *Spirit-Baptism: A Pentecostal Alternative.* Lanham, Md.: University Press of America, 1983.

Hyatt, Eddie L. *2000 Years of Charismatic Christianity.* Dallas: Hyatt International Ministries, 1996.

Iverson, Dick. *The Holy Spirit Today.* Portland, Ore.: City Bible Publications, 1974.

Josephus, Flavius. "The Wars of the Jews." In *The Works of Josephus,* translated by William Whiston. Lynn, Mass.: Hendrickson Publishers, 1980.

Judge, E. A. "Antioch in Syria." In *The Zondervan Pictorial Encyclopedia of the Bible,* edited by Merrill C. Tenney. Vol. 1. Grand Rapids: Zondervan, 1975.

Kärkkäinen, Veli-Matti. *Pneumatology.* Grand Rapids: Baker Academic, 2002.

Keller, Phillip W. *Rabboni . . . which is to say, Master.* Old Tappan, N.J.: Fleming H. Revell Co., 1971.

Kistemaker, Simon J. *New Testament Commentary: Exposition of the Acts of the Apostles.* Grand Rapids: Baker Book House, 1990.

———. *New Testament Commentary: Exposition of the First Epistle to the Corinthians.* Grand Rapids: Baker Books, 1993.

Kydd, Ronald A. N. *Charismatic Gifts in the Early Church: An Exploration into the Gifts of the Spirit During the First Three Centuries of the Christian Church.* Peabody, Mass.: Hendrickson Publishers, 1984.

Ladd, George Eldon. *A Theology of the New Testament.* Grand Rapids: Eerdmans, 1974.

Lampe, G. W. H. "The Holy Spirit in the Writings of St. Luke." In *Studies in the Gospels,* edited by D. E. Nineham. 1998.

Lamsa, George M. *Gospel Light: Comments on the Teaching of Jesus from Aramaic and Unchanging Eastern Customs.* Rev. ed. Philadelphia: A. J. Holman Co., 1936.

Lederle, H. I. *Treasures Old and New: Interpretations of "Spirit-Baptism" in the Charismatic Renewal Movement.* Peabody, Mass.: Hendrickson Publishers, 1988.

Lenski, R. C. H. *The Interpretation of the Acts of the Apostles.* Minneapolis: Augsburg Publishing House, 1934.

Lockyer, Herbert. *All the Divine Names and Titles in the Bible.* Grand Rapids: Zondervan, 1975.

Long, Zeb Bradford, and Douglas McMurray. *Receiving the Power: Preparing the Way for the Holy Spirit.* Grand Rapids: Chosen Books, 1996.

Lovelace, Richard. "Baptism in the Holy Spirit and the Evangelical Tradition." *Pneuma: The Journal of the Society for Pentecostal Studies* 7, no. 1 (fall 1985), 101–23.

Lovett, C. S. *Lovett's Lights on Acts.* Baldwin Park, Calif.: Personal Christianity, 1972.

MacDonald, William G. "Pentecostal Theology: A Classical Viewpoint." In *Perspectives on the New Pentecostalism,* edited by Russell Spittler. Grand Rapids: Baker Book House, 1976.

Mare, H. Harold. "1 Corinthians." In *The Expositor's Bible Commentary,* general editor Frank E. Gaebelein. Vol. 10. Grand Rapids: Zondervan, 1976.

Marshall, Catherine. *The Helper.* Waco: Word Books, 1978.

Marshall, I. Howard. "The Gospel of Luke: A Commentary on the Greek Text." In *New International Greek Testament Commentary.* Grand Rapids: Eerdmans, 1978.

Maynard, James. *I Believe in the Holy Ghost.* Minneapolis: Bethany, 1965.

McDonnell, Kilian, ed. *Presence, Power, Praise: Documents on the Charismatic Renewal.* Vols. 1, 2, 3. Collegeville, Minn.: The Liturgical Press, 1980.

McKenzie, John L., S.J. *Dictionary of the Bible.* New York: Simon & Schuster, A Touchstone Book, 1965.

McQuilkin, J. Robertson. *Understanding and Applying the Bible.* Chicago: Moody Press, 1983.

Meloon, Marion. *Ivan Spencer: Willow in the Wind.* Plainfield, N.J.: Logos, 1974.

Menzies, William. "Synoptic Theology: An Essay on Pentecostal Hermeneutics." *Paraclete* 13, no. 1 (winter 1979): 14.

Metzger, Bruce M. *A Textual Commentary on the Greek New Testament.* New York: United Bible Societies, 1971.

Meyer, Joyce. *Filled with the Spirit: Understanding God's Power in Your Life.* Tulsa, Okla.: Harrison House, 2001.

Montague, George T. *The Holy Spirit: Growth of a Biblical Tradition.* New York: Paulist Press, 1976.

Morgan, G. Campbell. *The Acts of the Apostles.* Fleming H. Revell Co., 1924.

———. *The Crises of the Christ.* 1903. Reprint, Old Tappan, N.J.: Fleming H. Revell Co.

———. *Great Chapters of the Bible.* London: Marshall, Morgan & Scott, 1946.

Moule, C. F. D. *The Holy Spirit.* Grand Rapids: Eerdmans, 1978.

Moulton, James Hope, and George Milligan. *The Vocabulary of the Greek Testament Illustrated from the Papyri and Other Non-Literary Sources.* Grand Rapids: Eerdmans, 1976.

Mullins, E. Y. "Holy Spirit." In *The International Standard Bible Encyclopedia,* general editor James Orr. Vol. 3. Grand Rapids: Eerdmans, 1974.

Munck, Johannes. *The Anchor Bible: The Acts of the Apostles.* Garden City, N.Y.: Doubleday and Co., 1967.

Niswander, Dwight L. *Handbook on Christian Terminology.* Author's publication, 1974.

Offiler, W. H. *God and His Name: A Message for Today.* Seattle: Bethel Temple, 1932.

Osteen, John H. "Pentecost Is Not a Denomination: It Is an Experience." *Full Gospel Business Men's Voice* 8 (June 1960): 4–9.

Packer, J. I. *Keep in Step with the Spirit.* Grand Rapids: Fleming H. Revell Co., 1984.

———. *"Tekton."* In *The New International Dictionary of New Testament Theology,* edited by Colin Brown. Vol. 1. Grand Rapids: Eerdmans, 1975.

Parker, Joseph. "Acts I–XII." In *Preaching Through the Bible.* Vol. 23. Grand Rapids: Baker Book House, 1978.

Pink, Arthur W. *The Holy Spirit.* Grand Rapids: Baker Book House, 1970.

Plummer, Alfred. "The Gospel According to St. Luke." In *The International Critical Commentary.* 1896. Reprint, Edinburgh: T & T Clark, 1951.

Prince, Derek. *The Holy Spirit in You.* New Kensington, Pa.: Whitaker House, 1987.

Ramm, Bernard. *Protestant Biblical Interpretation.* Grand Rapids: Baker Book House, 1970.

Rea, John. *The Holy Spirit in the Bible: All the Major Passages About the Spirit.* Lake Mary, Fla.: Creation House, 1990.

Richards, Lawrence O. *The Illustrated Concise Handbook.* Nashville: Thomas Nelson, 2000.

Riggs, Ralph M. *The Spirit Himself.* Springfield, Mo.: Gospel Publishing House, 1949.

Robeck, Cecil M., ed. *Charismatic Experiences in History.* Peabody, Mass.: Hendrickson Publishers, 1985.

Robertson, A. T. *Word Pictures in the New Testament.* Vols. 1, 2, 3. Nashville: Broadman Press, 1934.

Schaff, Philip. *History of the Christian Church.* Vol. 1. Grand Rapids: Eerdmans, 1950.

Shady Grove Publications. "Baptisms." In *First Principles.* Grand Prairie, Tex.: Shady Grove Church Publications, 1989.

Sheen, Fulton J. *Life of Christ.* New York: McGraw-Hill Book Company, Inc., 1958.

Shephard, J. W. *The Christ of the Gospels.* Grand Rapids: Eerdmans, 1939.

Sherrill, John L. *They Speak with Other Tongues: The Dramatic Story of the Age-Old Miracle Coming True Today.* Old Tappan, N.J.: Fleming H. Revell Co., 1964.

Shibley, David. "Four Christian Wonders." *Update* (Nov.–Dec. 2002): 1.

Simpson, A. B. *The Holy Spirit: Power from on High.* Camp Hill, Pa.: Christian Publications, 1994.

Smith, Wilbur. *Peloubet's Select Notes on the International Bible Lessons 1961.* Natick, Mass.: W. A. Wilde Company, 1960.

Spittler, Russell. "Glossolalia." In *Dictionary of Pentecostal and Charismatic Movements,* edited by Stanley M. Burgess and Gary B. McGee. Grand Rapids: Zondervan, 1988.

———, ed. *Perspectives on the New Pentecostalism.* Grand Rapids: Baker Book House, 1976.

Sproul, R. C. *Knowing Scripture.* Downers Grove, Ill.: InterVarsity Press, 1977.

Spurgeon, Charles. *Holy Spirit Power.* New Kensington, Pa.: Whitaker House, 1996.

Stanley, Charles F. *Charles Stanley's Handbook for Christian Living: Biblical Answers to Life's Tough Questions.* Nashville: Thomas Nelson Publishers, 1996.

Stedman, Ray C. "The Gift of Tongues: True or False?" *Theology, New and Notes* (March 1974): 18.

Stott, John R. *Baptism & Fullness: The Work of the Holy Spirit Today.* 2d ed. Downers Grove, Ill.: InterVarsity Press, 1964.

Stronstad, Roger. *The Charismatic Theology of St. Luke.* Peabody, Mass.: Hendrickson, 1984.

Swete, Henry Barclay. *The Holy Spirit in the New Testament.* 1910. Reprint, Grand Rapids: Baker Book House, 1976.

Synan, Vinson. *The Century of the Holy Spirit: 100 Years of Pentecostal and Charismatic Renewal, 1901–2001.* Nashville: Thomas Nelson, 2001.

Thompson, Torger G., and Zola Levitt. *The Miracle at Pentecost: Creation of a Masterpiece.* Dallas: Biblical Arts Center, circa 1981.

Torrey, R. A. *The Baptism with the Holy Spirit.* Minneapolis: Bethany House Publishers, 1972.

———. *The Person and Work of the Holy Spirit.* New Kensington, Pa.: Whitaker House, 1996.

Truscott, Graham. *The Only Foundation.* 3d ed. San Diego: Restoration Temple, 1987.

———. *You Shall Receive Power.* Poona, India: New Life Centre, 1967.

Turner, Max. *The Holy Spirit and Spiritual Gifts.* 1966. Reprint, Peabody, Mass.: Hendrickson Publishers, 1998.

Vine, W. E. *Expository Dictionary of New Testament Words.* Westwood, N.J.: Fleming H. Revell Co., 1966.

Wagner, C. Peter. *Acts of the Holy Spirit.* Ventura, Calif.: Regal, 1994.

———. *Spheres of Authority.* Colorado Springs: Wagner Publications, 2002.

Ward, Kaari, ed. *Jesus and His Times.* Pleasantville, N.Y.: Reader's Digest Association, Inc., 1987.

Williams, J. Rodman. "Pentecostal Theology: A Neo-Pentecostal Viewpoint." In *Perspectives on the New Pentecostalism,* edited by Russell Spittler. Grand Rapids: Baker Book House, 1976.

———. *Renewal Theology: Systematic Theology from a Charismatic Perspective.* Vol. 2. Grand Rapids: Zondervan, 1990.

Wuest, Kenneth S. *Wuest's Word Studies from the Greek New Testament.* Vols. 1–4. 1973. Reprint, Grand Rapids: Eerdmans, 2002.

SUBJECT INDEX

Acts, 160–61, 167–68, 172–73, 179–92, 193–209, 222, 223–28
adoption, 152
Africa, 109
Aland, Kurt, 252n26
Alexandria, 216, 259n3
Ananias, 186, 187, 196–97, 198–99
Anglican church, 230
anointing, 43, 49, 165, 169
Antioch, 182, 212–15
Apollos, 216, 259n4
Apostolic Church, 236
Aquila, 216
"ascetic model" of Christianity, 160
Asch, Sholem, 72, 247n3
Asians, 194
Assemblies of God, 236, 237–38, 251n18
authority, 49

Balaam, 44
baptism, 142, 159
of fire, 94, 253n6
    into Moses, 144–45
    in the New Testament, 142–43
    twofold fulfillment, 96–97
baptism with the Holy Spirit, 13, 15–16, 18, 43, 75, 94–95, 100, 106, 120, 128, 139, 140, 141, 157–75, 208, 218, 219–20, 223
Barclay, William, 57, 91, 179
bar-mitzvah, 29
Barnabas, 212–13
Barnes, Albert, 58, 63, 64
Barnett, Donald Lee, 248n20
Basham, Don, 117, 161
Bennett, Dennis, 109, 118, 219, 231, 238–39, 255n32
Bennett, Rita, 255n32
Bereans, 222
Bethlehem, 26, 27
Bezalel, 44
Bible:
    inspiration, 53, 222, 225
    as literature, 224–25
    organic unity, 226
blasphemy, of Holy Spirit, 52
Bloesch, Donald G., 232, 237, 238
blood, 144, 165, 253n7
Body of Christ, 147
born again, 14, 34
    see also conversion
Brown, Raymond E., 32
Bruce, F. F., 56, 188, 192, 201, 202, 245n4(2), 248n20, 256n4, 257n13

Brumback, Carl, 115, 116, 186, 198
Bruner, F. Dale, 113, 184, 243n3
burial, 142, 153
burning bush, 87

Caesarea, 200, 205–7
call, 40–42
candelabra, 100, 258n8
Canty, George, 115
casting out devils, 214
Catholic Church, 207, 230
Catholic Pentecostal movement, 239
charismatic gifts, 131–32
charismatic movement, 11, 163, 238, 240
Charismatic Presbyterians, 239
Chinese, 108, 110
chrismation, 231
Christ (title), 24, 43, 254n18
Christenson, Larry, 124, 225, 238, 250n5(2)
Christian baptism, 218
Christian and Missionary Alliance, 232
Christian (name), 24
church, 50, 100
caste system in, 133
    established, 163
    and Holy Spirit, 60
    maturity, 131–32
    persecution of, 195
Church of God (Anderson, Indiana), 232
Church of God in Christ, 236
Church of God (Cleveland), 236
Church of the Nazarene, 232
circumcision of heart, 154
cleanliness, laws of, 202–3
cleansing, 150, 253n6
comforter, 57, 58
condemnation, 153–54
confirmation, 230, 231
Conner, Kevin J., 149, 168, 171, 226, 257n12
conscience, 153–54
consoler, 58
context, 226
conversion, 18, 139, 140, 141, 148, 149–52, 158, 162, 165–67, 235
    as form of baptism, 142
Corinth, 130, 183, 215

Cornelius, 169, 182, 191, 200–207, 213, 255n14
Council at Jerusalem, 200, 211–15
counselor, 57, 58
counterfeits, 126
Court of the Gentiles, 78
Court of Israel, 79
Court of Prayer, 79
Court of the Priests, 79
Court of the Women, 78–79, 113
covenant renewal, 83
cross, 132
cults, 126

Damascus, 195
David, 45
Dayton, Donald W., 234
deeper life movements, 163
devil, and tongues, 126
Diaspora, 72, 80, 88, 90, 92
disciples, 55–56, 165–66, 217
doctrine, 180
Doeve, J. W., 31
dove, 43, 88
Dunn, James D. G., 83, 187, 190, 202, 204, 206, 243n3, 249n28, 255n14, 256–57n9, 257n23, 259n8
du Plessis, David, 12, 106, 160
Duquesne University, 239

early rain, 163
earnest, 169–70
Eastern Orthodox Church, 230
Edersheim, Alfred, 28–29, 83, 248n9
edification, 134
Elijah, 48
Elisha, 48
Elizabeth, 25–26, 35
Emmert, Athanasios F. S., 230
emotions, 125–26
empowerment, 159, 162, 164, 171, 241
encounter, with Jesus Christ, 106
encourager, 57
endowment with power, 18
enduement, 170
energy, 174
enthusiasm, 97

Ephesus, 129–30, 169, 183, 214–19
Episcopal Church, 231
Erickson, Millard J., 152
Ervin, Howard M., 133, 148, 196, 243n3, 256–57n9
Ethiopia, 192, 194
Ethiopian eunuch, 182, 185, 187, 189–92, 199, 201, 202
evangelicals, 235, 240
Ewert, David, 86
Exodus, 144–45
experience, 162, 180
Ezekiel, 44

faith, 127
falling upon, 170
family of God, 152
Feast of Tabernacles, 82, 174
Feast of Weeks, 82, 165
feasts, 82, 174
Fee, Gordon D., 17, 117, 118, 163, 170, 172
"filled with the Spirit", 17, 24, 44, 89, 97–98, 111, 128–29
filling, 128, 171
Finney, Charles G., 164, 216, 232, 233–34, 241
fire, 86–87, 88, 89, 93–102, 233, 253n6
firstfruits, 171
flesh, 132
Fletcher, John, 164, 232
Forbes, Christopher, 251n6
forgiveness, 154
Foursquare Gospel, 236
freedom, 47
Free Methodist Church, 232
friend, 57
fruit of the Spirit, 111
Fuller, Charles E., 14
Full Mention Principle, 168, 227

Gabriel, 25–26, 41
Galatia, 215
Garrard, Alec, 78
Gee, Donald, 167
Gelpi, Donald L., 239, 249n25
Gentile Pentecost, 209
Gentiles, 113, 194, 199, 200–209

gibberish, 108, 250n5(2)
gifts, 118, 171
gifts of the Spirit. *See* spiritual gifts
giving, 118
God:
    authority, 154–55
    divine presence, 99
    of fire, 98
    habitations of, 99–100
    will, 124
grace, 151–52
Graham, Billy, 235–36, 241
Great Commission, and tongues, 112–13
Greeks, 194
Green, Michael, 60, 64
Gresham, John, 233
Gromacki, Robert, 166, 235, 249n27

Haggai, 101
Hall, William Phillips, 254n18
Hartill, J. Edwin, 226, 227
harvest, 82
Hayford, Jack, 108
healing, 48, 50
Hebrew prophets, 85, 113
helper, 57, 61, 62
    see also parakletos
hermeneutics, 221, 222–28
Herod, 27, 75, 200
Higher Life movement, 165
historical narrative, 225
Holdcroft, L. Thomas, 44, 172, 253n6
holiness, 154
holiness churches, 163, 231–32, 240
Holy Spirit:
    in Acts, 172–73, 179–92
    as "another Jesus", 60
    and baptism, 146–48
    and church, 60
    descent of, 80–81
    divine characteristics, 45–46
    how to receive, 173–74
    illumination of, 101
    in Old Testament, 44, 53, 85
    outpouring of, 75
    prayer in, 116–17
    proceeds, 65

promise of, 53
as prosecutor, 65–66
as revealer, 66–68
as teacher and remembrancer, 63–65
witness of, 65, 150
see also baptism with the Holy Spirit
Horton, Stanley M., 96, 167, 188, 253n10,
    256n33, 259n8
Hunter, Harold D., 243n3
Hyatt, Eddie L., 232
hypocrites, 127

illegitimate identity transfer, 227
illumination, 65, 101
image of God, 151
immediate evidence, 237
incarnation, 150
Indonesia, 108
indwelling, 63, 171
initial evidence, 167–69
inspired worship, 112
Irving, Edward, 164
Iverson, Dick, 166

James, 213
James, Maynard, 249n31
Jerusalem, 29–30, 71–72, 73–74, 78, 168,
    182
Jerusalem Council, 200
Jesus:
    baptism, 42–43, 98, 128
    baptism with the Holy Spirit, 33, 34,
        88, 165
    as bridegroom, 152
    childhood, 22–23, 27–32, 34
    death and resurrection, 153, 223
    dedication, 79
    deity, 222
    Farewell Discourse, 61–68, 74
    glorified, 54
    humility, 23–24, 33
    incarnation, 23–24
    intercession in heaven, 62, 66, 246n23
    Lordship, 196, 218, 254n18
    messianic consciousness, 35–36
    ministry in the Spirit, 25–37, 46–48,
        49–51

miracles, 49–50
obedience, 34, 54
personal return, 223
presence made universal, 59–60
second blessing, 128
speaking in tongues, 50–51
teaching on Holy Spirit, 16, 24, 51–54,
    74, 246n22
in the Temple, 35
Jews, 194, 199
John, gospel of, 17
John the Baptist, 25–26, 35, 40–42, 88,
    94–95, 142, 152, 159, 208, 216–19,
    253n4, 259n9
Joppa, 203
Jordan, 42–43
Joseph (husband of Mary), 26–32, 33, 79
Joshua, 44
joy, 174, 191
Judge, E. A., 212
Judges, 44
judgment, 96, 99
justification, 151

Kärkkäinen, Veli-Matti, 230
Keller, W. Phillip, 30, 47
Keswick movement, 164, 165, 236
keys of the Kingdom, 206
Kingdom of God, 42, 51, 253n4
Kistemaker, Simon J., 146, 191, 205, 256n5
Kydd, Ronald A. N., 131

Ladd, George E., 94, 96
Lampe, G. W. H., 191
lamps, 100–101
Lamsa, George M., 40
languages, 90, 92, 107, 114, 118, 237,
    250–51n5
last days, 81
Last Supper, 55, 59
latter rain, 164
Lederle, H. I., 160, 237
Lenski, R. C. H., 84, 188, 201, 248n22,
    258n25
Levitical system, 165
liberation, 48
lifestyle, 162

Lockyer, Herbert, 86
Long, Zeb Bradford, 239
Lovett, C. S., 111
Luke, 17, 173, 180, 198, 201, 223–24,
    256n2
Lutheran Church, 231
Lydia, 182, 186

MacDonald, William G., 116, 168
marriage, 152
Marshall, Catherine, 56, 59
Marshall, I. Howard, 29, 48
martyrdom, 84
Mary (mother of Jesus), 25–32, 33, 35, 79
McDonnell, Kilian, 239
McGregor, Jeffrey, 248n20
McMurray, Douglas, 239
McQuilkin, J. Robertson, 224, 226, 227
Meloon, Marion, 109
Messiah, 24, 35–36, 41, 46, 217, 254n18
Methodist Church, 163, 232
Metzger, Bruce M., 257n27
Meyer, F. B., 99
Meyer, Joyce, 159
miracles, 49–50, 131, 188, 222
missionaries, 108–9
Montague, George T., 56, 256n9
Moody, Dwight L., 164, 232, 234, 241
Moody Bible Institute, 234
Morgan, G. Campbell, 24, 81, 84, 90, 189,
    259n5
Moses, 144–45, 254n18
Moule, C. F. D., 57
Munck, Johannes, 201

Nazareth, 22, 24, 27, 28, 32, 34, 47
Nee, Watchman, 225
neo-Pentecostals, 239, 240
new beginning, 149–50
new birth, 18, 43, 51, 235
new covenant, 154
new heart, 151
new life, 86, 149, 235
Nicodemus, 47, 51, 86
Niswander, Dwight L., 169
nutrition, 12

Offiler, W. H., 254n18, 259n9
oil, 101, 165, 169
old life, 153, 154
Old Testament, 44, 53, 165, 217
Olford, Steven, 236
"on fire for God", 93–94, 97
Open Bible Standard, 236
Osteen, John, 162, 237
outpouring, 170, 171
overflowing, 171
Ozman, Agnes, 167

parakletos, 56–58, 60, 61, 74
Parham, Charles, 167
Parker, Joseph, 72, 98, 203
Passover, 29–30, 82, 144–45, 165, 174,
    253n7
Patterson, W. W., 108
Paul, 17, 33, 212–13, 214–19, 254n19
    see also Saul
Paul VI, Pope, 230
peace, 174
Pentecost, 16, 17, 50, 61, 65, 72, 80–92,
    94, 95, 105, 114, 160–61, 165, 174,
    182, 197, 208
    agricultural significance, 82–83
    historical significance, 83
    practical significance, 83
Pentecostal century, 243n1(1)
Pentecostal hermeneutic, 223
Pentecostal Holiness, 236
"Pentecostal model" of Christianity, 160
Pentecostal movement, 11, 115, 162, 163,
    167, 236–38, 240
personal evidence, 111–12
Peter, 197–98, 202–9, 213–14
Peter Pattern, 17, 139–55, 163, 173, 174–
    75, 181–83, 193, 201, 206, 217,
    219, 224, 226, 228, 252n1(2), 258n5
Philip, 183, 185–86, 187, 188–92, 201
Philippi, 182, 183
Philippian jailer, 186
Philippines, 207
pietism, 163
Pink, Arthur W., 249n27
Plummer, Alfred, 31

Polybius, 258n13
power, 86
power encounter, 187
powers of evil, 47
praise, 112
prayer, 84, 106, 112, 116–18, 134, 161
preaching, 49
Presbyterians, 239
Prince, Derek, 59
Priscilla, 216
proclamation, 48
promise, 171
prophecy, 53, 114, 188
prophets, 45, 85
Psalms, 36
Puritans, 164

Ramm, Bernard, 224, 226
Rapp, Eugene, 250–51n5
Rea, John, 24, 56, 247n2, 248n20, 249n32,
    257n21
rebellion, against Holy Spirit, 46
receiving, 172, 173–74
Rees, Paul S., 102
Reformed Sealers, 164
regeneration, 75, 86, 149, 162
rejoicing, 191
renewal, 151
repentance, 42, 140, 152, 154, 217, 218,
    253n4
restorationist movement, 163
resurrection, 150, 153
revival, 216
revivalists, 164, 232–35, 240
Riggs, Ralph M., 188
Robertson, A. T., 31, 46, 90
Rodale, J. I., 58
Roman Catholic Church, 230
Romans, 194
Ryken, Leland, 225

sacramentalists, 229–31, 240
sacrifice, 99
salvation, 18, 74, 151
Salvation Army, 232
Samaritans, 168, 182, 183–87, 188, 191,
    194, 199, 256n7, 257n23

Samaritan woman, 47, 52
sanctification, 18, 154, 161, 164
Sanhedrin, 195
Satan, 46–47
Saul:
    conversion of, 168–69, 182, 194–97
    reception of Holy Spirit, 187, 197–99
    speaking in tongues, 197–98
    see also Paul
Saul (king), 44
Schaff, Philip, 194
sealing, 172
second blessing, 128, 158, 164–65, 231–32
Sell, David, 110
seminaries, 11
Sermon on the Mount, 36
service, 18
shamans, 126
Sheen, Fulton J., 59, 88
Shekinah, 87
Shepard, J. W., 30, 73
Shibley, David, 151
Simeon, 35
Simon, the magician, 187–89
simony, 187
Simpson, A. B., 57
Smith, Wilbur, 57
Solomon's Porch, 79, 84
Son of Man, 244n4
sorcery, 187
sound, 91
South America, 145
Spencer, Carlton, 109
Spirit-baptism. See baptism with the Holy
    Spirit
spiritual birth. See new birth
spiritual gifts, 50, 131–32, 223, 251n22
spiritual language, 108
spiritual maturity, 131–32, 140
spiritual truths, 64–65
Spittler, R., 107
Sproul, R. C., 224
Spurgeon, Charles, 64–65, 101–2
Stanley, Charles, 130, 134
Stedman, Ray C., 235
Stephen, 195
Stevens Street Mission (Spokane, Wash.), 14

Stott, John R. W., 235, 252n2(2)
Stronstad, Roger, 227, 237, 249n29
subsequence, 162–66, 237
Swete, Henry, 47, 60, 83
synagogue, 48
Synan, Vinson, 120, 164, 243n1(1)
Syrians, 194

Tabernacle of Moses, 100
tarrying, 256n33
Temple, 30, 80, 248n9, 258n22
Temple of Herod, 73, 75–79, 84–85, 100
Temple of Solomon, 100
temptations, 46–47
testifying, 65
testimony, 155, 161
Third Wave, 239
Thompson, Torger G., 247n9
three-stage Pentecost, 258n11, 259n2
  see also Peter Principle
tongue, 111
tongues, 11, 13, 16, 50, 89–90, 92, 106–21,
        158, 188–89, 219, 237, 258n8
  and "caste system", 133
  in epistles, 129–30
  as lesser sign-gift, 134
  objections about, 123–35
  and prayer, 116–18
  as sign of the Holy Spirit, 238
  and spiritual life, 119
tongues of fire, 85, 86–87, 89
Torrey, R. A., 164, 232, 234–35, 239
transformation, 150
translation, 151
transplanting, 151
truth, 67
Turner, Max, 63
two-stage patterns, 164
  see also second blessing

union with Christ and the Spirit, 160
United Pentecostal Church, 236
universal truth principle, 227–28
Upper Room, 55, 62, 75, 84–85, 248n20
utterances by the Spirit, 189, 198, 251n10

Vine, W. E., 107
Vineyard movement, 214, 239
virgin birth, 26, 35, 222

Wagner, C. Peter, 82, 110, 113, 201, 247n2,
        251n22, 252n26
walk in the Spirit, 162
Walker, David, 110
washing, 150
water, 144
water baptism, 13, 18, 43, 139, 140, 141,
        152–55, 162, 217
Wesley, John, 231–32
Wesleyan churches, 164, 231–32, 240
Williams, J. Rodman, 166, 229, 247n24
Wimber, John, 239
wind, 85, 86, 88, 91, 258n8
wisdom, 32, 53
witch doctors, 126
witnessing, 15, 65, 237
women, 113
world, 63
world evangelization, 82, 84
worship, 50, 51–52, 90, 100, 112, 113, 127
Wuest, Kenneth S., 57, 58, 82, 86
Wycliffe, John, 57

Zacharias, 25–26, 35, 41
Zechariah, 101

SCRIPTURE INDEX

Genesis

1:2   45
2:7   45, 249n25
6:3   45, 46
11:1–6   114
11:8   114
17   154
41:32   204

Exodus

3:2   99
3:14   254n18
6:3   254n18
12   253n7
12:24   253n7
12:51   83
13:21   98
19   83
19:1   83
19:18   98
23:16   247n3, 248n11
24:17   98
31:3   44
34:22   248n11
35:31   44

Leviticus

8:12   44
9:24   100
14:14–17   165
14:16   254n18

23:15–21   248n11
23:16–17   247n3

Numbers

11:1   99
11:17   44
11:25–26   44
11:29   44
16:35   99
23:19   171
24:2   44
28:26–31   248n11

Deuteronomy

4:24   98
16:9–12   248n11
23:1   190
34:9   44

Joshua

27:18   44

Judges

6:34   44
11:29   44
13:25   44
14:6   44, 170
14:19   44
15:14   44

1 Samuel

10:6   44
10:10   44
11:6   44
16:13   45
16:14   46
19:20   45
19:23   44

2 Samuel

23:2   45

1 Kings

8:10–11   80
8:41–43   192
18:24   98
18:38   99

2 Kings

2:9   45
2:15   45

1 Chronicles

12:18   45
21:26   98
25:1   249n32
28:12   45

280

2 Chronicles

5:11–14   249n28
5:13–14   102
7:1   100
7:1–3   80
15:1   45
20:14   45
24:20   45

Ezra

7:6   45
7:9   45
7:28   45
8:18   45
8:22   45
8:31   45

Nehemiah

9:20   45
9:30   45

Job

27:3   45
33:4   45
34:14   45

Psalms

2   245n23
8   245n23
16   245n23
18:28   101
22   245n23
23:5   171
40:6–8   36
45   245n23
50:3   99
51:11   45
51:12   45
55:17   258n22
68:31   192
69   245n23
72   245n23
89   245n23
96   113
97:3   99
104:4   89, 95
104:29–32   45
106:33   46
110   245n23
117:1   113
118   245n23
132   245n23

139:7   45
139:14   125
143:10   45

Proverbs

1:23   45
3:1–14   244n20

Isaiah

2:3   78
4:2   245n24
4:4   45
6:4   248n21
6:6–7   99
7:14   26
11:1   245n24
11:2   36, 46
11:10   245n24
31:3   45
32:15   44
40:3   259n4
40:3–5   41
40:7   45
40:13   44, 45
42:1   36, 46
42:1–4   245n22
42:5   45
44:3   44
48:16   36, 46
49:1–6   245n22
50:4–9   245n22
52:13–53:12   245n22
53:2   24, 245n24
53:7–8   190
56   192
56:3–7   192
57:19   112
59:19   45
59:21   46
61   48, 97
61:1   36, 46
61:2   97, 245n8
63:10   46
63:11   44

Jeremiah

17:9   151
23:5   245n24
29:13   128
31:31–34   151
33:15–16   245n24

Ezekiel

1:3   41
2:2   44
3:24   44
4:14   204
11:5   45
11:19   44
13:9   249n32
36:25–27   254n1
36:26   151
36:26–27   44
37   86
37:1   45
37:9–10   45
37:14   44
39:29   44, 254n1

Daniel

6:10   258n22
7:9   98
7:17   204
8:20–21   204

Joel

2:28   254n1
2:28–29   44
2:28–32   97

Amos

1:4   99
1:7   99
1:10   99
1:12   99
1:14   99
2:2   99
2:5   99
9:11–12   213

Micah

2:7   45
3:8   45
5:12   249n32

Haggai

2:5   45

Zechariah

3:8   245n24
4:6   45, 47, 101
6:9–15   245n24
7:12   45

10:2 249n32
12:10 44
13:1 253n5

Malachi

1:11 113

Matthew

1:20 26
2:10–11 27
3:3 259n4
3:5–6 253n4
3:7 96
3:10–12 94
3:11 87, 94, 141, 147, 158,
  169, 218, 246n22, 252n1
3:11–12 96
3:16 88, 170
4:1 46
5 67
5:14 101
7:29 245n9
10:5–6 186
10:20 53, 170
12:18 170
12:31–32 52
12:40 141
13:55 28, 244n6
13:55–56 28
16:16 165
16:19 206
19:27 165
20:22 252n3
21:12 78
21:23–24 245n9
21:27 245n9
22:43 53
23:38 73
27:51 79
28:19 53, 113, 152, 155

Mark

1:3 259n4
1:4 253n4
1:8 94, 141, 142, 147, 158,
  169, 218, 246n22, 252n1
1:10 88, 170
1:12 253n10
1:13 46
1:22 245n9
1:27 245n9
3:27 47
3:28–30 52

6:3 24, 28, 244n6
7:21–23 151
10:38–39 252n3
11:17 248n21
11:28–29 245n9
12:36 53
12:42 79
13:11 53
16:9–20 252n26
16:12 244n2
16:15–18 141
16:16 151, 152
16:17 50, 107, 120, 126

Luke

1:1–4 223
1:3–4 180
1:15 171
1:35 26
1:41 171
1:67 26, 171
2:25 170
2:25–35 27
2:27 79, 253n10
2:39–40 28
2:40 34
2:41–52 29
2:48–49 31
2:50 32
2:52 34
3:1–2 40
3:7–18 94
3:8 42
3:16 87, 94, 141, 147, 159,
  169, 218, 246n22, 252n1
3:21 43
3:22 43, 88, 170
4:1 171, 253n10
4:14 47
4:14–15 47
4:18 169
4:18–19 48
4:19 97
4:32 245n9
4:36 245n9
9:51–56 184
10:20 165
10:21 50, 52
11:9 124
11:9–13 255n31
11:13 124, 171, 246n22
11:51 248n20
12:10 52
12:12 53

12:50 252n3
19:46 248n20
20:2 245n9
20:8 245n9
22:12 248n17
22:31–32 247n23
22:32 149
24:49 74, 170, 171, 246n22
24:52 74
24:53 74, 84, 166, 248n20

John

1:1 23
1:11 62
1:12 141
1:25 253n4
1:29 253n5
1:32 42, 43
1:32–33 88, 170
1:33 94, 141, 147, 159, 169,
  245n2, 246n22, 252n1
2:14 78
2:16 248n21
2:20 73
2:22 63
3–7 61
3:1–5 141, 151
3:3 51
3:3–6 150
3:5–6 51, 149
3:8 51, 86, 149
3:16–17 62
3:17 151
3:22–23 253n4
3:34 49, 171
4:10–14 141
4:13 246n22
4:23–24 50, 51
5:19–20 24
5:43 62
6:44 149
6:63 49
6:69 62
7:38 171, 246n22
7:38–39 53
7:39 52, 141, 172, 246n22
7:45–46 245n9
10:9 151
12:16 63
12:31 63
13:7 64
13:10–11 166
13:13–14 62
14–16 55, 61

14–17 67, 74
14–20 61
14:5 63
14:6 62
14:8 63
14:10–11 50
14:12 59
14:13–14 255n31
14:15–23 150
14:16 56, 171, 246n22
14:16–17 61, 255n31
14:16–23 171
14:16–26 63
14:17 62, 63, 141, 246n22
14:18 56, 246n22
14:20 141
14:21–23 56
14:25–26 63
14:26 56, 61, 62, 63, 171,
  208, 246n22, 255n31
15:1–5 141
15:3 166
15:4–5 141
15:7 255n31
15:14 166
15:16 166, 255n31
15:18–26 62
15:26 56, 61, 62, 63, 171,
  246n22
15:26–27 65
16:7 54, 56, 59, 61, 63,
  246n22
16:7–8 62, 65
16:8 149, 246n22
16:8–11 62
16:12–15 66
16:13 62, 246n22
16:14 112, 246n22
16:15 246n22
16:20 62
16:23–24 255n31
16:26 255n31
16:27–28 62
17 62, 246n23
17:1 246n23
17:9 246n23
17:11 246n23
17:13 246n23
17:15 246n23
17:17 246n23
17:20 246n23
17:21 246n23
17:21–23 247n23
17:24 247n23

17:26 247n23
18:37 62
20 249n25
20:2 182
20:19 84
20:22 54, 166, 246n22,
  249n25
20:26 84
20:30 50
21:25 50, 63, 252n26
29:19–22 75

Acts

1:2 54
1:4 171, 246n22
1:4–8 74
1:5 74, 94, 96, 147, 159,
  169, 172, 246n22, 252n1,
  253n4, 259n31
1:8 65, 141, 166, 170, 172,
  179, 183, 192, 246n22
1:12 74
1:13 84
1:14 84, 166
1:15 83
1:15–22 166
1:21 166
2 11, 82, 92, 99, 162, 165,
  186, 194, 214, 249n25
2:1 217
2:1–4 141
2:1–8 81
2:2 84, 91
2:4 14, 89, 107, 112, 125,
  141, 171, 172, 182, 184
2:4–5 217
2:5 91, 218
2:6 92
2:8 92
2:8–11 90
2:10 91
2:11 90, 112
2:16 161
2:16–18 85
2:17–18 114, 171, 172
2:17–21 97
2:21 151
2:22 33
2:32–33 160
2:33 54, 62, 141, 171, 172
2:38 17, 141, 153, 154,
  155, 171, 172, 181, 182,
  217, 219, 228
2:38–39 139, 141

2:39 112, 115, 171, 207,
  219
2:41 182
2:47 151
3 79
3:19 149
4:8 89, 171, 172
4:13 89
4:27 172
4:31 89, 128, 171, 172
5:32 171, 172
6:3 89, 171, 172
6:5 89, 171, 172
6:8 141
6:10 170, 172
7 89
7:47 248n20, 248n21
7:49 248n20
7:55 171, 172
8 185, 194, 214
8:4 185
8:5 185
8:5–8 141
8:12 155, 182, 185
8:14 185
8:14–17 183, 231
8:14–18 182
8:15 172
8:16 155, 170, 172, 185
8:17 172
8:18 171
8:18–20 172
8:19 172
8:20 171
8:21 189
8:26–39 182
8:26–40 190
8:29 247n24
8:35 190
8:37 185
8:38–39 190
8:39 172
8:40 201
9 194, 203
9:1–19 182
9:3–5 195
9:5 155, 196
9:11 197
9:17 89, 171, 172
9:17–18 194
9:22 182
9:26 182
10 186, 194, 214
10:1–48 182

10:13   204
10:16   259n31
10:37–38   205
10:38   33, 49, 169, 172
10:43–44   205
10:44   170, 172
10:44–46   141, 184
10:44–48   199
10:45   141, 171, 172
10:46   111
10:47   171, 172
10:48   155
11:1–18   182
11:14   151
11:15   170, 172, 184, 208
11:16   94, 141, 147, 159,
   169, 172, 246n22, 252n1,
   253n4
11:17   171, 172
11:20   212
11:24   89, 171, 172
11:26   212
13   194, 212
13:9   89, 171, 172
13:48–52   182
13:52   89, 171, 172
15   200
15:1   213
15:7–9   182
15:8   171, 172
15:8–9   213
15:28   213
16:6   247n24
16:14–15   182, 186
16:30–31   151
16:30–33   183, 254n18
16:33   155
16:33–34   186
17:11–12   222
18   215, 252n5
18–21   217
18:8   183
18:23   259n6
18:24–19:7   259n5
18:25   216
18:27   259n6
19   186, 194, 215, 220, 226,
   252n5
19:1   259n6
19:1–7   183
19:2   141, 172
19:5   155
19:6   130, 170, 172, 184
19:9   259n6

19:10   259n7
19:20   215
19:30   259n6
20   226
20:1   259n6
20:7   259n6
20:28   172
20:30   259n6
20:35   252n26
21:4   259n6
21:8   201
21:16   259n6
22   194
22:8   196
22:10   196
22:16   141, 150, 153, 154,
   186
24:2   85
26   194
26:15   196
26:18   151
34:27   169

Romans

2:28–29   154
2:29   141
3:25   253n7
4:19   98
5:5   171
5:9   253n7
6:3   155
6:3–5   141
6:3–14   141
6:4   141, 142
6:4–5   153
6:5   141
6:23   141
7:4   152
8:1–11   51
8:9   141
8:11   54, 171
8:15   141, 149, 152, 167
8:15–16   141
8:16   150
8:23   171
8:26–27   117
8:26–28   151
8:34   62
9:1   150
10:9   116, 195
10:9–13   151
10:10   116
10:12   115
10:17   153

12:2   151
12:6   127
12:10–11   98
13:14   141, 154
15:11   113

1 Corinthians

1:5   257n21
1:6   133
1:11   133
1:21   63
2:4   170
2:13–16   64
3:11   133
5:7   82, 165
6:11   150, 151
6:19   151
10:1–2   253n7
10:2   144
10:16   253n7
11:25   253n7
11:27   253n7
11:32   63
12   148
12–14   124, 129
12:1–9   141
12:3   148, 195
12:9   148
12:10   107, 118
12:13   139, 142, 143, 144,
   146, 147, 148, 156, 250n1
12:31   141
13:1   108, 250n1
14   50, 107, 118, 119, 126,
   130, 134
14:1   124, 141
14:1–5   117
14:2   107, 119
14:4   107, 119, 125
14:5   119
14:14   107, 119
14:14–15   117
14:14–19   117
14:15   119
14:17   119
14:18   118, 119, 182, 199
14:19   107, 119
14:27   107
14:39   119, 124
15   150
15:3–4   141
15:6   74
15:45   149, 150

2 Corinthians

1:21   169
1:22   170, 172
3:6   49
4:4   63
5:5   170
5:17   141, 196
5:21   151
8:7   257n21
12:9   170
13:1   204

Galatians

3:2   172
3:3   92
3:26–28   115
3:27   141
4:5   152
4:5–6   149
4:6   167
4:19   56
5:22–23   111, 141
6:2–3   161
6:5   161
6:15   151

Ephesians

1:3   141
1:3–6   151
1:5   152
1:7   253n7
1:13   141, 166, 172
1:13–14   170, 219
2:1   141
2:6   141
2:13   253n7
2:13–17   112
2:18   112
2:22   171
3:5   253n10
3:14   141
3:16–17   150
3:19   141
4:5   143
4:23   151
4:30   247n24
5:18   148, 171
5:23–32   152
5:26   150
6:17–18   117, 121
6:18   130
6:19   257n21

Philippians

2   33
2:5–8   23
3:3   154
3:9–10   154

Colossians

1:13–14   151
1:14   253n7
1:20   253n7
1:27   150
1:29   170
2:11   141
2:11–12   142, 154
3:9–10   141
3:10   151
3:11   115
3:19   257n21

1 Thessalonians

1:5   170
1:7–8   253n6
4   150
4:8   171
5:19   98
5:23   141, 154
5:27   130

2 Thessalonians

1:7–8   96
1:8   96, 99
3:14   130

1 Timothy

1:17   99
3:16   33, 49

Titus

3:5   141, 149, 150, 154
3:6   171

Hebrews

1:1   45
1:7   89, 95
1:9   169
2:9–11   253n3
2:10   33
2:11–12   33
2:14   33, 253n3
2:17   33, 253n3
4:14–15   62
7:25   62

8:8–13   151
9:14   54
11:6   256n34
12:29   98
13:15   112

James

3:8   111
5:20   149

1 Peter

2:21   165
3:18   54
3:19   54
3:21   141, 153
4:14   170

2 Peter

3:15–16   130

1 John

1:9   142, 253n5
2:1   56, 60
2:20   64, 101, 169
2:27   64, 101, 169
3:8   49
3:10   126
3:18   56
5:1   141
5:4   141
5:10   141
5:14   116, 255n31

Jude

3   145
15   97
20–21   117

Revelation

1:4   129
1:5   253n5
1:13   100
2:1–11   130
3:20   171
3:21   141
4:5   100, 129
5:6   129
7:14   150, 253n5
13   67, 204
19:7–9   152
19:13   253n5
21:24   151

Ordained at the age of 17, **Ernest B. Gentile** has been in active ministry for the past 56 years, including pastoring for 41 years. He speaks frequently at churches and conferences in the U.S. and 22 foreign countries. Ernest is noted for his prophetic ministry, inspirational preaching and teaching, unique biblical insights and transparent approach to today's practical problems. He serves on the Apostolic Leadership Team of MFI (Ministers Fellowship International).

After founding Christian Community Church in San Jose, California, and pastoring it for 33 years, Ernest and his wife, Joy, have been active in an extensive traveling ministry for the past 11 years. They have been married 54 years and have four children, six grandchildren and one great-grandchild.

Ernest has a diploma from Bethel Temple Bible School (Seattle), a B.A. from Whitworth College (Spokane), and an M.A. in Biblical Theology from Fuller Theological Seminary. He is the author of *Your Sons and Daughters Shall Prophesy* (Chosen Books), *The Final Triumph* (Chosen Books), *Charismatic Catechism* (New Leaf Press), *Awaken the Dawn!* (TEC Publications) and *Worship God!* (City Bible Publications).